CW00825562

THE WINTER GAME

To Dad

Happy 65th Birthday

I hope this gives you
as much enjoyment as
watching Wales at the
Millenium Stadium.!!

Love

Beth xxx

Ben & 😊

xxx

To Stephanie – for sharing much of this journey with me, for fully supporting me and for providing the inspiration.

THE WINTER GAME

Rediscovering the Passion of Rugby

TODD R. NICHOLLS

MAINSTREAM
PUBLISHING
EDINBURGH AND LONDON

First published in Great Britain in 2005 by
MAINSTREAM PUBLISHING COMPANY (EDINBURGH) LTD
7 Albany Street
Edinburgh EH1 3UG

ISBN 1 84018 915 0

A catalogue record for this book is available from the British Library

Typeset in Frutiger and Janson

Printed in Great Britain by
Clays Ltd, St Ives plc

CONTENTS

ACKNOWLEDGEMENTS

First, I would like to thank my family for supporting my love of rugby down the years and never sighing when I put rugby above more profitable activities. Thank you also to Stephanie and the Woods family for their help and assistance.

My sincere gratitude to Skye Bothma of WordsWorth editing services, who provided much needed editing, editorial advice and support. She was a star. I would also like to thank Brian Hallinan of Sumner Ink!, Stephanie Woods, Ron Palenski, Derek Royal, Spiro Zavos and Stephen Jones for reading the manuscript and for making valued comments. Any factual mistakes remaining are, of course, mine.

Hugh Cottrell from Cottrell Law was a supportive employer when I told him that I needed a month off to get an insight into British and Irish rugby. Many thanks to him.

Stephen Smith, a best friend if ever there was one, assisted me no end when I was in England, picking me up at Heathrow in the early hours of a cold Monday morning being a good example of his support.

Neil and Debbie Uprichard in Belfast, Northern Ireland, and the Cosgrave family in Dublin, once again helped me out with a writing project. What can I say but many thanks for everything and that you are very special friends of mine.

James Parkinson in Auckland and Kent Nicholls and Derek Royal in Sydney provided friendship and support and their contribution is hopefully outlined in the following pages.

Bill Campbell from Mainstream helped initiate this idea and his incredible team helped foster it. Many thanks to them for their belief in this project and in me.

Andy Haden and the team at Sporting Contacts in Auckland,

New Zealand, assisted with contacts, while Sean Wallace very kindly provided tickets for the first All Blacks–Lions Test in Christchurch.

I would like to thank the various media managers and player agents who provided assistance. Special thanks to Kim, Jo and Joanne from the Canterbury Rugby Football Union who were obliging, helpful and always professional. I would also like to thank Brian Finn and Scott Campton from the New Zealand Rugby Football Union. Thank you also to the various photographers, newspapers, photo agencies and individuals who have assisted with illustrations.

I would especially like to thank the players (past and present), coaches, administrators and journalists who made themselves available for interviews and general discussions.

Those individuals included: Richard McCaw, Hamish Riach, Alan Whetton, Andy Dalton, Ron Palenski, Anton Oliver, Robbie Deans, Rueben Thorne, Russell Watkins, John Hart, Stephen Jones, Nick Cain, Paul Morgan, Graham Henry, Wayne Smith, Tana Umaga, Dennis Young, Steve Hansen, Darren Shand, Warwick Roger, Spiro Zavos, Justin Marshall, Jack Kyle, Bob Scott, George Naoupu, Michael Johnson, Luke O'Donnell, Ken Scotland, Tiny Hill, Lawrence Dallaglio, Warren Gatland, Craig Dowd, Colin Meads, Willie John McBride, Jim McKenzie, Simon Taylor, Barry John, Ian Kirkpatrick, Brian O'Driscoll, Michael Reid, Ken McDonald, Andy Irvine, Tane Norton, Gareth Edwards, Mervyn Davies, Bob Norster, Martyn Williams, Gavin Hastings, Ollie Campbell, Sean Fitzpatrick, Sir Clive Woodward, Bill Beaumont, Daniel Carter and Chris Jack.

If ever there was any doubt that rugby was a special game, then these individuals dispelled it.

PROLOGUE

> Some people mark significant moments in their lives by a particular song. I mark the passages of my life with the memories of great rugby teams, players and matches . . . From the time I saw the All Blacks run on to the park that first time, like a spill of black opals on green baize, I was hooked for life.
>
> Spiro Zavos

ALL BLACKS V. LIONS, CHRISTCHURCH, NEW ZEALAND, 25 JUNE 2005

Some match days you remember more than others. For so many reasons, this was a memorable one for me and one I'll never forget.

The day started around noon, when I'd uncharacteristically headed for an Irish pub called The Bog in Cashel Mall in downtown Christchurch. The centre of the city was buzzing with a vibe that I'd never previously felt in this part of the world. Hundreds of Lions fans were milling around like bees to a honey pot, most nervously anticipating the game that night.

They were a delightful blend of the old and the young, all united by a passion for rugby. There was plenty of good-natured fun going on and there was a clear collective purpose: beat the All Blacks.

Down Oxford Terrace, some 20 metres north, the bar proprietors and the Christchurch City Council had established a temporary food court that reinforced the feeling that this day was one big party.

The Bog was an appropriate place to meet Sean Wallace, a friend of mine from Limerick who was following the tour in what he said was a 'bloody stinking and cold campervan'. Sean and his mate had a rule in the campervan, however: you could do whatever you wanted but no number twos. It seemed a very sensible rule to me.

Sean is a corporate lawyer and as he has lived most of his life in New Zealand, he regards himself as a staunch All Black supporter. He wore his All Black training jersey this day, although in this pub he was outnumbered by Lions supporters by at least ten to one.

The Lions supporters came in all shapes and sizes and were inherently linked by their liking for a good time. They seemed not to like New Zealand beer, although it appeared that as long as it was wet, they would take what they could get.

Sean and his travelling companion – another corporate lawyer from Dublin – had met up with two other travelling fans, one of whom Sean played rugby with at a club in Limerick.

The other bloke, who was from Donegal in Ireland, admitted that he wasn't crazy about rugby but had decided to blow a bank loan that he'd earmarked for a new kitchen on a trip to New Zealand.

The young guy from Limerick spoke about a rugby trip to Brussels that he had shared with Sean and his club. Apparently more beer was drunk than rugby played and there was some trouble. I believed him.

The bloke from Donegal outlined how he decided, on a whim, to take his summer holidays in cold New Zealand. His boss was expecting him back in two weeks, although he'd be back in four and a half.

He didn't know where he was staying in Wellington the following week, while he continually got mixed up about his next port of call: Christchurch or Queenstown.

These lads weren't confident the Lions would win later in the day but they didn't seem to care too much. The lad from Limerick and the bloke from Donegal had after all only arrived in the country the previous day and had met for the first time on the bus going into the city.

As the pints flowed, we shared plenty of craic about rugby, travel and life. Each of the guys had different stories to tell and although we were all thinking about the rugby later in the evening, it seemed secondary to being here and having a good time.

When the afternoon drew to a close, we got photos of our little informal group. It was symbolic of the fact that rugby can open doors and allow you to meet people that you wouldn't otherwise have met.

When I arrived home, my own enthusiasm was building and I felt as if I was going to play the game myself. Sean had very kindly given me two stand tickets and so my girlfriend Stephanie and I were going along.

I'd spent NZ$370 on a corporate hospitality package months earlier but for all of that money I would still have ended up in the uncovered DB Stand with half the 'Barmy Army'. No, the stand and the free tickets were the better option.

Steph was appropriately dressed for the cold and wet night: she was rugged up and looked splendid in her All Black scarf and hat. For someone who isn't mad about the sport, she looked like an earnest All Black fan and I loved her for it.

It was ironic that on the biggest rugby occasion in Christchurch for years there was no problem finding a parking space. In fact, it was much easier than the average Super 12 match, as few Lions fans were travelling with cars.

When we parked my Ford Festiva (affectionately known as 'Mehrts' after the All Black first five-eight Andrew Mehrtens) and wrapped up again for the conditions, I was literally feeling sick. I had been looking forward to this match for months and I just couldn't wait for kick-off.

When Brian O'Driscoll and Tana Umaga led their teams onto the field, to what appeared to be equal roars, I was shaking with nerves, something Steph innocently put down to the cold.

When the teams lined up for, respectively, their anthem and song, I felt like my country was united to a man and woman, the atmosphere was that electric. Yet I felt bonded in a positive sense and so very proud to be a New Zealander.

When the TV camera panned down the Lions line as they played that awful anthem 'The Power of Four', it stopped for a moment and captured the facial expression of the captain, Brian O'Driscoll.

O'Driscoll, so much the modern player, combining natural brilliance with the charm of a Jack Kyle or a Tony O'Reilly, had a look on his face that will live with me for ever. It was a look that simply stated that he was born for this moment and that all roads leading up to now had been about this moment. It was simplistic, it was peaceful and it was inspiring.

In some ways, I knew how he felt. This game, this contest, this moment, had been on my radar for months and here and now in Christchurch it was happening and it felt fantastic.

For months I had hoped that this match would be the occasion when my love and passion for rugby would be rekindled. I'd hoped that I would be able to look at the faces of the players and see real responsibility, real nervousness and pride in the teams they were representing.

I'd hoped that I would be able to stand when they played the national anthem and scream 'God Defend New Zealand' like I used to do when I was a kid.

I wanted to feel the crunch of a big hit and sigh when we came close to scoring a try. I wanted the whole thing to matter and for me to be affected, one way or the other, by the result.

I wanted to see my reflection in the faces of the All Blacks and feel connection and identity. I wanted to embrace the men in black as if they were my brothers.

I didn't want to think that, regardless of what happened, 'rugby was the winner', as was often said in this politically correct age. Despite my fondness for O'Driscoll, I wanted the All Blacks to destroy the Lions and I wanted to enjoy every minute.

This may seem childish and yet there is a reason. You see, some two years ago I was beginning to think that rugby didn't mean anything to me any more and that the sport's unique ethos had been lost in the maze that was professionalism.

Rugby had traditionally reflected what it meant to be a New Zealander and, if I'm honest, it had been central to my own sense of identity.

Yet since the full effect of professionalism had been realised, I had begun not to care about rugby in general or about whether the side I supported won or lost. You could say I was disillusioned.

There would be nights when New Zealand played Australia in yet another Tri-Nations match somewhere when I would choose to go out rather than watch the rugby.

I would rarely get up to see the All Blacks play in the northern hemisphere and yet getting up with Dad to watch rugby and drink Milo in the middle of the night was a staple of my childhood.

I knew the players would always give their best, especially when they were representing their country, but they often spoke of being bored playing in the same competitions each year against the same opponents. I knew how they felt: I was bored watching it.

I also sensed that professionalism was destroying rugby's special ethos and that money was becoming more important to players than the honour and pride in playing for their club, province or country.

Special ethos you say. What's that? It's an indefinable entity but let me give you one example.

Brisbane, Australia, 1999. Ireland had just been beaten by the Wallabies. In the visitors' dressing-room, debutant Irish centre Brian O'Driscoll shook hands proudly with midfielder Tim Horan.

Horan (one of the greats of the game) handed O'Driscoll his own sweat-soaked jersey, the way that international players did after a Test match.

O'Driscoll accepted the jersey gracefully and then, without hesitation but with a little sadness (it was his first Test jersey after all), handed over his own.

Horan then looked O'Driscoll squarely in the eye.

'You keep it,' he said genuinely, knowing that O'Driscoll's jersey had been earned and should be kept by the man himself. The smile on O'Driscoll's face said it all.

Go back ten years to 1989. Eden Park, Auckland. Horan was standing in the Wallabies' dressing-room. Aged 19, he'd just made *his* debut for his nation.

Standing in front of him was Joe Stanley, the All Black midfielder who made his own debut in 1986. Stanley handed over his jersey but then when offered Horan's, he turned it down. Like Horan ten years later, he knew the debutant deserved to keep it.

You see, traditionally there was always something about rugby that made the game special. More particularly, there was something about a rugby man that made him distinct.

It was, as it were, a brotherhood of sorts which meant that regardless of where you were in the world, rugby was a common currency that was reflective of good manners, teamwork and sportsmanship. The result was important all right but there was something more.

Yet it appeared to me that this unique ethos was no longer so prominent and that rugby was becoming no different to any other professional sport.

Since the advent of professionalism, the top players (and their agents) seemed to regularly talk about contracts and appearance fees and not merely about the pride in representing their communities.

Where once the players were part of their communities, now they were part of the new rich who were invited to swanky parties and who graced the covers of fancy magazines.

Administrators now jabbered on about television rights and bums on seats and not about serving the people who had made the game great.

You went to a major ground for a match these days and early in the first half the crowd would often burst into a Mexican wave. It reflected the fact that rugby had become entertainment and a competitor for the discretionary dollar.

In the modern era, corporate hospitality had become code for making money by offering tickets and free drink to business types. Yet how many of them belonged to rugby clubs?

Regardless of how you looked at it, professional rugby had changed rugby's ethos and I was sick of lamenting the impact that it was having on the sport that I loved more than any other.

So I decided (after some sleepless nights and England's World Cup victory) to undertake an 18-month odyssey to try and discover whether my assumptions were correct.

I wanted to find out whether the changes that had occurred had made rugby a better game or whether they were just reflective of any professional sport.

I wanted to know whether that special ethos that set rugby apart from other sports had been lost or whether it still existed but in a different form.

To determine how rugby's special ethos had changed, I decided to focus on the build-up to the Lions tour of New Zealand in 2005 and the tour itself.

This tour, I figured, would be the ultimate combination of traditionalism and professionalism and would give me a clearer picture of what impact professionalism had had.

I decided to focus on certain potential Lions, their coaches and some of the All Black players and coaches who might play a part in the series and follow their journey up to and including the tour itself.

On my odyssey, I also planned to talk with administrators, writers and icons of the game, all of whom would hopefully provide me with diverse perspectives.

I also wanted to track the changes that had occurred since the advent of professionalism by comparing the 2005 tour with past Lions tours of New Zealand.

I hoped that by talking about the game with many of the past greats of the sport and getting their take on modern rugby, I'd rediscover some of the romance of rugby that I reckon we've all been missing since the start of professionalism in 1995.

If I'm honest, my odyssey was also personal. I desperately wanted to rediscover my passion for a sport that used to be as important to me as air and water.

I make no bones about why I undertook this journey but then again I figured that I probably wasn't the only rugby fan who felt this way.

Who am I? Well, I could give you my biography and if you're keen enough you'll probably read it elsewhere in this book. Yet it doesn't matter.

I could tell you that Canterbury and the All Blacks have become part of me like Arsenal had become part of Nick Hornby or the Boston Red Sox a part of Bill Bryson and yet it doesn't matter.

All that matters is that rugby's fundamental ethos is still alive and that since the start of professionalism, the sport's heart remains as healthy as it was when I was a kid.

It's here that I'll begin and over the next few pages I'll show you what rugby, and specifically Lions tours of New Zealand, has meant to me and my country.

After that, I'll examine the Super 12, the international season in New Zealand and the Tri-Nations competition before heading to Europe to look at the issues there.

After reviewing rugby in the four home unions, I'll look at the All Blacks' end-of-year tour to Europe, the Six Nations and then the build-up to the Lions tour itself. I will also look at the Lions selection and the economics involved in this massive sporting event.

The last part of this book will look at the tour itself, an adventure that Clive Woodward optimistically called the biggest sporting event of 2005.

By examining the build-up to the tour and some of the main issues involved in the game, it was my hope that I could perhaps shed some light on why what happened happened.

Regardless of who won that series, my odyssey would be a success if at the end of it I could say that, although maybe not solely a winter game any more, rugby remained the game that they might play in heaven.

BACKYARD RUGBY

CANTERBURY V. LIONS, 25 JUNE 1977

I will never be asked to name my favourite rugby player. If I were, I would say Grant Keenan.

Grant eventually ended up playing for a Canterbury XV and Hawke's Bay B. This is impressive but not the type of rugby résumé that would place him above Blanco, Campese or Fitzpatrick in most people's estimation.

Grant, or 'Sandy' as he was known, had a love for rugby that was as natural as running after daffodils in spring. It was a passion demonstrated in what he spoke about, the way he walked, the tatty posters on his bedroom wall. He was the perfect example of the New Zealand rugby kid and he was my hero.

It's funny the things you want when you're six. Grant's ripped Sid Going and Grant Batty posters – not two of the handsomest All Blacks it has to be said – captivated and stimulated me as if they were beautiful pieces of fifteenth-century Italian art.

I would sit at the foot of Grant's bed and stare dreamily at them as if they were Greek gods. Dream, perhaps, that one day I would also be an All Black. (Grant's mum thought this behaviour somewhat odd and it made me realise for the first time that women cannot *really* understand the beauty of rugby.)

To me, the posters of Going and Batty symbolised the 1977 Lions tour. I didn't know Phil Bennett's sidestep from Graham Price's scrummaging but I was captivated like someone experiencing falling in love for the first time.

One of my first clear memories is reading a copy of a Lions tour book that was published shortly after the 1977 tour had finished. The stunning scarlet of the Lions jersey, nicely matched with the crisp white shorts and the auspicious dark-blue socks with the lush emerald-green top, drew me like a bee to pollen. I was hooked.

The Lions were the catalysts but Grant was the reason. To copy my hero's habits seemed as obvious as disliking school and as natural as feeling a southern autumn chill on Anzac Day in April.

Grant's favourite number was nine. Mine too. Grant, not

surprisingly, played half-back. I wanted to be a half-back. Grant played club rugby for the Lincoln club and school rugby for Lincoln Primary. I wanted to do the same. The only problem was that neither the club nor the school thought a perky (yet energetic) six year old was ready for the vigours of Under-10 rugby.

Grant's parents bought him his red and black striped Lincoln club jersey (*exactly* the same colours as Canterbury, which I was eternally grateful for . . . I couldn't have imagined playing in the Southbridge club's blue and white, the same colours as Auckland) at Duffel's drapery in the village. I would go into the store and stroke the material as if it were Arabian silk. If I'd had the money, I would have bought a jersey and worn it to bed like a first-time All Black was rumoured to have once done.

We lived across the road from the Keenans but it wasn't close enough and at every opportunity I would try and find Grant. It was Grant whom I turned to (he understood my pain) when I mistakenly put ALL BLACKS 12 MUNSTER 0 on my *Listener* Follow-the-All Blacks tour poster in 1978. It was as if he were the older brother that I never had.

When I found Grant, I would badger him to play footy on his front lawn. For him, it must have been a novelty having a groupie. I loved hearing Grant's heroic tales of taking on Waihora at Tai Tapu some six kilometres away, of playing rugby under the hills at Little River on the Banks Peninsula. His were romantic stories of two mighty armies (albeit of ten year olds) fighting each other on mud-covered pitches. Not surprisingly, the good guys normally won.

There was beauty and drama in his stories, the way next week's tactics would be worked out in precise detail. We would practise his passing with my well-greased Adidas leather ball that became symbolic of my burgeoning love for the sport. We would talk about our rugby heroes if they embodied all that was good in the world and about how we hated the boys who played for Waihora. Winter and summer, we played for hours.

Eventually Grant became a teenager and not surprisingly I became a headache. Grant discovered Wendy Hillyer down the road and pop music, and although he still loved sport (especially cricket), I became nothing more than an annoying kid.

Grant's mum also got sick of me, although his dad was always nice. One day a few years on when I was playing for the Lincoln Under-12s, he said to someone that all that practice on the front lawn must have paid off. God bless him. He was right in one sense, as it was on that front lawn that the most passionate love affair of my life began.

RED HERO

ALL BLACKS V. LIONS, CHRISTCHURCH, 4 JUNE 1983

He stood out because of his red hair, his lily-white skin and his ability to torment opponents with his pinpoint kicking. That kicking: yes, he could control a rugby ball with all the skill of Pelé and make it look so easy. How I wanted to be just like him.

He had the ability to beat my beloved All Blacks almost single-handedly the following day but, as he was my hero, standing here watching him train was my paradise. In fact, 80 minutes of Test rugby was going to be an anticlimax.

Like his rugby in general, he practised on this muddy training ground with great precision. He took kick after kick and instantly knew when the heavy leather Adidas ball was going to fly sweetly between the posts. He didn't appear to mind that the conditions were both damp and depressing and that Dublin was probably basking in summer sunshine.

My fact file on the 1983 British and Irish Lions said Seamus Oliver Campbell was 5 ft 10 in. tall but before I saw him in the flesh I swore he was at least 10 ft and walked on water. I knew he was Irish but, as I was 11 (nearly 12), he could have been from Mars. He was a rugby legend and that was all that mattered.

Almost 12 years after Barry John had tormented New Zealand, I was on the brink of my adolescence and another number 10 was the centre of national attention.

Peter Barkle, the headmaster of Lincoln Primary School, had stormed into our classroom just before lunchtime. It being Friday, he didn't beat about the bush. 'Who is going to the Test on Saturday between the All Blacks and the Lions?' he asked.

All these young lads quickly put their hands up – Lancaster Park (although renamed Jade Stadium these days, it will always be Lancaster Park to me) was obviously the place to be the following afternoon. I had my dad to thank for my hand shooting up as quickly as anyone's. He'd managed to get his hands on two Number Three Stand tickets and he was taking me, the world's greatest 11-year-old rugby fan, along to the footy.

I was delighted with Mr Barkle – we were being taken out of class and avoiding the joys of Form One maths. No girls either, just us lads. Pleasure personified. I could have fallen in love with the headmaster then and there, although this adventure was going to get even better.

Around 20 of us walked down to Lincoln College, about a kilometre away, and who should we find there but 30 Lions training their hearts out in preparation for the ultimate test the following day. We were obviously more delighted to see them than they us but what did that matter?

Cautiously at first, growing more confident as every priceless second passed, we inched closer to watch these great men train. I had my eyes open for Campbell, the Irishman whom everybody the length and breadth of New Zealand was talking about. He was the star, the five-eight, and the kicker. Campbell had to be stopped tomorrow but today all I wanted to do was to get close to him and maybe get a word, an autograph and an acknowledgement.

Before we had settled in, a large man wearing a red tracksuit came over. I knew this man was another bloke who had played a bit of footy in his time – Willie John McBride was his name and he was the manager of the side. He told us you didn't play rugby competitively in Ireland until you were a teenager. Right now, though, he was preventing me getting close to Ollie Campbell.

'Can we go over and get autographs?' I blurted out to Willie John, who close up was bigger than Texas and still looked as though he could have packed down in a scrum or two. By making such a request I was neglecting the fact that the Lions were training and had the first Test to prepare for.

Naturally, my inappropriate request was turned down, although Mr McBride compensated to some degree by signing his own name. When it came to signing autographs, he must have hated having a long name.

No player autographs but there was still no way I was going back to school this afternoon. I quietly snuck away from my classmates, who were watching the Lions pack do battle with a scrum machine, moaning and groaning and trying to improve each time.

I moved slyly across to the second field where Ollie Campbell was practising his goal kicking. Just him, the cold wind from the south, the gloom of a Friday in winter . . . and now me. Initially, he didn't know I was watching him practise but after a while I was very difficult to miss, as I was by myself and my eyes were glued to him like he was the king of the world.

I figured he must have been used to kids watching him practise: he was Ollie Campbell after all. But such was his concentration and focus that if he did know I was there, it didn't seem to bother him. He kicked balls for the best part of 30 minutes and in that time I focused exclusively on my hero, still finding it hard to believe that he was right here practising his art in Lincoln.

This was heaven. After a while, he came over to collect his balls one final time, smiling at me in the process and making my day, my year. He looked a very nice man and although I now knew he wasn't 10 ft tall, it didn't mean I respected him any less.

My paradise was broken by the sound of my friends coming over, laughing like kids who had seen what they wanted and now lost concentration. Not me, though; I could have stayed there all day watching Ollie Campbell – if, of course, he had practised all day and I hadn't been told in no uncertain terms that it was time to head back.

I walked back to school on such an enormous high. I just couldn't wait to get home and tell Mum and Dad, to savour my Willie John autograph. That night I imagined that Ollie Campbell was coming around for tea. He never did show but then again I hadn't had the chance to invite him.

The following day, Dad and I watched the All Blacks beat the Lions 16–12 in the low-setting winter sun. The game could have gone either way, although Ollie Campbell was superb, and given that and the result, I couldn't have asked for more. The sight of Ollie leaving the field, his arm draped innocently around a child, a big smile on his face despite the loss, will live with me for ever.

Fast forward to 1999 and I was now working in sports journalism in Dublin on my overseas experience. A long way from Lincoln in some respects, although not as far as I may once have imagined. For obvious reasons, I wanted to interview Ollie Campbell. How to find out where he lived? Look in the phone book, dummy! There he was, one Ollie Campbell.

I rang and got an answer machine. Nervous as hell, I left a message and asked him to contact me. When he did later that evening, he was confident, polished and unbelievably nice. We talked for over an hour, my hero and me, and covered as much rugby as we could fit in. I felt 11 again, actually talking to my hero this time and yet still feeling as though he was a rugby god.

He was everything I imagined he would be. In his tone and manner, he was distinctly Irish, while he was polite, analytical and, like me, deeply in love with rugby. In short, he was everything I had wanted him to be. I didn't have the guts to ask him whether he remembered me, because I am sure he didn't and that would have broken my heart.

I told Ollie that he was probably respected more in New Zealand than in Ireland, and that in some shape or form he had changed my life. He appreciated my comments and was as gracious as any hero should be.

In Dublin, so long after that fateful Friday in Lincoln, I felt inspired again by my red-headed hero. I was fundamentally the same person as I was when I was 11 and, thankfully, he was still the man I had worshipped back then. I was on a high for the next few days. Childhood heroes can do that to you.

A FAMILY AFTERNOON

CANTERBURY V. LIONS, 28 JUNE 1983

Although my beloved Canterbury beat the Lions 22–20, the biggest coup of 28 June 1983 was my mum coming to the footy with us.

Mum wasn't the biggest rugby fan. Surprisingly, she put being with her friends on Saturdays above the plight of our provincial rugby team. (It is perhaps because of Mum's attitude that I now find women who are into rugby as attractive as baked beans.)

Why Mum agreed to come along beats me. Could it have been the ticket thrust on her by Dad, or was it simply the promise of an afternoon in the winter sunshine? I didn't care: she was coming and it was now a family afternoon.

Mum did have a point in some respects. There was a long graffiti-covered tunnel that we had to go through to reach the ground. Passing through it felt like going through a sewer, and that was where some of the language shouted appeared to originate from. I should have told Dad to park elsewhere.

Walking closely with my father and mother on one side and my brothers on the other, I felt the nervous expectation of the tightly squeezed Canterbury fans reverberate against the tunnel walls. We were united in our passion for our province, yet this did not make the tunnel smell any better.

Some yobbo in the distance yelled out something that I couldn't make out (I think it may have been CAN . . . TER . . . BURY and if it was, then that's fine) but we kept walking, realising that the faster we walked the quicker we would make the other side. For just a moment, I valued Mum's appreciation of other activities.

Eventually, daylight appeared and I felt a sense of euphoria, a rush that could only be caused by the fact that we were now just a few metres from the park. Lancaster Park. I'd been here a few times before but the novelty was still as raw as a stud mark.

I knew this Canterbury team was special. They had successfully challenged for the Ranfurly Shield against Wellington the previous season and I, like so many others my age, had gone along to see them take on Counties in the first challenge the following weekend.

What a match that was: Canterbury struggled for most of the game only to be saved when Counties winger Robert Kururangi was adjudged offside and Robbie Deans kicked the penalty to draw the match and save the shield for Canterbury.

It was on that day that I decided I wanted to be the next Robbie Deans. It helped that Mum said I looked like him. He was certainly a talent yet what made him special was his charisma. Before I had heard of Nelson Mandela, Gandhi or Martin Luther King, it was Robbie Deans who to me best represented the beauty of the human condition.

Yet Robbie was not alone. The 1983 Canterbury side was special for the quality of its individuals and its collective talent. There was the intellect of Wayne Smith at first-five (whom I met at the Canterbury Sports Depot one day and got his autograph); the brute strength of Dale Atkins off the back of the scrum; the humility of captain Don Hayes; the solid dependability of Warwick Taylor in midfield; the brilliance of wing Craig Green.

To me, these guys were instant heroes and, looking back, they deserved to be, for they were not only great rugby players but also, on the whole, great men. Perhaps most importantly, there was a solidarity about them as a team that was hard to beat. Rightly or wrongly, they reflected everything that was good about my childhood: solid, dependable, occasionally brilliant and yet, if nothing else, decidedly honest.

I'm not sure whether Mum appreciated the beauty of this side. Sure, she saw the boyish good looks of Robbie Deans no doubt and 'that very quick Craig Green who lives around the road' but the skilful boot of Wayne Smith and the classical lines run by Jock Hobbs were lost on her, as they were on most women.

Our family sat in the Number Three Stand (the best place to watch rugby as it was right in the middle) and I embraced it all – the rugby, the atmosphere, the sense of togetherness that comes from baying for British and Irish blood.

As the crowd filled the stands (later than those on the embankment as their seats were secure), I struggled to sit still. Mum noticed my nervousness and put her hand on my shoulder, as if to say that it was only a game, son. I looked at her and smiled, and then looked out to the sea of faces that shared my passion for the red and blacks.

Dad had been coerced into going to the tuck shop. When he returned with pies, Cokes and a couple of bags of pineapple lumps, he was as popular as Margaret Thatcher in Britain after the Falklands War.

As we sat there chomping, sipping and waiting, I looked across at Mum and witnessed a yawn. Not a full-blown yawn, rather a quiet sense of release. What was she thinking? Canterbury were playing the Lions! I stared at her and she looked away, as if embarrassed.

Dad was doing his best to entertain my eight-year-old twin brothers by describing the great matches he had seen at the park. They were listening intently to stories of (former All Blacks) Alex Wyllie, Fergi McCormick and Doug Bruce, and I am sure at their age they would not have realised the full implications of the fact that Dad had actually gone to school with Doug Bruce (I'd had years to think it over . . .).

We were delighted when Canterbury won. Irishman Hugo MacNeill missed a late conversion that would have drawn the match. Canterbury number 8 Dale Atkins and Robbie Deans had storming matches. I felt elated as the referee blew his whistle for the final time and we had beaten the Lions! Yes, *we* had beaten the Lions!

Just after the final whistle, I looked at Mum with a smile that suggested that there was no possible way she couldn't have enjoyed *that*! I mean, come on, Mum! Canterbury had just beaten the Lions in a nail-biter! She smiled, as if to suggest that that wasn't so bad after all!

After surviving the tunnel going the other way (this time with much more shouting of CAN . . . TER . . . BURY . . . and a couple of open cans of beer thrown), we drove home in silence, perhaps celebrating our togetherness as much as the victory.

THE INSPIRATION OF
WILL CARLING

CANTERBURY V. LIONS, 31 MAY 1993

'You cannot be serious?' she said directly.

You cannot be serious asking me whether I am serious, I thought, although dared not say. 'I'll return it in good condition and put petrol in it,' was all I could muster.

'What do you need to go to Leeston for anyway?' she asked, the redness of her cheeks reflecting her anger at my seemingly innocuous request.

'Look, the Lions are training down there and I can afford to miss a lecture,' I said innocently, failing to point out that my light-blue Mini would not have made the 40 kilometres from Christchurch to Leeston.

'So?' she asked firmly, 'Is it imperative that you're there?'

Duh! I mean, come on! Here I was, an honours student in politics (i.e. read plenty of time), with an opportunity to see the Lions train . . . what do you think I should be doing, luv? She was a pretty girl and we were living together but she had no idea when it came to rugby.

My girlfriend didn't like students (she figured they should all have jobs and be out earning real money). She didn't like light-blue Minis that kept breaking down either for that matter.

As for rugby, well, that wasn't amongst her top ten hates but she was no John Kirwan groupie (I did get her a signed picture of Frank Bunce when we were courting, although I suspect that her fascination wasn't because of Bunce's outside break).

I was eventually allowed to borrow the snazzy and dependable red Ford Laser for one afternoon and I drove it to Leeston as though my life depended on it, which in some ways it did.

Leeston isn't London; in fact, it's not even Christchurch. It is, rather, a small country town whose residents appreciate the more basic things in life. Yet the townsfolk know how to look after a touring rugby team, by providing a warm New Zealand welcome, a shower and a hearty feed after training.

This did not make me feel any warmer as I watched the Lions train on this cold Monday afternoon. The thing I noticed first was the redness of the training squad. The red tracksuits made it somewhat difficult to distinguish Rob Andrew from Scott Gibbs and Rory Underwood.

Still, there were some things that were clearly noticeable: Guscott's playful laid-back antics that indicated that he was not taking training or life too seriously; the grunt put into the scrummage by the likes of Richards and Galway; Carling's aloofness.

I knew that Will Carling was England's posterboy, the sturdy public-school midfielder with the dashing good looks who like a royal had begun his career in the army. I knew that he'd fallen in love with a TV presenter and that he'd been hailed as England's saviour after they'd made the final of the World Cup in 1991. In short, he was never going to be a favourite with egalitarian New Zealand.

I watched Carling intently, in my own mind mixing his presence with the idealistic political theories that were being drilled into me at university and the latest Duran Duran song that I'd listened to over and over again on the way south.

I was star-struck. In the 45 minutes I watched Carling lope around Leeston Domain, all my passions for travel and the excitement of a foreign land were symbolised by one man. Although I didn't particularly care for Carling's image in the media, to me he reflected the energy and opportunity of Britain. I wanted travel in my life and I wanted it now.

Being an aspiring journalist, I went over to Carling as he trudged from the training field, his kit less muddy than that of the forwards. It had, it appeared, been a routine day at the office. After introducing myself, I asked for the all-important interview.

'Sure, although can we do it after I've had a shower?' he said in his clipped tones.

What? Weren't you meant to tell me to piss off? Surely if your media image was to be believed you wouldn't have any time? Surely you should be selling shares on the London stock market, organising summer tea in the country house for when you return home in July, or spending time with your glamorous TV presenter partner who's flown over from Australia? Come on, Will, why did you have to be so nice?

So I waited until the English captain had showered before going upstairs in the clubrooms to do the interview. He was gracious, sincere and polite. He looked refreshed after his shower, well groomed, relaxed. He again seemed bloody nice. I didn't need to ask him these questions. I just needed to connect for a few short minutes with someone who, to me, had come to symbolise the thrill of adventure.

I was emotional as I left Leeston Domain, the well-being of the car now less important. That evening, I wrote a piece on Carling that reflected the difference between the man's image in New Zealand and my reality. I dropped the article in to him. I hope he read it and, if he did, I hoped he liked it.

'So how was it?' she asked when I picked her up from work that evening. I didn't know what to say. Should I have shared my awakenings with her, the same person who valued a steady job and a firm income above the adventures of overseas travel?

'It was OK,' I said mildly. 'Thanks for the use of the car,' I continued, moving across to kiss her gently on the cheek. As my lips brushed against her and I felt the tenderness of her skin, smelt her feminine scent and reflected on her day's effort, I realised our relationship would end sooner rather than later.

PART ONE
Made-for-TV Rugby

Rugby football was the best of all our pleasures: it was religion and desire and fulfilment all in one. Most New Zealanders can look back on some game which they played to win and whose issues seemed to them then a good deal more important than a lot that has happened since.

John Mulgan (New Zealand author)

THE BLESSED HERO OF KUROW

Wednesday, 25 February 2004

If I'm going to rediscover rugby's special ethos, then I'm going to need a real hero. A modern-day Sid Going or Grant Batty, if you like. Rugby needs heroes like Americans need apple pie: the models for the posters that young people put up on their walls, the champions who present the right ideals.

In New Zealand, we are currently debating whether sports stars are heroes and whether they should be role models as of right. One argument goes that a talented 19 year old who has arrived on the scene has no moral or social obligation to be a role model. He is a sportsman, not a social do-gooder.

Another argument goes that high-profile sportspeople by their very nature are role models. Professional sportspeople especially have an inherent requirement (often included in contractual form) to act in a way that positively represents their teams and their sport.

The best role models act in an appropriate way instinctively. As if they were born to do what they are doing. They are like artists who realise that their special gift gives them not only opportunities but also responsibilities. The very best role models inspire by being who they are naturally.

The best role models act gracefully on and off the field: poetry in motion when performing; respectful off the field like a ballet dancer tiptoeing through a minefield of journalists, sponsors and hangers-on.

Grace. It doesn't matter whether you are a top sportsperson, artist, dancer or poet. To be great, you have to have grace under pressure. Any modern-day hero must have this essential element.

To be fair, I've only experienced it live a few times: listening to Irish poet Seamus Heaney recite verse was one occasion, hearing Van Morrison play, another. Watching Richard Hugh McCaw throughout the 2004 Super 12 was another example – poetry in motion – and he quickly became a potential hero of mine.

I'm not saying that I haven't seen better rugby players in the southern hemisphere: who could forget David Campese at his best, the athleticism of Michael Jones, the amazing all-round talent that was John Eales. I'd even seen Andrew Mehrtens in 1998 dominate a Super 12 like I thought no player could.

What I'm saying is that during the 2004 Super 12, Richard produced rugby that was as consistently sublime as anything I'd ever seen. There was greatness about his work and yet it seemed that everybody was too busy in the collective to notice.

That's the beauty of rugby, I guess: everyone focuses on the team and the bigger picture rather than the individual. I can understand that but it shouldn't stop fans of all ages having heroes. People can relate to individuals. They can sympathise, remember and respect. We all want to be like individuals of quality.

Before the 2004 Super 12, I'd figured that Frenchman Oliver Magne was the best number 7 in the world. The figure of Magne running with ball in hand was one of the great sights of world rugby. I'd known he was the best in the world for years. I was loyal.

Yet Richard, also athletic, fantastic at the breakdown, one of the best scavengers in the game, is raising the bar. Before matches, he would stride out up and down Jade Stadium by himself, gradually raising the momentum, focusing his mind. It's preparation for his solitary work as an openside.

Once the game begins, he runs at a hundred miles an hour, black headgear firmly attached, socks often down like J.P.R., throwing himself at the opposition, whether on attack or defence. There are no half measures, no ifs or buts when the game ends. Yes, Richard has true grace on the field, grace under pressure.

Yet I want to know whether Richard has grace off the field. In my view, you can't be a hero without having that fundamental togetherness that comes from being a well-rounded person. Graham Mourie had it, Michael Jones as well. It's something more than just getting to the breakdown first and winning the ball for the team.

Before I even have a chance to say 'I'm here to see . . . ' one warm late February afternoon, Richard bounds over, dressed in training gear. He looks relaxed and, after the pleasantries, we talk.

They love him in his home province of Otago and in Christchurch where he plays. In Auckland, they appreciate his marketability. In Wellington, they accept his status. He says it in a boy-next-door fashion and the New Zealand public loves him for it.

This season he's vice-captain of the Crusaders. Sure to be the All Black number 7 come Test time. He also appears a shoe-in to be the All Black captain at some stage, perhaps as early as 2006. He's a made man and, as we start talking, I feel reverence.

I don't know what it is to begin with but the more we talk, the more it becomes obvious: it's the way he combines old-fashioned values (respect, tradition, giving your guts) with new-age reality (marketing, media interviews, satisfying sponsors).

It's a simple combination, sure enough, but one he appears to have mastered. I know it's got something to do with Kurow (in North Otago where he's from) but I'm not sure how.

It's reassuring to think that Kurow can produce a top-class All Black. Although Richard only grew up there, there is something innocent and pure about the notion. It's perhaps a New Zealand sporting version of the American Dream but no less important to a legion of rugby fans in a land where rugby is religion.

'I played for North Otago representative teams and then went on to Otago Boys' in Dunedin,' Richard says, doing his best not to yawn. 'I made the first XV there for a couple of years and then came to Lincoln [University] to do a degree.

'My old man went to Lincoln and it was always something that I was interested in. If rugby was going to happen for me, it was going to happen in Otago or up here. I had to put rugby out of the equation, although there was a rugby scholarship at Lincoln that helped me with the fees. As it turned out, it's probably the best thing that's happened to me.'

A middle-aged female colleague in my office has a huge poster of Richard displayed on her wall. She's like some star-struck teenager. She tells me she would prefer the real thing. I don't doubt her sincerity. Members of the opposite sex love the way he moves, the way he looks and the fact that he almost leaves part of his soul on the track.

'Yeah, it does worry me sometimes,' he says of the attention, 'but you can't let yourself get affected by it. It's a cliché but you're only as good as your last game and that's the way I'm trying to approach it. Sure, it's nice to see good things written about you but you have to remember that there will be times when things won't be so good.

'There are many, many examples around the world of players taking too much for granted and paying the price. Luckily, I have plenty of mates outside of rugby who keep me grounded.'

Still, he's not your typical rugby player. He's nearly finished a university degree in agriculture and also has his pilot's licence. A former professor of his had suggested that he could have become a Rhodes Scholar had he so chosen.

He tells me he was studying until recently but decided to put it on hold because he wasn't doing himself justice. 'It was cutting into my time when I should have been doing things like recovery and seeing physios.

'It just became a hassle and I thought that there was no point in doing either of them half-cocked. You only get one shot at rugby and so I chopped the study for the time being. It was the best thing I could have done.

'Then I went into the NPC campaign in 2002 and all I thought about was the rugby and I didn't get on too good. That's when I realised that having something else to think about was pretty important and that's why I decided to do my pilot's licence.

'It was right at the end of that campaign and we'd missed out on making the semi-finals. I was almost more looking forward to going flying than playing rugby and I realised that that wasn't right. So I took a break from rugby.'

Michael Jones and John Kirwan were Richard's heroes, he tells me, doing his best not to yawn again. 'Then at secondary school it was Josh Kronfeld who caught my imagination.' The same Kronfeld who criticised Richard's selection when he made his debut for the All Blacks against Ireland in Dublin in 2001.

'I was actually away when it came out back home. Someone actually told me about it. I thought, "I'll bloody show you" sort of thing but he later got a message back to me that he had been ambushed and that he wasn't talking about me, that he was talking more generally. Despite that, it didn't really bother me a whole heap. He's probably entitled to say that because he was around for so long.'

We talk about how my journey ends with the Lions tour in 2005. I momentarily stop and contemplate that having been born in 1980, he would only recall the 1993 Lions in New Zealand.

Still, I figure he will be one of the stars of the 2005 series. So I ask him about what he recalls about the Lions. He admits to 'not a whole heap'.

'I was in Australia three years ago with the Under-21s when the Lions were there. We saw all the hype that went with it. I guess playing against the Lions would be a great thing to do and certainly a challenge for any New Zealand rugby player.

'I remember watching them when they came here in 1993, although I can't recall too much about the hype.'

'Do you know many of the northern hemisphere players?' I ask.

'I've met a number of them on a number of occasions and had a yarn with them,' he says. 'To be honest, though, I haven't had a lot to do with them.'

He tells me that if he's come off the field having given his best, he's happy and that if his team's won and he's not performed, he's often grumpy. He says this is selfish but I reckon that can be excused.

'I remember a couple of years ago when we snuck home against the [ACT] Brumbies. I felt I played really poorly and I was more disappointed than I had been on several occasions when we lost.'

Someone's waiting for Richard on the field down below. It looks like a television reporter. Our time is up. We head down the stairs. The small talk is false. Our closeness has not lasted. The media are part of his job and everyone wants to be his friend. Separating the bullshit from the praise is a job requirement.

We talk again a couple of times over the course of the Super 12, mostly about how he's going, nod when we cross paths after matches. The last time we talk under the stands I give him a small box of chocolates as a means of saying thanks for his time. 'Gee, thanks, mate,' he says sincerely.

I've never given anyone I've interviewed a thank-you gift before. Every journalistic bone in my body is disgusted. Yet I know why I've done this. Over the course of a few weeks, Richard has become symbolic of my journey and a role model for the next generation, just like Graham Mourie was for mine.

He can play rugby like God intended and he embraces the sport like New Zealand heroes of yesteryear. He combines the old values with new realities. Perhaps most importantly, he can place the sport in its proper perspective. We all need heroes. Richard has become one of mine.

DOLLARS AND CENTS

Monday, 29 March 2004

If you read the official history, you may learn that Super 12 supposedly evolved out of the South Pacific Championship. That competition, involving teams from New Zealand, Australia and Fiji, was a pre-season competition that had all the atmosphere of an empty paddock.

The competition was relaunched in 1992 as Super 6s and then

expanded to become Super 10s when the South African provincial sides were readmitted to the international fold.

Yet the reality is that Rupert Murdoch and his News Corporation needed a product that they could sell to a public ready for the vigours of professional rugby. If Super 10s had not been created, rugby administrators would quickly have invented it.

Although the competition known as Super 12 as a concept had merit, it was merely a package that could be sold like soap and cream cheese to a public hungry for professional rugby. Whether it had been a saleable success or not depended on whom you spoke to.

Critics in the northern hemisphere suggest that it is powder-puff stuff and that it is mere show and not substance. Players who have participated in it say it is constant physical and mental pressure. I wonder whether there is truth in both views.

Some commentators are saying that the real issue is whether Super 12 is a viable commercial product that is able to keep rugby in the southern hemisphere financially strong. So I trundle along to the Canterbury Rugby Football Union (CRFU) this autumn lunchtime to find some perspective.

The faded red and black carpet has CRFU patterned on it and is a symbol of the province of Canterbury's rich rugby history. I'm standing at the counter of the CRFU offices waiting to be served and I'm filled with nostalgia. It might have something to do with the faded photos of Canterbury teams that line the walls like bridges to the past.

Hamish Riach, chief executive of the CRFU, is a happy man: the Crusaders won last Saturday and the ground was full. I can almost see his thin moustache glisten with satisfaction as a result of the success.

I've known Hamish for more than ten years. He was chief executive of the Selwyn District Council when I had my first job as a reporter with a community newspaper. I'd initially wondered what he knew about rugby before realising that the modern rugby administrator did not need to know a lot.

The CRFU has a joint role: making sure that rugby within its own province is strong, while managing the Crusaders franchise for the other six participating unions. Given that, I wonder what role the franchise has in the scheme of things for the CRFU.

'Super 12 [and the Crusaders] is critically important as we [the CRFU] are a 59 per cent stakeholder in the Crusaders and so it is financially important,' Hamish tells me. 'But it is also aspirational for players and because we have the management contract for the franchise it allows good people to come here and work full time across the whole year and that's really beneficial for the coaching and development of people.'

Super 12 also kept rugby at the forefront of people's minds at a time of year when the weather made night-time rugby still enjoyable.

The Crusaders region, made up of seven unions, has also significantly benefited from the success of the franchise on the field. The Crusaders had won the competition more times than any other franchise and each season the financial spoils had been significant.

In 2003, for example, the Crusaders franchise had made NZ$1.3 million, which had been shared between the provinces on the basis of player registration.

The critics of this system pointed out that while the New Zealand provincial unions that were within a successful franchise benefited financially, those that weren't didn't. The situation was made worse by the fact that the successful franchises tended to remain successful.

It was all well and good my club, Lincoln, receiving a bonus each year the Crusaders did well but what about similar clubs in Poverty Bay, Taranaki and Southland? Why should they be disadvantaged by being part of franchises that had under-performed over the years?

Hamish is well aware of the inequities of the system. A possible alternative, we both agree, is to pool the money into the New Zealand Rugby Football Union (NZRFU) in Wellington and then distribute it by need to the unions.

'What should happen is that Canterbury should pay a decent franchise fee to the NZRFU who own the franchise and then the NZRFU can distribute this [the revenue] on whatever basis they like. The money would then be flowing to where the need is rather than some geographical arbitrary line.'

While Super 12 has prospered, the competition has had a detrimental effect on New Zealand's National Provincial Championship (NPC). Where the kids of my generation aspired to play for Canterbury and Auckland, the new generation wants to play for the Crusaders and the Blues. Hamish tells me, however, that the fortunes of Canterbury rugby remain paramount to the CRFU.

'The bulk of our revenue is still associated with Canterbury rugby,'

Hamish explains. 'There are only 28 Crusaders, while we've got 13,000 players aligned to the Canterbury Rugby Union. And so the fabric of rugby is still very much provincially aligned, as is the revenue.'

That aside, who wanted to watch NPC rugby when the All Blacks were resting in preparation for big money-spinning encounters in the northern hemisphere in November and December?

'I think there is a real danger of that,' Hamish concedes. 'It hasn't been decided yet but what the NZRFU have said so far is that subject to there being adequate All Black games, then they wouldn't be available. So if there are for whatever reason no Tests during the NPC, then the All Blacks will still be available.'

To me, there was no way All Blacks could continue to play NPC and Super 12 rugby on top of a domestic international programme and end-of-year tour to the northern hemisphere. Their bodies and minds wouldn't allow it. Something would have to give and my brain (but not my heart) told me that it would be NPC.

A further frequent criticism of Super 12 is that the quality players in New Zealand are transferring their political allegiances to the five unions where the franchises are based and playing their NPC rugby there.

A good example was Corey Flynn, a talented hooker from the Southland province who, after two seasons playing for the Crusaders, had transferred to Canterbury. The result was that within ten months Flynn was an All Black. Yet had his move benefited Southland and New Zealand rugby?

This worrying trend had been addressed by the NZRFU to some degree, although it had become a complex legal issue involving restraint of trade and monopoly issues. Hamish is adamant that the steps taken by the NZRFU to keep the provinces on an even footing were good for no one.

'What you have to understand is that there is a level of professional rugby that is sustainable and beyond that it isn't. Wales has found that. There is a level of affordability and sustainability and that means that in the current set-up New Zealand has five franchises, which appears sustainable.

'Those five teams have to be based somewhere. If you're a good young player somewhere other than where the base is, you're going to have to be attracted [to go] there.

'It's absolutely inevitable and natural that players are going to be attracted to where the professional sides are based. The fact that these sides are based in New Zealand's biggest cities, where lots of young people are attracted anyway, is also inevitable.'

That aside, is it good for New Zealand rugby to have all of its top players concentrated in five metropolitan areas? The NZRFU had suggested a quota system to balance this uneven distribution.

Hamish says they've got to be careful about what they define as uneven distribution. At the end of the day, over 50 per cent of registered rugby players in New Zealand are in the five big unions anyway. So, he argues, you're fiddling with the distribution if you arbitrarily make players go to a union, such as Southland.

'Does it make sense saying to a young fellow making his way through the ranks, who needs a job or tertiary education, that we're going to send you off to where there is no university? It would be just insanity.

'What you have to do is encourage the players to be able to make choices for their own reasons as to where they want to play rugby. You shouldn't say to someone, "Sorry, we know you're born in Christchurch, we know that you want to go to university, your family is here, but we want you to go to Rotorua." How does that make sense? It doesn't.'

What Hamish is saying is that what the NZRFU has to do is encourage an environment outside the major centres where players want to move. He uses as an example former Canterbury winger Ryan Glover, who transferred to Southland.

'He's got a girlfriend there, he's got a job opportunity, he sees an opportunity to play his rugby there. I say great: a player making a decision for his reasons. He didn't have to be driven out of his own city.'

Critics of Super 12 also claimed that the competition has had a detrimental impact on All Black rugby. That the fundamentals that had made the men in black so dominant for so long were being eroded by the high risk, razzmatazz style of play that attracted the crowds but did not please the purists.

Yet such an explanation overlooked the fact that professionalism was always going to favour the English and the Australians, both of whom had greater player bases and financial resources.

'I think what's happened is that Super 12 has advantaged Australia far more than it has us,' Hamish says, 'because we were already at a very professional level and because it's our national game. English rugby has also benefited and what's occurred is that the gap between the top teams has been evened out by professionalism.

'And then you have to look at what would have happened had New Zealand Rugby not gone professional. Well, every decent player would have gone overseas or gone to [rugby] league. You can't wind back the clock. I feel that New Zealand has made a pretty good fist of it [professionalism].'

True enough, but I point out, however, that since the advent of professionalism dozens of former All Blacks and quality provincial players had still left the country for the lure of yen and sterling anyway.

Just that week, the NZRFU had pooh-poohed the possibility of New Zealanders playing outside of New Zealand playing for the All Blacks. In a move designed to protect the game locally, the union deemed that players had to be part of the system here.

'That [All Blacks playing offshore] would screw the domestic competition more effectively than anything else the union could do,' Hamish says. 'The young aspirational players know that to realise their dreams of a Super 12 contract and of perhaps becoming an All Black they have to do that here. If they can do that in London and Tokyo, there is no reason for them to stay and the lure of overseas experience for a whole lot of money that we could never match would be so great that our domestic competition would be hugely affected.'

I wonder about the reverse: overseas players of the ilk of Brian O'Driscoll, Jonny Wilkinson and Tom Smith playing in the Super 12. Hamish suggests that there is no sign that this will happen and that there would be no gain in having a whole host of Super 12 players who were not eligible for the All Blacks.

'All that would do is prevent someone who is eligible for the All Blacks playing Super 12. The only way I could see that happening is if the whole way that the All Blacks are selected is to change. In other words, to select them from overseas so it didn't matter who played domestically. I think that would be the worst thing that could happen.'

Undoubtedly, the Crusaders have been the competition's most successful franchise. Five titles and seven finals appearances in ten seasons is a terrific record in what is often a brutally physical competition. What's more, the Crusaders have developed a family-like atmosphere that has seen players drafted in from outside the franchise prosper and, in some cases, go on to become All Blacks.

Hamish has been CEO for only three years yet understands why it is that the franchise has been so successful.

'It's about people. Wonderful coaches who have got the best out of some great players and they've been successful. I don't think there's a silver bullet. I think it has been about trying to do everything as well as you can and no acceptance of second best, whether it be on or off the field. It's the same commitment to excellence.'

In other words, it is about promoting old-fashioned values within an environment that is outward looking, professional and realistic about what's commercially required. Getting the mix right (a term often used in the Crusaders) would appear to have been the key to success.

THEATRE OF DREAMS

Friday, 16 April 2004

There is an atmospheric fog that hangs across Eden Park in Auckland reminiscent of midday Mexico City in summer. Coming from Christchurch, it confuses me and makes me feel uncomfortable. I feel as though I'm in the tropics and there is nothing else to do but drink and survive.

Tonight there is no red and black, just blue in differing shades. This is a big city: there are plenty of other things going on in Auckland tonight and the rugby is but one option. It makes the city feel broader but for some reason it also makes me feel more than a touch apprehensive.

I have a ticket to a corporate box that former All Black captain Andy Dalton has generously given to me. Not having been to Eden Park before, I arrive two hours early. I'm like a kid in a candy store and I want to lap up the atmosphere, reflect on the parts of the ground where great rugby events have occurred and somehow connect my past with the present. Yet this all seems fresh and I'm left wondering whether the past ever really happened.

Inside the stadium, I momentarily stop and dwell on the boards that proudly display the names of the winners of the Gallaher Shield (the club championship in Auckland) and Auckland's All Blacks. They are like pathways to the past and I'm now filled with the glories of yesteryear.

I walk out onto the main stand and take an empty front-row pew. The curtain-raiser is between Ponsonby and Marist, arguably Auckland's two most famous clubs. The vast majority of the players are Polynesian, the rugby flamboyant and spirited as a result and never dull. I feel a long way from the more traditional and European Christchurch.

There is a delightful innocence about watching the simplicity of club rugby by myself, as if this was the way it should always be. There are a few spectators littered around the ground, while the odd media person prepares himself for the main game. I enjoy being alone and having time to appreciate the purity that many rugby fans fail to appreciate these days.

An elderly gentleman walking slowly over breaks my isolation. He is initially no threat but then the threat becomes real. 'I hope you're not going to be here long,' he says with a devilish smile, pointing out that my seat has been reserved. I explain myself and we start talking.

Bob Russell watched his first Test at Eden Park in 1930 and has missed only three in the subsequent 74 years. A former serviceman, Bob recalls watching the New Zealand servicemen play rugby against the South Africans during the Second World War.

'There was this huge festival of sport. We played the South Africans at rugby, there was a grid-iron game, they played hardball, while the Egyptian soccer team played the English soccer team.'

Sport, though, was the least of Bob's worries during those years. He'd been a prisoner of war for two years and, after escaping, had walked from the top of Italy to the south, where he had met up with the Canadian troops shortly after they had landed.

Settling back into New Zealand life after the war was not easy. 'It was the strangest thing,' Bob reflects as we sneak sly glances at the club rugby, 'as it took me a long time to get it [the war] out of my system. We should have had counselling back then.'

'Counselling wasn't the thing to do back then?' I ask sincerely.

'No, there was no such thing. I had something of a breakdown and my father must have rung up the army and said, "Come and get my son, he's in a bad way, you'd better get him into hospital," and so I was taken to the army hospital, where I spent a month under supervision. After that I came right.'

Bob's passion for rugby, in particular the Ponsonby club, runs deep. He'd played for the club as a boy and had followed the club ever since. It had been a passionate love affair. 'I never used to miss a club game but recently I had an operation on my right leg, which makes it difficult moving about. They also now play at Western Springs and it makes it hard walking over there.'

Given that Bob has front-row seats, it is not surprising that he has season tickets at Eden Park for both the cricket and the rugby. Bob admits rugby has continued to evolve.

'The positioning of the game has changed,' Bob reflects, as Ponsonby kick a penalty. 'You will probably see it tonight: the Blues full-back playing in the back line. The ball is kicked through and there is nobody at home. In our day, the full-back was a full-back.'

Bob likes Super 12 but feels that to some degree the competition is losing its way. Attendances, he figures, are an increasing problem. 'You'll probably see about 28,000 here tonight. The last time it was a day game and the people loved it.'

'You like the day games?' I ask.

'Oh yes,' Bob replies. 'I have two boys who come to the footy, too. They just say they love footy in the daytime. I'm not sure what the players think about it. It's television, isn't it? They demand it.'

'Do you think all this razzmatazz hurts the All Blacks' style of play?' I ask.

'Not really,' Bob replies, looking back at the club rugby. 'The players are there. I think you will find that the ability of the players is just as good as it was three or four years ago; in some cases there are better footballers around. I don't know how long you have been following it . . . '

'Not as long as you,' I reply as Ponsonby run in yet another try. Bob laughs loudly.

'Is the spirit of rugby still alive?' I ask.

'I can remember coming to rep and club games and the players before the match would have their jeans on. After the match, they would be nicely dressed with their blazers on. That sort of thing hasn't changed and it does a lot for rugby. I love it [rugby] and it will stay with me for ever.'

With that, I get to my feet, shake Bob's hand and thank him for his time and, perhaps, his inspiration. If ever I needed proof that rugby was still more than just about dollars and cents, then I had found it in Bob's passion.

I then retreat to the corporate box. Winding my way to the right box feels like, I would suspect, entering a brothel: plush corridors, service people walking quickly with their heads down, voices echoing off Mediterranean-coloured walls, a sense of expectation.

I quietly, shyly enter the box, consciously aware that I am a guest and don't really deserve to be here. Andy Dalton greets me and gets me a drink. The box is situated around the halfway mark and as I look out onto the field a thousand TV memories now strike me. It now feels like something akin to a homecoming and I finally start to relax.

The guests are, not surprisingly, corporate types, the chat naturally formal. Yet it is decidedly pleasant: the food and drink divine, the atmosphere civil. I feel conspicuous yet this all melts away like snow when the rugby starts.

The rugby itself is bizarre: the Blues are unable to hold onto the ball and by half-time are virtually out of the match as the Stormers savour the unpredictable nature of the home side.

Surprisingly, I have little sympathy – I am from Christchurch after all. So I sip my second orange juice of the evening, reflect on the roast meal that I've just savoured, chat intellectually to the former All Black captain sitting beside me and conclude that life isn't too bad.

As the match draws to an uneventful end, former All Black Alan Whetton comes over and sits beside me. Alan, who works for the same company as Andy Dalton, had been one of the stars of the 1987 World Cup-winning squad. Like everyone at Eden Park, he is shocked at what he is seeing. Still, his indulgence has made the night more bearable for him.

'Entertainment, that's what it's about these days,' Alan says reflectively, sounding like Spike Milligan. 'The excitement, the intensity is still there but when it comes to wins against losses maybe it is not as directly decisive as it was in my day when winning was everything.'

I look across Eden Park thoughtfully and ask Alan whether the glitz that is such a part of Super 12 is actually good for the All Blacks' style of play. Alan agrees that rugby in his day was more structured.

'Test match football is Test match football. We weren't playing this type of football. Rugby in my day was more structured, more patterned and so it was easier to fall into a team situation, as the pattern didn't change much. Obviously this sort of rugby is more erratic.'

'Would you have loved to have been part of this sort of rugby?' I ask.

'I can't comment on that. I mean, I was in a different era. Now money is involved, the players are bigger and stronger and faster, and you have to weigh that up against results.'

'If you had to make some changes to Super 12 rugby, what would those changes be?' I ask.

'I don't think I would change it, I just think it's the nature of the style of rugby. My only bugbear is that the consistency is not there. Time and time again we don't see that enough in the teams and it's a great shame.'

I wonder whether the lack of consistency was to do with the lack of stimulation some of the players have outside rugby.

'When I was playing, you would look forward to the two hours of training when you could forget about work,' Alan says, looking across the field. 'You had experience in the real world. I'm not sure the players of today have that.'

'How do you change that?' I ask.

'You can't. That's the nature of professional sport . . . that's the environment of professional sport and that's what happens when you bring money into sport.'

Alan says that, that aside, New Zealand rugby is in good heart with the Under-19s, Under-21s, the Sevens and the Super 12 sides generally doing well on the world stage. Still, the number of players making the step up from under-age representative sides to international rugby is a concern.

'We have to ask ourselves why players aren't making the leap from Under-19s and Under-21s to the senior level? Why aren't we dominating like we were in the past? I think money has a lot to do with it and the resources that the other unions, the likes of England, have invested. Whether we like it or not, we are now competing against countries with vast populations and vast wealth.'

We finish our conversation as the final whistle blows and I contemplate making my way through the horrendous Auckland traffic like a snail in a 100-metre dash. As I do, I wonder whether in 20 years' time today's crop of players will be as balanced as Andy and Alan are.

THE HOUSE OF RON

Saturday, 24 April 2004

It has been a long drive down from Christchurch but eventually the hilly northern suburbs of Dunedin appear like a beacon in the night. After struggling to find Carisbrook, I park my car and reflect briefly on one of New Zealand's premier sporting stadiums. It doesn't look that premier and reminds me of what Jade Stadium used to be like in Christchurch when it was the innocently named Lancaster Park: well worn, historic and, to be honest, out of date.

It is three hours before the Highlanders take on the Hurricanes in what the marketing people are describing as a benefit of sorts for Tony Brown, who is off to the greener (and richer) pastures of Japan. Brown has come to epitomise the spirit of the Highlanders: dogged, determined and gutsy.

Ron Palenski, chairman of the Otago Rugby Football Union and perhaps New Zealand's finest sportswriter, meets me at four o'clock at the unspectacular entrance to the union's headquarters on Burns Street. It looks like a trade union's headquarters and if you didn't know it was here, you could quite easily pass it without blinking an eye.

Ever since the publication of *Graham Mourie: Captain*, the biography of one of the finest All Black captains, I'd admired Ron. I'd devoured his columns in *The Dominion*, purchased his books religiously and agreed with most of what he'd written. He made rugby a higher art form and I respected him for it.

Here, amongst the Speights memorabilia and the manly stench of Otago rugby, I set about interviewing a man who had seen more rugby than most. It's always difficult interviewing journalists. They know the procedure and can evaluate your questions. Still, the upside is that they always know what you require.

'This is the ninth season of Super 12. Do you believe it has been a success per se?' I ask nervously, testing the waters like a pupil interviewing his master.

'I think there are two aspects to Super 12,' Ron answers reflectively, authoritatively.

'One is the type of rugby and the other is the type of entertainment it provides, and I think it has been very successful in terms of an entertainment package, certainly from a television and spectator point of view. It provides fast, spectacular rugby and it helps that it is played at this time of year when the grounds are hard and in the few day games you get the sun is shining. In that respect, it has been a big success.

'But I am not convinced the quality of rugby is sufficient to build a Test team on it. A lot of the play is too loose. Players play differently in Super 12 than they do in Test rugby and I think we have been shown that quite often by the northern hemisphere.

'Whereas the old system of clubs, NPC and Tests is a much better system of developing internationals, you can't turn the clock back. Super 12 is here, it's an integral part of the New Zealand Union's renegotiation with Newscorp and so it is here to stay and you just have to manage it the best way you can.'

It was indicative of this generally held view that new All Black coach Graham Henry had called for an All Black trial at the completion of the Super 12. The obvious connotation was that Super 12 was not appropriate pre-Test preparation for the All Blacks.

Northern hemisphere critics – Stephen Jones the most prominent – regularly suggested that the Super 12 was a major factor in what was commonly referred to as a deterioration of playing standards in the southern hemisphere. Does Ron agree?

'I know what Stephen's views are and I've discussed them with him several times. I must say that he writes like a lot of journalists: for effect. He sometimes writes things much more strongly than he would actually debate them in person.'

I push Ron to make a comparison between Super 12 and, say, the Heineken Cup. This on a semi-finals weekend in the Heineken Cup which sees two French clubs, an Irish province and an English club compete.

He says that regardless of how you look at it, the Super 12 teams are hybrid sides and don't naturally find an affinity with the public. That, he reckons, is best illustrated in Australia, where commentators talk about Wellington or Otago playing in the Super 12.

'The advantage Britain has is that they don't play on a regional basis and so it's all based on club rugby and all the clubs, except for the Scottish ones, have a long history and tradition that crowds readily identify with, just the same way as crowds here identify with an Otago or a Wellington or a Southland.

'In terms of rugby, it depends on what you want. I've seen Heineken Cup games that are played on grounds that New Zealand grounds used to be like, mudbaths, and the rugby is just appalling. Equally, I've seen games that you could have said were transplanted out of the Super 12. I think it is largely determined by the conditions.

'Also, because the Brits play in so many different competitions, sometimes the games are absolutely meaningless in terms of where they are on a points table or players deciding that they can afford, whether consciously or subconsciously, to drop a game, and [as a result] the quality of rugby suffers. Equally, the coaches will not run out their best team for every game, as they have to protect their players.'

I wonder out loud whether it is only a matter of time before some of the stars of the northern hemisphere start appearing for Super 12 sides. Gregor Townsend was playing for the Sharks this season, while Brian O'Driscoll had expressed an interest in playing for the Crusaders.

Yet while the prospect of seeing some of the best northern hemisphere players in action was appetising, there had been debate in New Zealand as to the impact this would have on the local game.

The NZRFU introduced a rule to the effect that overseas players were prohibited but then made a U-turn and allowed exceptions. So, for example, if union officials could state a case that there were no other wings in the country up to the required standard, then they could get an exemption. This normally resulted in a Polynesian flyer being signed.

'I disagree with unions bringing in players from Australia or South Africa to bolster their ranks during the NPC,' Ron says. 'What is that doing for their local rugby? So no, I wouldn't like to see Brian O'Driscoll playing here unless he was playing in the green of Ireland or the red of the Lions.'

I wondered about the impact of Super 12 rugby on the club competition in a place like Dunedin that had amongst its ranks such famous New Zealand clubs as University, Southern and Zingari-Richmond.

The problem appeared twofold. First, with up to six Super 12 games each weekend, the public was choosing to stay home and watch the professionals and, second, the nation's best players were hardly ever seen playing for their clubs.

'Super 12 is sometimes just a convenient whipping boy,' Ron says thoughtfully. 'I think Super 12 also does a lot of good for rugby in that it brings people to games who aren't committed rugby supporters. I don't think it necessarily distracts from club rugby, as most of the Super 12 games are at night and club games are in the afternoon. The hardcore will still go to both.

'From a club point of view, one negative impact is that during the Super 12 they only get their star players back when they are recovering from injury or something like that and that can be disruptive to what a club is trying to do. The clubs only get their players back for any length at the end of Super 12, assuming the players don't go on to the All Blacks or other national sides.'

Clubs, in Ron's view, have to move with the times in the sense that they have to realise that the halcyon days of last century when club games attracted large crowds on Saturday afternoons are long gone.

Despite this, no one at club level was complaining about the revenue that Super 12 rugby brought in to the city. Ron says that no study has been conducted on the impact that Super 12 has had on the Dunedin economy, although studies of the impact of Test rugby in the city have been carried out.

'Super 12 here is like rugby at any time: if your team is winning it has a bigger impact than when it's not winning. So 1999, for example, when the Highlanders hosted the final, was like a Test match in terms of the economic impact. Whereas this year and most other years is nothing like that.'

Although the incomes and haircuts of the players had changed down the years, to Ron the heart and soul of the individuals who played the game at an elite level have not changed one iota.

'Have they changed as people? I don't think so. I wasn't around in 1905 but I imagine the All Blacks were pretty much the same then as they are now in terms of being fit young men, being very good at what they do, being committed to what they do, conscious that they were playing not just for their country but for their teammates.

'I would challenge anyone to go into a team's dressing-room before a big game and see the players and say that the spirit of rugby has diminished. It hasn't at all.'

We finish our interview there and I leave the sparse offices of the Otago Rugby Union overwhelmed by the experience. Ron was present at some of the most memorable moments of my rugby childhood and I could almost smell his passion for the sport I loved. Role models, players or otherwise, should never be underestimated.

THE HONEST CAPTAIN

Sunday, 25 April 2004

I awake sheepishly in an expensive hotel room in Dunedin. It's Anzac Day – the day citizens Down Under stop and remember those who have fought for their country. My mind is on my grandparents and their sacrifices. I know I should be home paying my respects. Still, there is rugby to watch and interviews to do.

Last night, I went to the pub and watched the first half of the Crusaders–Bulls match in Christchurch. With the Crusaders safely ahead, I'd then walked down to Carisbrook, where I saw the Highlanders outclass the Hurricanes. It wasn't the match of the century. Far from it. The home side had, however, come away with a gutsy win.

Although the victory had pleased the locals, it had left me cold and without a bed for the night. When I eventually found one, I tuned in to see the Waratahs pip the Brumbies in the dying seconds in Sydney in what was arguably the match of the competition. I wished I'd been in Sydney, not cold, damp Dunedin.

This morning is icy clear. I find Logan Park easily enough and beneath rows of student flats and the almost reverent hush of Sunday quiet, I eventually find the Highlanders' training base.

I'm here to interview Anton Oliver. After making myself known to manager Des Smith, I am offered make-your-own coffee and the opportunity to sit in the team room and wait. It is an environment of positive vibe: 'unity', 'domination', 'defiance', 'respect for tradition', 'honesty' and 'trust' are emblazoned on the walls of the team room like William Wallace battle chants.

Half-back Jimmy Cowan relaxes by watching a replay of last night's match. Wing Aisea Tuilevu surfs the Internet. There is a feeling of quiet satisfaction as I sip my coffee and wait patiently. It was obviously a good night at the office for the boys.

Showered, Anton appears wearing jeans and a brown T-shirt. He too appears relaxed and satisfied. I'm looking forward to talking with him. *Really talking*, not powder-puff bullshit that you get normally from rugby players. He takes me to a room that looks like it's used for police interviewing: barren, minimalist and unoccupied. Too formal for a Sunday morning.

Anton's is an interesting story. The son of an All Black, some say he tries as hard as he can to be different from his father. Still, it must have been a no-win situation for him: if he succeeded, it was because of his genes. If he didn't, he would be seen as a failure.

'Early on, when I was about 15, it was happening quite a bit,' Anton says, looking me in the eye. 'You could see people stare at you. I decided to turn that into a positive. If I've got to be the son of Frank Oliver and people are looking at me, then that's quite good, as people are looking at me straight away and I don't have to do anything to impress them.'

'It must have been worse for your brothers?' I say.

'Far worse for my brothers. It's now a son of or a brother of. They don't have an identity at all, poor bastards!' Anton reflects.

Anton came to Dunedin to study for a health sciences degree at Otago University. He fitted right into the student scene, managing effectively the mix of study and rugby.

'It's a really interesting culture. Most of the student flats are situated in one area and as a result there is one concentrated mass of people all the same age, all doing the same thing. It's great.'

Study has always been important for Anton. He's ended up with degrees in physical education and finance. The last degree took him a while – fitting it in between Super 12, NPC and All Black commitments. Anton says it wasn't difficult being a virtual celebrity from the first day he stepped foot on campus.

'Everyone knows you. I remember when I was first at Varsity, Danyon Loader [double Olympic swimming champion] was rocking round just after he'd won his medals. Everyone was so cool that they didn't want to blow cover. I really enjoy that anonymity of university.'

As he has now finished university, I wondered whether Anton was tempted to leave the nest that was Dunedin for the heady commercial lights of Auckland or Wellington.

'I've had offers but I've never taken them. Dunedin is quite restricted in some ways. After a while, all your mates go, either touring around the world or doing something exotic, while I'm still here. It doesn't feel like I've accomplished anything. Then equally so you've got to say that you've just got to get off your arse: there is heaps of cool stuff to do here, especially in Central Otago.'

Anton's career had largely followed that of Sean Fitzpatrick. They'd been big boots to fill. While it was unrealistic to expect Anton's career to replicate Fitzpatrick's, I wondered whether Anton had felt pressure in following the career of a legend.

'It was probably always going to be difficult for me. I was never going to play 90-odd Tests and there was never going to be another Fitzy. Being young and impressionable, I wanted to display some of the traits that he had.'

Anton didn't have a lot to do with Fitzpatrick, the pair appearing together on only two tours. 'I was so off the pace,' Anton laughs. 'There were three hookers: me, Norm Hewitt and Sean. I wasn't very forthcoming to him either, so I guess it is a two-way street.'

'I guess you were competition?' I say.

'I guess so. That was the way he thought – self-preservation. That was why he was so good. Even though there was no way I was competition for him at that stage.'

While Fitzpatrick's career had up until the end been largely injury-free, Anton had ruptured an Achilles tendon in 2002. The injury saw Rueben Thorne establish himself as All Black captain and Anton struggle to make up lost ground. Did he feel as though his destiny had been taken away from him?

'No, I think it was given to me. That was my destiny. I have learnt a lot about myself during that time away. I'm incredibly thankful. For my rugby destiny it wasn't so good but for me personally it was tremendously fulfilling.'

'Did it change you as a person?' I ask. 'Did it make you more balanced?'

'It made me more centred. There was a lot of shit going on in my brain that I hadn't addressed. I was able to put it into compartments that I was able to sift through and understand. That break was the first time I was able to think about things.

'Rugby is a bit like a fucking circus. You pack up, you go to another game, you pack up . . . you don't know who you are after a while. I've played 97 games for the Highlanders . . . fuck knows where they have gone! I've got no idea. It's worrying when you start to forget whole seasons. It was about time that I was forced to redress not only what I'd done and where I'd been but also who I was now and where do I want to go and what do I want to do.'

Anton is prepared to say what he thinks. It makes him refreshing but not always the flavour of the month. The previous season, he'd almost led a player revolt against Highlanders coach Laurie Mains. The new ways had appeared to clash with the old.

'I've gone through the whole resentment, anger, fury stage. Just sad about the reality of stuff. The thing that will be lasting on me is the intensity of the cynicism about a lot of stuff in rugby these days – media, sponsors, coaches. It has moved away from what I thought was great about rugby.'

'You won't have a future in administration?' I ask rhetorically.

Anton bursts into laughter. 'That's what the guys say – they call me a fish head because I can't keep my beak out of the issues. Perhaps if I have children I might cut the oranges or do the jerseys if they want to play rugby.'

I ask Anton about his omission from the All Blacks, Tri-Nations and World Cup squads in 2003. It appeared to me that not only had he had to deal with the personal pain of being dropped but also the public reaction. It can't have been easy.

'I didn't want to go out in public at all,' Anton says honestly, for just a moment taking time to find the right words.

'I just wanted to crawl into a hole and wallow in self-pity for a while. I thought, "Fuck, I've got nothing to hide. I'll just say what I think. I don't hate anyone. I'll have to be guarded with what I say as I don't want to say anything that is going to be harmful to other people or me."

'But people were great and if they came up to me and were being kind and friendly, why couldn't I take the time to do the same to them? That said, all the speculation in the media was tough. The whole nation knows that you are getting fired.'

'But you're not *really* getting fired, are you?' I ask.

'Well, I was in the job and then I was out. If that's not getting fired, what is it?'

'Well, the All Blacks are the best team,' I reply.

'Let's put it in context: I was in the best category for seven years and so I consider myself to be the best. So when I'm not there, I'm fired, I'm out.'

'So how motivated are you to make it back?' I ask.

'It was very strong to make it back into the World Cup squad. When I didn't make that, I went really downhill. I'd played some really good footy at the start of the NPC and at the end it was getting a bit much . . . '

'What about this year?'

'Because I've been captain of the Highlanders this year, it [the All Blacks] hasn't been a huge focus.'

Anton is contracted to the NZRFU until the end of the season. If he doesn't make the All Blacks in 2004, he may be tempted to look elsewhere.

'I don't know what it would mean to be an All Black now,' Anton says. 'I haven't been part of the set-up for the last two years, really. I feel a bit abstracted from it.'

'So what priority does rugby play in your life now?' I ask.

'Priority in terms of what?' Anton asks.

'Would you put it number one priority?' I say, ducking the question to my question.

'No,' Anton replies.

'Where would it rank?'

'I've never really thought about that . . . Rugby is a vehicle for the things that are most important in my life. That's like continually seeking new stuff, being challenged and questioned and exposing myself to new experiences and challenges. Because I've done so much of that, it can't actually give me much more of that. I've been to South Africa 17 times!'

'I guess the reality is that you are good at it [rugby] and people do what they are good at,' I suggest.

'Yeah, that's right,' Anton answers. 'The way I prioritise my life wouldn't be in terms of a functionality thing like rugby, doing dishes, playing guitar. Things that are imbued inside that.'

Which is maybe partly why Anton is so honest with his public comments. While other captains rolled out cliché after cliché, Anton was normally insightful and, sometimes, controversial. Had that been held against him?

'It does in some quarters. Every now and again I say something that people don't like. In this country, we often espouse honest, straight talking. We really don't. You actually say what you think and you back it up and people then say, "He's rocking the boat" and "What did he say that for?"'

I keep harking back to Anton being an All Black again. It may be obsessing me more than him.

'It would be kind of fairy-taleish if I got back in again, it really would, but I am not going to have my life ruled by selections of teams and things like that. At the end of the day, it is trivial.

'I don't want to be 70 and think to myself, "Oh, I didn't make that team." It's just not my destiny to be worried about that. When I finish with rugby, I'm just going to close the chapter in that book and put it away. I won't be commentating on TV3! I don't want to be defined as a rugby player.'

'So how do you want to be defined?' I ask, intrigued.

'I'm not too concerned about how people want to define me but it's how I want intrinsically to be defined. I want to stretch the boundaries. At the moment, there are not too many levels in rugby where I can grow from.'

'But how do you walk away from something that has been such a big part of your life?' I ask.

'You walk away because you have to continue to grow as a person. You don't want to live other people's dreams. That's what other people want you to do. I'm not doing this for you, I'm doing this for me and the team.'

'But that's why you get the benefits from it?' I suggest. 'Everyone lives their dreams *through* you. You get the benefits from that: the adoration, the people lining Carisbrook after the game.'

'Yeah, but that doesn't do it for me. I like the little things: getting anonymous letters from people who say amazing things. Signatures and all that is great, women and all that is meaningless, but that's not what makes me tick. It's going to the fish and chip store and finding that you have an extra piece of fish that you didn't order, the butcher who looks after you with a few extra sausages – things like that are quite special. That's people being nice.'

Anton continues on that theme and tells me that the debt he owes to rugby is huge.

'Rugby has given me everything. It has given me a large chunk of my friends, it's made me the person I am through the experiences I've had, through the highs and lows, wins and losses, meeting people and sharing stuff. I don't think I would have ever mixed with Fijian, Samoan and Tongan cultures as much. Establishing connections where I can go and stay in their little villages where they don't have power has been really good.

'Obviously rugby has given me money and financial security but money to me is just the opportunity to do other things that other 28 year olds perhaps couldn't do, like cruise around the world for six months and not worry about money.'

'How would you like to be remembered – as a player and as a person?'

I ask. I'm not writing Anton's obituary but it seems like the perfect question to wrap up a wide-ranging and insightful conversation.

'Respected,' Anton immediately replies. 'As a player by my peers and as a person. Respect doesn't change from the Middle Ages to now. It's an enduring quality.'

It is not hard to respect Anton, as to me he fits the mould of what a good rugby player should be: thoughtful, dedicated, determined. Far from a New Zealand stereotype in rugby's professional age.

OLD HEROES

Thursday, 29 April 2004

I've read somewhere that someone – I think it might have been Willie John McBride – said that when he was playing, the coach was the thing the players used to get between the hotel and the ground.

Of course, the game has moved on from those days. Still, you've got to wonder whether the game has been made more complicated than it really is.

Coaches to me often get something of a bum rap. If their side win, the players get all the credit; and if they lose, the coach is normally shown the door. Although this is not unique to rugby, you have to wonder about the justice of it all.

When I was growing up, Alex Wyllie was the coach of Canterbury. A big gruff former All Black, Wyllie told his players that there were only two excuses for missing training: a death in the family or docking on the farm. In this politically correct age, that comment would have been considered discriminatory against townsfolk.

Despite his image, Wyllie was surprisingly modern in his approach. Tactically, he was underrated, while he had a homespun method of working out which players to needle and which to leave alone. He also knew when his side needed to relax and when they needed a jolly good flogging.

Robbie Deans was one of Wyllie's troops and as they were from the same club, he knew the man better than most. They even used to farm in the same area of North Canterbury and drink beer at the Omihi pub.

Wyllie and Deans are, in their own individual ways, symbolic of the changes that have taken place in coaching. I'd known Robbie since around 1994, when he coached the Canterbury Country side. It was clear then that he was destined for bigger things and that this was only a stepping stone.

I'd always respected Robbie. He'd been a star of that successful 1982–85 Canterbury side and as a kid I'd put a poster of him up on my wall. As a young journalist, I'd impressed him when, on a Country tour I was reporting on, I'd quickly named Paul Mitchell as the manager of the 1983 All Blacks tour of England and Scotland (you remember these things).

Robbie had coached Canterbury from 1997 to 2000 and been manager of the Crusaders in 1998 and 1999 before taking over the helm in 2000. He'd led the franchise to three titles and two other finals appearances. Robbie had also been assistant coach to the All Blacks during John Mitchell's reign. When Mitchell was deposed in late 2003, Robbie went with him. No one was better placed to comment on how rugby had evolved.

As a coach, Robbie, like the Crusaders generally, encompasses the appropriate blend of professionalism and old-fashioned values. If there is a reason why he has been successful then I reckon this is it.

'We go to great lengths [with the Crusaders] to try and recreate an environment that is effectively amateur in its outlook and that [allows] people [to] derive the same satisfaction from the same things we did,' Robbie says.

'The reality is that in the long run, in terms of how you enjoy your experiences in the game, it has got nothing to do with the money. It's the experiences that make it up and what you earn from those experiences is totally irrelevant.

'If players ever get to the stage where they think of what they are being paid for the actions they do, then they will be as good as history, because the guy that is motivated through being part of something bigger than himself is going to be the better player.'

Fair enough, but surely loyalty is more difficult for coaches these days? After all, coaches often have to make the tough calls. This season, Robbie had dropped Canterbury favourite Andrew Mehrtens from the Crusaders' starting line-up for much of the Super 12.

'That's not really changed,' Robbie replies coyly. 'That [selection] has always been the domain of the coach, because whether you like it or not, you do establish bonds. In the amateur era as well, players came and went and I would suggest that the turnover wouldn't be too dissimilar in the professional era, so that's one of the challenging areas for coaches.

'That's where you've got to be motivated by the right reasons in the decisions that you make and consistent in your delivery, because there is the possibility of being clouded by peripheral issues, such as livelihood or whatever.'

As he had played for Canterbury between 1979 and 1990, and been an All Black between 1983 and 1985, I wonder whether Robbie saw any further similarities between the game that he played and the one he now coaches?

Surely the games were diametrically opposite? To be honest, I didn't see much similarity between the game I watched as a kid in the 1980s and the game I'm watching these days. Heck, even the name of the stadium in Christchurch had changed.

'I guess I was lucky in that my experiences in the game in terms of the group of players that I played with and a large extent of the coaching I experienced wasn't that dissimilar,' Robbie says quietly.

'Expansiveness was encouraged, involving every player, and that's where we are now. You just can't hide on the field of play. If you have a weakness in your skill-set, teams will find it and persecute you. Particularly through the early 1980s, we were encouraged to get involved and use the skills that we had. To that end, the game isn't that dissimilar.

'The biggest distinction is obviously the ability of players to prepare to play. They can now dedicate themselves to prepare to play. The best evidence of that is in the body shapes. They are bigger, faster and stronger, and the impact is greater. In terms of the methods of the game, the principles are similar.'

A part of me lamented the fact that players of yesteryear were now sitting back and watching their successors receive the sort of salaries that they could only have dreamed of. I felt particularly sad for the players who had missed out on professionalism by only a few years. Surely they would be kicking themselves at not only the salaries but also the opportunity to train and play full time and, perhaps, reach their playing potential.

Robbie had been lucky to some degree: he was earning a living out of rugby. Undoubtedly, his playing exploits had proved useful in helping him reach his coaching goals. Still, he was probably being paid less than many of his players.

'I didn't have a choice,' Robbie replies when I ask him whether he would have preferred to have played in his era or now, 'and I certainly don't have any regrets. In fact, a comment was made to me just yesterday by an ex-player who had the good fortune to go offshore and ply his trade. He implied to me that perhaps I was unlucky that I didn't have that opportunity.

'I don't see it that way at all. I see myself as being hugely fortunate to have played when I played and to have had the experiences that I had, and in many ways I have had the best of both worlds as I have seen the transition from amateur to professional. It's been enriching, really, to see both sides.'

Enriching, too, for his family. Robbie, like most professional coaches, has a family that shares with him the ups and downs and peculiarities of professional sport. They undoubtedly see not only the good times but also the heartache and stress.

Robbie agrees that the families go through the highs and lows with the players and coaches. A technique that he has used to remain balanced is to try and make a clear division between work and home life.

In other words, whether the Crusaders win or lose that weekend, after the game is over, it's over. It allows him some sanity, he tells me, while it also gives him balance and allows him to put the occasional loss into perspective.

It's particularly important at this time in the season when the Crusaders (more often than not) prepare for semi-finals rugby. For most franchises, making the semi-finals would be regarded as a success. For the Crusaders, this is as standard as mud in winter.

It all seems a long way away from the days when I used to stand in the kids' enclosure at Lancaster Park and watch Robbie win matches for Canterbury. Professionalism came at a cost and maybe that was rugby's loss of innocence. Maybe, like the sport in general, I've lost mine.

IN SEARCH OF RUEBEN

Tuesday, 18 May 2004

The week leading up to the Super 12 final is, in Christchurch at least, akin to getting married for the second time: you know that you should be excited but it is proving extremely difficult as you have been here before and you know it could all end in tears.

The Crusaders are taking on the Brumbies in Canberra. This was the bookies' bet at the start of the season: the two sides had met twice in the final of Super 12, once in Canberra, once in Christchurch, with the New Zealanders winning both times.

I'm at Rugby Park in Christchurch again and, to be frank, I don't really want to be here. I should be at work rather than trying to obtain an exclusive quote. Still, I vow to get in and out as quickly as I can. The overcast wintry weather might have something to do with my pessimism. The last media session of the campaign is being conducted and I'm on the lookout for Rueben Thorne.

The Crusaders' captain personifies the Kiwi personality: strong, quiet, a person who lets his actions do the talking. Yet for some reason many New Zealanders have failed to embrace him.

Still, I admire Rueben. Not only is he a no-nonsense type of player but he's invaluable in the sense that he makes players around him look good. I know he's one of the reasons why Richard McCaw has been outstanding this Super 12. He also seems oblivious to the hoopla that so characterises modern rugby. His answers at press conferences may not be enlightening but I would follow him over the trenches.

Throughout this Super 12, I've often stared at Rueben during press conferences and sensed his vulnerability. I've only been brought back to reality by the realisation that he's a professional athlete who has spent the last 80 minutes pushing his body to the limit. That aside, Rueben would be the ideal best friend: honest, sincere, solid.

There is no sign of Rueben yet. A dozen journalists are, however, interviewing Daniel Carter, the current wonder boy. 'What do you visualise before you kick the ball?' one of the female journalists asks.

'Just the ball sailing through the posts,' Carter replies deadpan.

Bored, I lean against the signage, turn, and there Rueben is! Sadly there will be no one-on-one interviews today: not surprisingly everyone wants to interview the captain. He's quickly changed into his training gear and looks oblivious to the waiting media and their questions.

'Is the captaincy issue of the All Blacks a distraction for you at the moment?' is the first question Rueben is asked.

'It's the last thing I'm thinking about at the moment – I'm just focusing on the Brumbies,' Rueben replies, as if he'd heard the question too many times before.

Rueben is asked all the obvious questions: what the weather in Canberra will be like, the strengths of the Brumbies, the tactics on Saturday. I wonder how rugby fans would have learnt anything from either the questions asked or the answers given.

'This is your sixth visit to a Super 12 final. Has anything changed in your preparation to the build-up at this stage of the week?' a local radio journalist asks.

'I can't remember that long ago,' Rueben laughs. 'We just do the same things: prepare as well as we can, do our homework, tighten up on a few things and get ourselves ready for the battle.'

Like vultures that had picked the guts out of their prey, one by one the journalists leave the shivering captain. Until it is Rueben, a local print journalist and me. I've never interviewed Rueben individually. I want to hug him like a lost son, tell him to believe in himself and that I think he should be All Black captain this season. I doubt he would care what I think.

'Is this type of intensity good for international rugby down the track for the players lucky enough to make it?' I ask authoritatively. It is starting to rain.

'Yeah, I think so,' Rueben replies. 'Especially the Tri-Nations. It is a real step up. It is fast and physical and they [the Brumbies] are a really well-drilled side and we have to do our homework. They've got all sorts of tricks up their sleeves that they can pull out at any time and so we really have to be aware of everything.'

I've moved on to the international season but Rueben is not surprisingly thinking about the Super 12 final on Saturday.

'Are you personally playing better rugby than you've ever played?' I ask, now clearly overwhelmed by my new friend. Rueben chuckles quietly to himself.

'I don't know. I'm certainly enjoying my rugby. It's hard to really measure. I'm certainly enjoying being with the team.'

I deserve that answer: my questioning has become as clichéd as that of the other scribes this cold Tuesday morning. Still, Rueben is my potential best friend and I want to tell him my problems. I try again soon after.

'Looking back at the New South Wales loss earlier in the season you must be delighted, regardless of the result at the weekend, about how the team has done?'

Rueben almost cracks up and I'm pleased I'm being so entertaining. 'For sure. It certainly wasn't the way we wanted to start but the guys have made progress and worked hard to improve throughout.'

'One thing I noticed after that press conference,' I continue, 'was that you were very relaxed. There was no sense of desperation . . . '

'I think having been through that before [helped]. We'd made bad starts in the past and it's a long competition and so you've got time to fight your way back into it. We always believed we could.'

'There is a great photo of the 1997 NPC Canterbury side in the Canterbury Supporters Club, a side which you were in, of course,' I say. 'You must feel that's a long time ago.'

'That was my first taste of success at the top level in New Zealand,' Rueben replies reflectively. 'That seems a while ago now.'

'I interviewed Anton Oliver a couple of weeks ago and he said that your public persona is the real you. Is the public Rueben Thorne the real Rueben Thorne?'

'I try and . . . yeah, I like to have my privacy, so I don't give away too much. I just keep them separate, my private life and my rugby life. The guys will tell you I'm just like this, normal and just myself, I guess.'

We leave it there. Rueben has to train. I have to get back to work. The rain is starting to settle. As he jogs away to join up with his teammates, I reflect on a man who's been much maligned outside Canterbury. He's had his career highs and lows conducted in the public arena. For a private man, it must have been difficult. Yet he appears resolute in character and I admire him for, at the very least, being true to himself.

HOME IS WHERE THE HEART IS

Saturday, 22 May 2004

The weather in Canterbury has not improved any during the week. While the Crusaders contemplate playing the final of Super 12 against the Brumbies in Canberra, I leave the sanctuary of home for Lincoln Domain. It is a walk of less than half a kilometre but to me it feels like going back in time.

I would love to be in Canberra. Yet work and the small matter of a spare NZ$1,000 makes it impossible. So on the day Rueben and his troops play in the Super 12 final, I go back to my roots and my home club.

It's Under-19s final day at Lincoln. By the time I arrive at the Domain, the players have retreated to the changing-sheds. As I walk across the wet grass, the barren emptiness of a thousand memories hits me. Two young fellows walk towards me, one texting furiously. Times have changed.

The clubroom is packed with Under-19 players, their girlfriends, officials and club stalwarts. As I walk into the club, I immediately feel at home. I did not expect to feel such immediate identity, yet I quickly remember that this club is part of who I am. The number of people I know reinforces this feeling: people who work voluntarily behind the bar, people who clean the changing-sheds, people with a similar affinity.

President Russell Watkins is part of the club's rich fabric. Now 42, he's turned out for the club since he was knee high to a grasshopper. Today, he's played for the club's senior Bs, returning to the club this afternoon to help behind the bar. He's a third-generation Watkins who has played for Lincoln and couldn't imagine wearing any other club colours.

We shake hands and, as the Under-19s mingle, we start talking rugby. I want to know about the impact of Super 12 on club rugby. On a more personal level, I want to know whether this is the same club that I had grown up with. If that was unrealistic, I want to know whether the same spirit exists.

'There have been two different influences that Super 12 rugby has had on club rugby,' Russell says, sipping his twelve ounce of Tuis beer quietly.

'One, is raising the profile of rugby. We've got hundreds of kids aged seven, eight, nine wanting to play rugby. There are clubs around with two Under-11 sides and two Midget grade sides who are struggling to field a senior side. So Super 12 has increased the profile of rugby quite a bit.

'Then you've got the financial side. The Canterbury Rugby Union is putting a lot of the money they've made from the Crusaders back into club rugby. The last three or four years with the Crusaders doing really well have been great. The union gives money to the clubs depending on the number of players they've got. So we got NZ$5–6,000 last year, as did most clubs in Ellesmere. That's a great boost for grass-roots rugby.'

The Lincoln club plays in the Ellesmere competition. Ellesmere is one of the three components of Canterbury Rugby – North Canterbury and Christchurch Metropolitan being the others. Lincoln is probably one of the top two or three clubs in the sub-union, being especially strong in the junior grades. Like the passionate administrator that he is, Russell rattles off to me how each Lincoln side is doing.

Russell is undeniably positive about the future. There is no denying, however, that the numbers playing senior rugby are not increasing. The fact that Russell himself is lacing up his boots each Saturday is proof of that.

'A lot of people are choosing to give the game away a lot earlier,' Russell explains before being interrupted by the dong of a large golden bell. It's prize-giving time.

'I wish you guys the best for the next round,' the Prebbleton Under-19 captain declares, sounding like a young Sean Fitzpatrick. 'You did well. To my guys, we had a goal of making the top four, we got there, and now we have to move on. I'd like to thank the ref for his services, the touchies who did a good job out there, the fire service with the first aid, the bar staff, and my team I'd like to be upstanding for the opposition.'

The Prebbleton players get to their feet and toast the opposition before the player of the day is announced.

The captain of the Lincoln team then speaks, issuing similar noble sentiments. From the club life members choosing the player of the day, through to the obvious signs of sportsmanship, the whole occasion is remarkably innocent. Yet these are old New

Zealand values on display. Just like when I was growing up. It feels terrific.

After the formalities, Russell and I continue talking.

'Work commitments have definitely had an impact,' Russell says over the din of the Lincoln player of the day sculling an alarmingly large quantity of beer. 'And this has led to a lot of players giving the game away earlier than they may have in the past. These days, a lot of guys are pulling the pin at 26 or 27.

'The thing with work commitments is that they have had an impact not only on playing numbers but also on the administrators, the committee members and stuff like that. A lot of clubs are in the same boat. They are struggling to find people to come back into the game after they've stopped playing. It's just the changing times.'

Russell's major concern is the growing number of players being lost to the game between the ages of 17 and around 20. Twenty years ago you played rugby and that was it. Nowadays kids play rugby and then they get to 16 and 17, they get a driver's licence and they realise there's so many different things they can do.

While changes in society have challenged senior playing numbers, some things haven't changed. The desire of the junior ranks to emulate their heroes remains strong. They still want to be All Blacks, sure enough, but now they also want to be Crusaders.

'Ten or twenty years ago, the All Blacks were there but they only played three games a year or whatever. These days, young kids get to see Crusaders play ten, twelve weeks and that really raises the profile and they aspire to be like their role models.'

Still, I lament the fact that where kids of my generation were able to go and watch the best players in the province play club rugby, kids of today could not. 'It's probably sad in that it was a great thing for a club if they had an All Black,' Russell says. 'I remember back when the Southbridge club had Alby Anderson, who was an All Black. Alby would play half to three-quarters of competition games for Southbridge. Players were able to play alongside and against an All Black. It could only have been good for the depth. Unfortunately, that's something that clubs have had to accept in the professional era.'

Yet despite the changes that have taken place, Russell is convinced that the spirit that has characterised New Zealand rugby in the past remains.

'People like me have a passion for rugby. You look at what happened in Wellington a couple of weeks ago when they were able to fill the Cake Tin [Wellington's home ground] despite [the Hurricanes] having a bad season. The passion for rugby in this country will never die.'

There is no better advertisement for the passion of rugby than Russell. To him, rugby is not just a sport, it's a way of life. Along with the family connection, Russell has grown up side by side with his mates on Lincoln's playing fields. Rugby has been a sort of ritual for him.

· 'Lincoln had an Under-19 side that was quite good. They then brought in the Colts grade. I was in those sides with a lot of my mates. We had all gone through school together. We then went on to play either in the senior As or Bs. By the time we were in our mid-20s, out of the 20 of us who were in the Under-16s together, there was probably 17 of us still with the club. Today, you look at the Under-16 team and there might be 5 jokers who will carry on right through.'

I shiver with emotion as I leave the club, as I know I belong here. This club is part of me and regardless of where I will end up and what I will do, the red and black of Lincoln is engrained in my soul.

Later in the evening, the Brumbies show their all-round class to beat the Crusaders 47–38 in Canberra. The home side score 33 points in the first 19 minutes, effectively shutting the visitors out of the match. The Australians deserve their victory.

On Monday, the All Black trial teams are announced. Richard McCaw is in the Probables but bracketed because his shoulders need a rest. Tana Umaga is the new All Black captain. Rueben Thorne, the selectors say, is not sure of his place. They tell him at 9.00 a.m. He takes it with dignity. The merry-go-round that is professional rugby continues even after a finals defeat. Regardless, the 2004 Super 12 is over and my focus is now on the first Lions squad that toured New Zealand in 1930.

* * *

A DINNER JACKET, PLEASE

The 1930 British and Irish side that toured New Zealand was the third team from the United Kingdom to tour there but the first to be known as the Lions.

The squad was not the strongest. The great Wavell Wakefield, who was expected to be tour captain, was injured, while Scots Ian Smith and Phil Macpherson and Irish trio Mark Sugden, Ernie Crawford and Harry Stephenson were all unavailable.

Under the captaincy of Doug Prentice, the Lions were more of a cross-section of society than previous British touring sides, some members still hardly having left their villages or valleys. Team members were required to have a dinner jacket (so they could dine on the boat out), together with £80 spending money.

The manager looked after the £80 on behalf of each player and when money was required, he would provide the players with it. The players did receive a daily allowance of three shillings but it was not received in money, rather in chits from the manager.

The Lions were farewelled at a dinner at the Savoy Hotel by New Zealanders resident in London and over 400 guests were present, including the Duke of York (later King George VI). The squad sailed from Southampton on 11 April and travelled to New Zealand by passenger boat via the Panama Canal, arriving in Wellington on 17 May.

When the squad arrived at Wellington, the New Zealand government steamer Janie Seddon, carrying New Zealand Rugby Football Union officials, went out to meet the tourists and brought them to Pipitea Wharf, where the shed had been decorated with British flags and greenery.

After arriving, the Lions held a training session in Wellington before leaving the following day to prepare for their first match against Wanganui.

In Wanganui, a continuous stream of country people converged on the small town from the early hours on the morning of the match, with business in the town virtually coming to a standstill in the afternoon.

A MAN APART

By the time the 1930 Lions arrived in New Zealand, George Nepia's star *was already in the next stratosphere. Selected at 19 as the only full-back on the 1924–25 All Black tour of Great Britain, George played in all 32 matches and performed outstandingly.*

George was called to the final trial in Wellington to select the All Black team to take on the 1930 Lions. At the ripe old age of 25, he was being talked about as a veteran. In his own words, he felt he could still bring off some good catches and tackles and make some good kicks.

Not surprisingly, George was selected for the first Test but couldn't stop Welsh winger Jack Morley scoring in the last 30 seconds of the game to give the visitors a 6–3 victory.

'I had had success in my career in bundling two or three runners together or in persuading the ball-carrier to hang on too long and I was to perform this feat again – but against Jones and Morley, I had no chance whatsoever,' George told his biographer, Terry McLean.

George must have felt powerless and gutted like the rest of the All Blacks as the Lions scored to win the match. He'd played most of the match cold and although the old skills were certainly still there, he couldn't stop Morley.

'Out of admiration, as footballers, for those two Welshmen, I think we All Blacks willingly conceded them the match. I know the crowd did. The yelling and cheering as Morley and Cooke ran stride for stride in the corner, with Cooke perhaps gaining an inch at a time, could be heard all the way to Port Chalmers [and] the whole ground went cuckoo.'

George's day did improve. At the dinner that evening, the manager of the Lions, James Baxter, claimed that George was the most magnificent full-back that it had ever been his privilege to see. Although chuffed with the compliment, I am sure George would have swapped it for a win in the first Test.

THE RETURN OF THE ALL BLACKS

The All Blacks were lucky to win the second Test 13–10. The Irish half-back Paul Murray dislocated his left shoulder in a hard tackle just before half-time, forcing Ivor Jones to come out of the scrum to substitute. Although he performed adequately, his passing did not have the same speed as Murphy's and as a result the Lions backs did not have that extra metre of space.

Where George had been unable to stop the Lions backs from scoring the match-winner in Dunedin, he made amends in Christchurch.

This time he was faced with the imposing figure of Carl Aarvold, later to become a judge at the Old Bailey. The outstanding centre ran towards George with a try looming.

Back-pedalling, George succeeded in making Aarvold misjudge the *distance between them and then instantly made a crash tackle, catching him ball and all. 'You bastard,' Aarvold said. 'Who taught you that trick?'*

'It always seemed to me the right thing to do,' George said before the pair continued with the game.

HOW TO WIN FRIENDS

Welsh captain Harry Bowcott must have been an unassuming bloke. He made himself unavailable after the original selection but, due to an injury to another player, eventually made the squad. The Lions were lucky to have him, as he quickly formed a lethal combination with fellow centre Aarvold.

Rugged, quick and with toughness that came from playing in the competitive Welsh league, Harry was the type of person that the New Zealand rugby public instantly respected. The same could not be said for James Baxter, the Lions manager.

'He slaughtered them in one of his speeches after dinner and one sensed that they became afraid of him,' Harry told former Lion turned writer Clem Thomas.

That speech was after the very first match in Wanganui and the issue was the play of the wing-forward (later flanker). Baxter, described as a cultivated English gentleman of the old school, was in many respects the prototype of cricketer Douglas Jardine, who would cause such a sensation in Australia in 1932–33.

'The ordinary man who plays wing-forward is nothing more or less than a cheat,' he said. 'He is deliberately trying to beat the referee by unfair tactics.'

These comments not surprisingly went down like a lead balloon and ensured that Baxter became public enemy number one to New Zealanders.

Baxter also became incensed with various interpretations of the rules and insisted that the tour agreement said that the matches were to be played under IRB laws.

He was also deeply unhappy about the seven-man scrum and the fact that New Zealand played a 'rover', who just happened to be the All Black captain Cliff Porter.

The rover put the ball into the scrum and then stayed on his feet to either harass the opposition backs if they won the ball or support his own backs if his side won the ball. Calling Porter a cheat was never going to win Baxter many New Zealand fans.

Regardless of the controversy, the players continued to have fun. 'We were no better and no worse than the young men of today in our behaviour,' Harry told Clem Thomas.

'*We drank a bit and enjoyed female company but we tended to carouse only after matches. Standards of behaviour were left to the individual. I would not say that the manager, Jim Baxter, could not care less, for he was a typical RFU man.*'

Harry was also a tour selector. '*The teams were selected by the senior people in the side, including one from each country, and I was the Welsh representative. Scotland, for a number of reasons, had only one man on the tour, Bill Welsh from Hawick, and even after seven months we could not understand what he was saying!*'

Harry was one of the undisputed stars for the Lions in the third Test at Eden Park, scoring a magnificent try after 13 minutes to give the visitors the lead and a sniff of victory.

Stung by Harry's try, the All Blacks scored before half-time and the sides went into the break 5–5. Two tries and a drop goal in the second half put the home side out to a 15–5 lead before Aarvold restored some pride for the Lions with a splendid try under the posts.

IN SEARCH OF HARRY

I'd wanted to talk with Harry badly, as I knew he was the last of the 1930 Lions alive. My calls to the Welsh Rugby Union started in September 2004 and continued when I was in Europe the following month. No one seemed to know how to get hold of Harry and, given that I was on a tight schedule, I did not persist.

I would have loved to have spoken with Harry about what he really thought about James Baxter, how he formed such a lethal combination with Aarvold, whether he had a chance to chat with George Nepia at any stage during the series. Yet I left Wales without meeting the oldest living Lion.

Fast forward to 17 December 2004 and news came that Harry had passed away, aged 97. I regretted that I had not tried harder to find him, although I wonder whether he would have been in a position to talk with me about the greatest rugby tour of his life.

All up, Harry played only eight Tests for Wales between 1929 and 1933, playing out of Cambridge University, Cardiff and London Welsh. He captained his country against England in 1930 and was one of the main catalysts in Wales's first victory at Twickenham in 1932.

After his playing days ended, Harry became one of Welsh rugby's leading administrators and was a civil servant throughout his working life. He is undoubtedly one of the great names of Welsh rugby.

PLAYER POWER

Player unionism almost prevented the fourth Test from being played. The issue was match tickets. The All Blacks got just one a game and this, according to George, was yet another example of the fact that 'you had to have all the worst characteristics of Ebenezer Scrooge in mid-season form' to be appointed to the union's board.

Captain Cliff Porter got his team together. 'This is the story, chaps,' he said, before suggesting that unless the ticket allocation increased, the All Blacks would not take the field. 'Are you with me?' he asked after stating his case. The All Blacks answered yes to a man and so Porter went back to the powers that be and not surprisingly their ticket allocation increased.

The match itself was less dramatic. Although the Lions were only one point behind with half an hour to play, New Zealand ended up winning comfortably 22–8 to seal the series 3–1.

The Wellington crowd poured onto the field after the match and cheered the players off, the police having to provide a passage for both teams.

At the dinner after the game, Baxter was gracious and complimented the All Black forwards especially on their performance. At least he had ended the tour on a high note.

Before the Lions left New Zealand, official farewells were tendered by the government and by the NZRFU. Baxter spoke over the radio to express the thanks of his team to the people of New Zealand and he was joined by Prentice and Porter. A large crowd gathered at Wellington's Queen's Wharf to bid farewell to the Lions as they left for Australia. Baxter aside, they had in general been warmly received.

While Harry spent his life after finishing playing in the civil service and in rugby administration, George became a national icon. This series was his last in international rugby. After a temporary retirement, George returned in 1935 in a trial for a place on the All Black side to tour Britain. Although he was playing the best rugby of his career, he was not selected.

With depression gripping New Zealand as much as the rest of the world, George went and played rugby league for two seasons, representing New Zealand in that sport. Reinstated to rugby after the Second World War, George played for East Coast in 1947 and in 1950, aged 45, captained an Olympians club side against the province of Poverty Bay, a side captained by his son George.

Although his performances for the All Blacks were outstanding, George became an iconic figure in New Zealand as much for other reasons. Due to his humility, his reverence and unassuming nature, he reflected the beauty of Maoridom. Through his trials and tribulations, he became symbolic of his generation in New Zealand.

His crowning moment on the international stage after his retirement came in 1982 at St Helen's in Swansea. Before the New Zealand Maori played the home side, George was introduced to the crowd. There he stood, this gentle man who had been through so much and who had starred on that very field nearly 60 years earlier, his cap in hand, being recognised for being great.

Although he never made a fortune out of rugby, the sport helped make George the man he was. Yet George gave far more to the game than he ever received and his legend and contribution to New Zealand rugby is almost unprecedented. His life was also testimony to the undoubted truth that it is far more important to be a great man than a great player.

PART TWO
The International Season

The Rules may be modified, and, alas, evaded but the
game in general will never alter.
A.C. Swan, *History of New Zealand Rugby*

A RETURN TO THE
GOOD OLD DAYS

Despite being third in the world at the 2003 World Cup and winning the Tri-Nations and the Bledisloe Cup that season, new All Black coach Graham Henry promises changes. A return to the good old days, it is said, when the All Black forwards were feared and when physicality was the name of the game.

The changes are reflective of the general feeling in New Zealand society. The amount of political correctness is stifling. Conservatives are sick of tiptoeing around. They want recklessness. Leadership. Likewise, the New Zealand rugby public can accept loss yet it cannot stomach a lack of guts and wishy-washy rugby. They want their All Blacks to be real men. Eat raw steak and all that.

It is ironic that Graham Henry was a principal at one of Auckland's biggest secondary schools in the 1980s: political correctness had been introduced into the nation's education institutions in that decade. Partly as a result, New Zealand has become a nation of followers rather than leaders.

Graham gets it right by reintroducing the All Black trial. The trial, held in Auckland, is impressive but it unearths some worrying signs: the Possibles scrum decimates the Probables, a number of brave selections in the shadow Test side prove to be not quite ready, while the Probables only just win.

Still, it's a step up from Super 12 and more like the demands of international rugby. It also shows, as some northern critics have suggested, that playing rugby at the start of February in the southern hemisphere is different to slugging it out in the mud in the depths of June.

It's telling that, although Graham's Probables back line is selected for the first Test against England in Dunedin, only one player from the Probables pack makes the starting XV. Although injury has kept Richard McCaw and Chris Jack out of the trial, the point is that Super 12 rugby hasn't given the All Black selectors what they require up front.

The All Black squad is an eclectic mix of youth and experience. The youth is reflected by the selection of Samoan New Zealanders Sam Tuitupou and Mose Tuiali'i and is symbolic of a new era. The hope must be that these players peak at the World Cup in France in 2007.

The experience partly comes in the shape of Andrew Mehrtens. If ever a sportsman could be called mercurial it was Mehrtens. He is a sportswriter's dream: boy-next-door looks, quick-witted, intelligent, immensely talented. Yet also incredibly frustrating. A moment's brilliance can be undone by an attempt at the impossible. He could have been French.

His season has reflected his mercurial nature. On the outer for the Crusaders for most of the Super 12, his performance against the Brumbies in the final was inspirational, his cameo in the All Black trial proof that Canberra was no fluke. So there he is, the Wednesday morning after the trial, a 2004 All Black. It is a comeback of epic proportions after not being selected for the national side in 2003.

Great sportspeople come back after being dropped. For many reasons, Mehrtens deserves the tag of greatness. He plays the game with the vitality and inspiration that gives rugby fans the knowledge that rugby is, as they regularly used to say in the valleys of Wales, the chosen game. There is an energy about his play that when on song is almost unparalleled. Great men, it is said, are dreamers. Mehrtens often plays rugby like that. As if there were no rules.

At the All Black trial, you sense that there is a positive atmosphere within New Zealand's rugby elite. The aura around the new regime is undoubtedly partly responsible. There is confidence that in Graham, Wayne Smith and Steve Hansen New Zealand has the coaching expertise to compete with the world's best. It is ironic that all three have developed their craft greatly in the northern hemisphere.

England come to New Zealand after losses to Ireland and France in the Six Nations and without Jonny Wilkinson and, more importantly, Martin Johnson. Still, they are world champions and that hurts the New Zealand rugby public. Besides, there is never a second-rate All Black side, so why should there be a second-rate England squad?

Clive Woodward is full of enthusiasm about the trip, although you get the feeling he could put a positive slant on a natural disaster. 'With six world champions now retired and four others recovering from injuries, there can be no better opportunity for some of our existing young talent to come to the fore,' he says optimistically.

While it is difficult not to respect Clive for all he has achieved in life and in rugby, it is also not hard to see why he does not endear himself to many New Zealanders. While Martin Johnson is revered in New Zealand for his character and his no-nonsense approach, Clive appears the archetypal upper-class Englishman that Antipodeans hate so easily.

It's just the small things: staying in Auckland until the Thursday before the first Test in Dunedin, bringing a support entourage of 19 (including a Queen's Counsel) to New Zealand, making brash comments that can't be backed up by fact. He is, some say, unique.

While the Englishmen remain in Auckland until the Thursday, Dunedin is in Test mode. I'd been there for a Super 12 match earlier this year and am not looking forward to my return date with the cold. But as this is Test weekend, I hope that the hearty spirits that go along to Carisbrook will soften the city's southern chill.

THE LONELY ROAD TO DUNEDIN

Saturday, 12 June 2004

I rent a car and spend five hours driving south. In my splendid isolation, with only Roxy Music and U2 for company, I reflect on the extent to which New Zealanders love rugby. It's as if the sport is an expression of ourselves, our need for national identity. Driving south, I feel that direct need for identity and an earthy oneness with the land.

When I arrive in Dunedin, I quickly find a phone box and call Stephen Jones ('call me Steve'), the well-known rugby writer for the *Sunday Times* in London. I've read Steve for years, not always agreeing with him but always respecting his views. I want to meet him in the flesh and see the whites of his eyes.

We eventually meet at the Scenic Circle Hotel. He is about to lunch. I wait 45 minutes before he returns. He hasn't finished but he kindly asks me to join him and his colleagues.

Walking with Stephen Jones on the streets of Dunedin before a Test is the closest I'm going to get to dancing with Mick Jagger this afternoon. Almost everyone recognises him, tooting, whistling, commenting. What immediately strikes me about Steve, ironically, is his shyness.

Waiting for us at the near-empty restaurant are Jones's colleague, Nick Cain, and Paul Morgan from *Rugby World*. A smorgasbord of rugby opinion. My mouth waters, I ooze with questions. I feel more than a touch intimidated. In the past, I might have obtained confidence from the fact that the All Blacks were the world leaders in rugby. Now England are the world champs and I can almost feel the glow of superiority amongst these talented rugby journos.

Being away from home makes you feel more patriotic, more passionate about your own nationality. These guys are clearly warriors for English rugby (despite Steve being Welsh). I can sense their passion not only for the sport in general but also for the English side. They would not have been human if they hadn't identified with Clive's troops. After all, they follow them around the world.

So we talk. With the wine flowing and as we tuck into bangers and mash, there is a clear consensus amongst my colleagues that Super 12 is overestimated in the minds of the New Zealand rugby public.

'People always came here to watch rugby,' Nick Cain suggests, referring to the local fans. 'To say that you've got to have one form of rugby that is high on entertainment and that what people then go and see at Test level is a different product is wrong. You go and see in club rugby or provincial rugby the type of rugby that you are going to get in Test rugby.'

'When Super 12 started, the coaches and the referees got together,' Steve adds, 'and they decided what people wanted to see and what was entertaining and [that] was the greatest patronising of an audience in the history of sport in any country.'

I wonder whether Steve is totally serious or whether, as Ron Palenski had suggested to me earlier this season, he was saying it more for effect. Before I can push him further, I'm politely offered a glass of wine, which I decline.

'I put it to you,' I say, 'that if you were getting 9–6 scorelines you wouldn't get half the attendances that you do get in Super 12.' Surely rugby has become in part entertainment and a competitor for the discretionary dollar?

'If you think about the great touring sides that have come here and you think about the great games in the Ranfurly Shield,' Nick says, 'it wasn't necessarily about the scoreline, it was about the event, it was real rugged competition. Super 12 has now become somewhat manufactured. You've got the billeting of players, so they don't build any genuine rapport with the people who live there.'

We turn to the state of English rugby. I want to know why English rugby has become the hotbed of the sport internationally.

'The thing about it is, is that there is always the concept [that] winning the World Cup makes absolutely everything rosy in the garden,' Nick says. 'That's never the case. There is still a gap between the clubs and the national union and everyone wants their slice of the cake, which means that the demands on players every season get ever greater.

'What's made English rugby competitive is a competitive league structure. An element of that is that some of the Premiership owners want to ring-fence the Premiership and that is a serious battle that is not likely to go away.'

The problem, Nick suggests, is the difference in money between the Premiership clubs and the division clubs. Without a moneybags backer who is prepared to invest large sums, the chances of fluidity between the divisions are small.

Steve feels that the major issue in English rugby is that, amazingly, they cannot build stadiums fast enough. 'Three years ago, Wasps were getting 3,000 people along to their games. Now, they are getting 10,000 sell-outs.'

Paul agrees. 'Leicester have a maximum capacity of 15,000 and three months before the start of the season they have sold 11,000 season tickets.'

The guys concede that England's World Cup success increased the demand, although the strength of the Zurich Premiership is there for all to see.

We move to the here and now. Tonight, the All Blacks are playing England and in some ways it's Graham Henry up against Clive Woodward. I remind Steve that he's written that both gentlemen are the best coaches in world rugby.

'Woodward's not so much a coach but the head of a big conglomerate,' Steve says. 'He's the best tracksuited chief executive in sport . . . possibly not even Woody himself would describe himself as a coaching wizard but he fronts up this incredible [organisation].

'I think [Graham] Henry in a man-to-man battle of the coaches would eat Woody alive. Not many people would agree with this but

I think Graham's a really intelligent, clever, funny bloke and I think he's a very fine coach. All things being equal, if it was Clive's team against Graham's team, I would pick Graham's team to win.

'But you can't take away from what Clive's done. In a way, then, it doesn't matter what you think of him individually, as he's won the tournament [the World Cup].'

Steve refutes the notion that Clive is arrogant and claims that he is in actual fact a decent bloke. Nick says he doesn't know enough about him but what he admires Clive for is the fact that he had the courage of his convictions and that, at the end of the day, in 2003 he was successful.

'If he'd lost in the final, he would have been butchered,' Steve concurs, 'and he was courageous . . . Clive said we are proudly English, we are coming down here to win the World Cup. It wasn't easy, it took some doing.'

I wonder whether comparisons can be drawn between the loss of aura that currently surrounds New Zealand rugby and the Welsh situation in the 1980s.

Steve says it all comes down to being in a commercially viable arena, although he admits that it's far worse in Wales.

'Wales is a country with slightly narrow horizons and we hate elitism. If you're in a village and there are ten boys and one of them becomes a Billy Elliot, the others will say that he's getting too big for his boots.

'We were terrified of professionalism in Wales. Instead of having 350 clubs, all of which were exactly the same, we would have had 10 clubs and people would have said, "Who the hell do they think they are?" I don't think New Zealand is as bad. In New Zealand, people are more comfortable with elitism. They want the All Blacks and their Super 12 side to be pretty good. In Wales, we don't mind you being crap, as long as we are all crap together.'

Steve says that, as in Wales, it will now be 20 per cent harder for the All Blacks to win, as, whether New Zealanders like it or not, the heart of commerce in rugby terms is based in Sydney and London, not in Auckland. Connected with that, each gentleman agrees with me that New Zealand needs a world-class national stadium.

Despite the Test match feeling in Dunedin this cold Saturday, this all feels like the calm before the storm, especially without Wilkinson and Johnson in the English line-up. Next season, the Lions are coming and that will be the real test for the All Blacks. Was this just the curtain-raiser?

'Woodward's great strength,' Steve says after some thought, 'is that every game is a one-off. It's nothing to do with the future or the past. I think Clive would say that it's a different ballgame next year and I think that's dead right.

'Tonight, England are playing the All Blacks. The world champions are playing the greatest rugby nation. If that's not a great one-off match, what is?'

Lions tours, rather than becoming a relic of the amateur era, are now a huge sporting spectacle.

'Try telling the 21,000 people who came down to Australia in 2001 that Lions tours are a thing of the past,' Nick says, 'or the people who are waiting to get on the waiting list to come down in 2005. Will Carling aside, the players love them and they just go from strength to strength.'

'There is still an aura about playing for the Lions and it is considered to be the pinnacle for a rugby player in the British Isles. Why else would Woodward, for example, want to be Lions coach?'

These guys have seen more rugby than I have. They have reported on it, followed it, embraced it, lived it. It may have become a second family to them, a mistress even. They have undoubtedly seen the changes since the advent of professionalism in 1995. Was the spirit of rugby still alive?

'Everything changes in life,' Steve says reflectively. 'There used to be steam engines. I have to say that I've got an unbelievable affection for the old days of touring, for the egalitarian nature of it where the players would always be at the bar after a match. That's not completely gone but the game's moved on.

'It's very professional but as far as the spirit of it goes, I still think that a rugby man is a rugby man regardless of whether you meet him in Greenland, Lapland or South Africa, or Soweto, or Dunedin. There's no shame in doing it better than what you were. After 20 years on the *Sunday Times*, I can still count the number of people who I don't like easily on one hand.'

'When you're talking about the spirit of rugby, you're talking about the good old amateur days,' Nick says. 'I still think that [despite the changes] rugby has an underlying goodness that continues to exist as strongly as ever. I don't think that that goodness is mutually exclusive to the brave new professional world.'

I'm exhausted. It's always difficult interviewing journalists as sometimes they can ask the questions better than you. Yet these gentlemen, once they put their Super 12 prejudices aside, displayed the passion for the sport I loved. It was an inspiring afternoon and as I left the restaurant, I felt an overwhelming sense of understanding, not only of New Zealand rugby but of the sport as a whole.

* * *

Tonight, I sit with around 30,000 rugby fans in the cold of Dunedin in a decrepit stadium watching a game of rugby. It's mad and yet when they play the national anthem and I can feel a nation unite behind the foggy haze of a thousand breaths, it feels incredibly natural.

Graham Henry is feeling nationalistic more than most. This is his first Test as All Black coach, something which he has said in the past was his ultimate ambition. What's more, he is facing off against Clive Woodward, a man who bitterly criticised his appointment and performance as Lions coach in 2001.

The position of All Black coach is more prized than that of prime minister but, ironically, it has been characterised by some unusual selections down the years.

The NZRFU has always been an earnest body of men, yet has regularly failed to appoint the right person. From the non-selection of Vic Cavanagh in 1949 through to the premature appointment of John Mitchell in 2001, the appointment of All Black coach was often a haphazard political affair with common sense sometimes overlooked.

Yet in December 2003, the NZRFU appeared to get it right with the choice of Graham Henry as All Black coach. While John Mitchell's regular dismissal of sponsors, the media and many at the NZRFU ended any realistic chance of him continuing in the role, Henry's was always the stronger résumé.

Graham's rugby story began in the musty halls of Christchurch Boys' High School in the 1960s. Although he was a useful rugby player and cricketer, from an early age he had an ambition to coach. This was reflected in his vocation as a teacher of physical education and, later, a secondary school headmaster.

'I grew up as an amateur coach,' he says, 'and started coaching seriously in 1975 at Auckland Grammar. When you grow up as an amateur coach, you haven't got a lot of time to do a lot of amateur coaching.

'I mean Wayne [Smith] and Steve [Hansen] are better individual coaches than I am and they are very good at that. My strength, if I have one, is that I am good at seeing the bigger picture and working out the team gameplan and the opposition.'

Graham achieved success almost everywhere he went. From the 3A side at Auckland Grammar, through to the first XV at that same school, then on to the Auckland University club side and then the Auckland senior side and the Auckland Blues, Graham established himself as one of the best analysts of the game.

His move to coach Wales was brave given his desire to one day coach the All Blacks. The NZRFU put in place a rule preventing New Zealand coaches who coached national sides overseas from coming back to coach the men in black. And there was the chance that Graham might still have coached the All Blacks at some stage had he remained in New Zealand.

'I may have got the job when [John] Harty resigned. He had a bad run for a season [1998] and it may have been an opportunity for me then. But I made my decision and that was to go to Wales. I was quite happy with that.

'When I went to Wales, I thought that was the end of that [coaching the All Blacks], as there was a pretty negative reaction from the administrators and they brought in the Henry law to stop coaches coming and going.'

Despite the eventual parting of ways, Graham was a success in Wales. He restored a level of pride to Welsh rugby and, although the results tapered off, his contribution is still highly regarded in the valleys.

His appointment as Lions coach in 2001 was inevitable. Although it is questionable whether a foreigner should have been appointed, no one would have quibbled with that had the Lions won the third Test. Player burnout and a huge injury toll appeared to be the major reasons why the series was not won.

'There were some problems on that tour,' Graham concedes, 'which have been highlighted in great detail. From an experience point of view, it was the best experience I have ever had. From a rugby touring, coaching experience I learnt the most from [it].

'It was very difficult because I was a New Zealander coaching the Lions. That had never happened before and there was a lot of opposition to that.

'But my position was that I was asked to do the job and I accepted. I can understand the opposition. Yet as a tour it was an incredible experience and I have no doubt that it has helped me in my future coaching and my philosophy towards my coaching.'

Graham returned to New Zealand and almost immediately re-established his credentials as a defence analyst with Auckland Rugby. When the All Black position became open after the national side was bundled out of the World Cup in 2003, there was only one realistic choice for the NZRFU.

As it was his lifetime dream, Graham had no hesitation in putting his name forward for the All Black job. Against him was the fact that five of the last six All Black coaches had worn the silver fern as players.

'It's probably a definite help for the coach if he's played at that level,' Graham says.

'Look at John Bracewell with the national cricket side. It probably takes guys like me a little longer to achieve the goal than it would take a guy who's had that sort of experience really.

'I had no problem with that and I understood that. I realised that it was something that I would have to overcome if I wanted to coach in international rugby.'

Reflecting his experience, Graham chose his assistants wisely. Wayne Smith should never have been dumped as All Black coach in 2001, going on to furnish an outstanding record with Northampton. His re-emergence within the All Black set-up was a coup.

Cantabrian and former Welsh coach Steve Hansen had worked with Graham in Wales and was a forwards specialist. His return to his homeland completed a trio that was remarkably experienced and competent.

Graham was like a breath of fresh air. After John Mitchell's reluctance to communicate with the public on his journey, Graham was open and willing. His common sense and maturity enabled New Zealand to immediately fall behind him.

Tonight, though, is the first Test. Graham admits that he's nervous but he sees the bigger picture.

'Coaching a rugby side is a big deal for a lot of people, not a big deal for just one person. Obviously, you're delighted that you've achieved your goal, just like a guy who makes the All Black team. But you soon get over that and you start working with 30 or 40 other people to produce something that you are all very proud of. It becomes a collective thing.'

This is not a forerunner to the Lions series, Graham says quickly. There's no Martin Johnson, no Jonny Wilkinson. This is an English side that has played a lot of rugby and has injuries.

'The Lions will be the biggest tour this country has ever seen,' Graham says, although avoiding any suggestion that it's a major duel between himself and his perceived arch-nemesis, Clive Woodward.

'A lot of people think about this as an individual competition. When you're involved in a team sport, you are dealing with teams and not individuals.

'When you're involved with the All Blacks, everything that you do, whether it is the Lions or the Tri-Nations, or the World Cup, is very important. The next thing is always the most important.

'I think the thing that we are about is trying to build a team that reaches its potential. I think this side has huge potential and that's what motivates this group of people. It certainly motivates Wayne Smith, Steve Hansen and me.'

Tonight, though, it's about beating England. Graham realises the pressure and responsibility and accepts that it goes with the territory of being All Black coach.

'I think the only way you can deal with it and do your very best,' he says of the pressure, 'is to work as a team and if a team is good they will gain strength from each other and become something that is pretty special.

'I don't think individually we can handle those pressures but we can handle them working together and helping each other, and I think that's what sport is all about.'

Graham sits in a box above the stand waiting for his team, the nation's team, to do the haka. Nearly 30 years of coaching and a dream is being realised.

Cometh the hour, cometh the man. This is Graham's time and in many respects it's not too much different from one of those many cold mornings at schoolboy rugby in Auckland.

Then, Graham always had his gameplan sorted and understood clearly what he expected from his players. Believed in them. His is no overnight apprenticeship but you get the feeling that no man has been better prepared. Win or lose, this night is as much about Graham as it is about the players.

As I try to spot Graham from the stands, a rousing haka is performed. The game kicks off. Joe Rokocoko scores. The All Blacks blitz England in the first half to lead 30–3 at the break. They go on to win 36–3. It's convincing and for once the winter night air in Dunedin doesn't feel so cold.

As I drive back to Christchurch, I hear Graham's after-match comments on the radio. He says the right things and puts it all into perspective. The reasons why the All Blacks won are obvious. It's as if he knew all along what the end result would be.

As I reach Oamaru, I conclude that Graham has the goods. He's intelligent all right and seems a good joker. He is well-rounded, testimony to 30 years of coaching. He also appears to understand the big picture and the fact that, at the end of the day, rugby is just a game played by mere mortals.

The All Blacks appear in good hands. Yet this is Test one for Graham and his crew. The question is whether Graham will be able to deal with the relentless pressure that goes with the top job. As I turn the ignition off and complete my five-hour journey home, I conclude that I think he will.

SCRAPBOOKS OF YESTERYEAR

Tuesday, 15 June 2004

I quickly make my way through the deserted streets of Rangiora, a town situated some 25 kilometres to the north of Christchurch. It's just before 6.00 p.m., pitch black and I'm hopelessly lost. I stop at a Shell service station and ask for directions but they don't seem to know where my intended destination is and so I keep driving until I eventually find the right road.

Now 15 minutes late, I find the right house after some further searching and, out of breath, I sprint to the door feeling like a groom late for his wedding. When the door opens, former All Black Dennis Young must wonder what stands in front of him. I smile gently, apologise for being late and enter his warm, inviting home.

As is often the case in rugby, Dennis wears more than one hat. He's currently president of the Canterbury Rugby Football Union and a former partner in a travel business that specialises in sport, while he's also a former All Black. In total, Dennis played 61 games for New Zealand, including 22 Tests.

This Saturday, the All Blacks are playing England in the second Test in Auckland. Dennis played against the 1963 English touring squad and I was interested to know, 41 years on, whether the game that he played then was the one we were seeing now.

'We knew some of the names,' Dennis reflects when I ask him about the 1963 English squad, 'but typical of the way I approached the game, I only thought about the front row. They had a good one as it turned out.

'We were late in our build-ups,' Dennis says of the preparation for the Tests, 'nothing like the time they spend together now. There was a limit on the number of days you could assemble before a Test match, set down by the IRB. I'm not saying that wasn't broken occasionally but it was generally stuck to.'

The first Test in 1963 was played in Auckland and, although the English applied plenty of pressure in the first half, the All Blacks eventually won 21–11.

'They gave us a bit of a shock in the first half,' Dennis recalls, 'although to be fair we didn't know much about them. We could get built up [to play] against South Africa, the British Lions, a little bit against Australia, but with England coming out here, I don't know. Yet when we finished the game, I'd developed a lot of respect for them, especially their front row.'

Bonds were formed between the sides after the matches and for Dennis that meant making acquaintances with the impressive Coventry hooker Herbert Godwin.

'I went to visit him ten years later,' Dennis recalls, 'when I was over that way with a supporters group. Unfortunately, he had the flu and was in bed. As if to demonstrate the difference between amateur and professional eras, he was living in this box of a house. There were these narrow wee stairs leading to a tiny bedroom. Here he was, a top international living in a place that was substandard.'

According to Dennis, there was a camaraderie between the international hookers that lasted well after the final whistle. 'We used to swap blazers,' Dennis recalls, 'although some of them used to be too big for me,' referring to his relatively small stature.

'There was in those days, perhaps more than there is today, a close affinity between you and the person you played against and if there was a chance to continue it further outside the game, you took it.'

The second Test was closer, the All Blacks winning 9–6 in Christchurch, thanks to colossal All Black full-back Don Clarke succeeding with a 65-yard kick from the mark, held by his brother Ian.

As with the first Test, the teams got together after the match, which in Christchurch meant a dinner at the Clarendon Hotel, where overseas teams used to stay, along with royalty, the Beatles and other notables. They were joyous, innocent times and rugby was the thing, not commercial considerations.

'You make comparisons,' Dennis says when I ask him about the differences between the game in 1963 and the game today, 'but not too many because there have been so many changes.

'I think the size of the players today amazes players of my generation. People often think that I was the typical size of a hooker in my day, which I was not. I was short, even in those days. But in those days hookers were hookers and if you had the skill to win the ball from scrums it didn't matter what physique you were. These days hookers have different skills. I jokingly call them "beefed up darts players".'

Training for Dennis meant two sessions during the week and then again on a Sunday, with the game on Saturday.

'You had to come home from whatever your job was and get your gear and go out on a cold night. In those days, you were a player of the people. You mixed with the public and most of us guys would have a beer after training on Thursday, where you rubbed shoulders with blokes in your club.'

That mixing also meant walking with the fans to get to a representative game at Lancaster Park. 'I would walk with my wife and my mother and it was great as people would take you to heart. It certainly gave the people that warm, fuzzy feeling when they knew that they could come close to their players.'

The rugby calendar was structured and orderly in Dennis's day. You would have your club opening day in the middle of April, while two weeks later you would have your first club game. At Queen's Birthday [in June], the Canterbury provincial side would travel across to the West Coast, before the players came back into club rugby. Representative rugby would start in August and from then it would be provincial.

I get the feeling that Dennis is not totally happy with the way the game has progressed.

'I enjoyed the game in Dunedin last weekend,' Dennis says, 'because I saw elements of the old game. I don't like forwards being spread against the paddock. If they were supporting as a second line, that would be OK but otherwise I think it spoils the game. Still, I admire a lot of their players, their fitness and such like.'

Another of Dennis's concerns is that many of New Zealand's second tier of players are leaving the country to further their careers in Europe or Japan, where they can make good money. It's affected the depth here, Dennis feels, and he couldn't imagine ever spending a year or two playing overseas after finishing his career.

It strikes me that Dennis is a realist about the changes that have taken place in the sport but also in many ways is still a rugby romantic. As a result of this practical combination, I like him immensely.

'While I was waiting for you there, I picked up a pictorial book of the 1963–64 tour,' he tells me reflectively. 'It's shots of us at Buckingham Palace and all that sort of stuff. They miss that today. We were there [Britain and France] for four and a half months and got very close, very tight-knit. We also weren't being watched by media all the time, a bit but not much.'

I ask Dennis whether he would have preferred to play in the modern era. 'If life treats you well, and I think that life has treated me well, then I've got the best of both worlds: good living, a loving family and this to look back on,' he says of his time in the All Blacks.

With that, he asks me to pull out a big black book that is situated behind me. It contains clippings and memories of one of Dennis's tours with the All Blacks that had been kept for him in England.

We sift through the contents and reflect on the beauty and magnificence of days gone by. For a moment I feel sad, as many of the people included in this tome have now passed away. Yet I return to embrace the moment and once again give thanks for having the opportunity to sit and talk rugby.

THE DREADLOCKED CAPTAIN

Saturday, 19 June 2004

While Dunedin was a baptism of fire for Graham Henry, it was no less the case for the new All Black captain, Tana Umaga.

From the tossed dreadlocks to the quiet, thoughtful way he answers questions, there is something unique about Tana and the fans love him for it ('oh, ah, Umaga' and all that).

It's a given that he's a talent on the field. Having started his All Black career as a winger in 1997, he's slowly moved closer to the pack as he's aged.

He's what some commentators describe as a vital player, sure enough, but when you meet him you realise that the man's got presence and an inner strength that is a part of only the finest athletes.

Still, if you were asking which of the 1997 All Blacks was going to captain the All Blacks some seven years later, then Umaga would have been near the bottom of the list.

To be fair, Tana took time to find his feet as an All Black. A drunken episode on the streets of Christchurch after one Test did his public image no favours.

Yet Tana matured and he's become a rugby superstar. He's also become a trailblazer in the sense that he's the first Polynesian New Zealander to captain the All Blacks on a long-term basis.

If there is an example of the New Zealand Dream it is Tana. His parents, rich in ambition but little else, arrived in New Zealand from Samoa and set about establishing a better life for their family.

Tana's brother, Mike, played for Wellington and Samoa before moving to rugby league. Tana's appointment as All Black captain was a clear symbol that rugby was reflecting the cultural changes taking place in New Zealand society.

'I think it shows the changing face of New Zealand,' he says of his appointment as All Black captain, 'and the diverse cultures that we have here.

'Of course, it's not just the Pacific Islanders that are making an impact in New Zealand society. We've got people from all around the world settling here, the Pakistanis, the Iranians, the Somalians [for example], it's just the changing face of the world, I think. People are always emigrating.'

Tana knows that becoming All Black captain in New Zealand is almost akin to becoming president in the United States. It is something that reeks of history. Tana's appointment was a positive symbol not only to other Samoans but also to other minorities in New Zealand.

'Hopefully [my appointment] gives others who are not originally from New Zealand a bit of hope that they can achieve in sport and other aspects of life. If [my appointment] does help them, then that's fantastic.'

Tana was appointed All Black captain for a number of reasons: he was sure of his place in the Test side; he had the respect of the other All Blacks; he had been vice-captain in 2003; and he was immensely popular with the New Zealand public.

Determining how he got himself into this position is a little more difficult to work out. I figure it had something to do with his background and the fact that his brother Mike paved the way in many respects.

'At the time I didn't really see him [Mike] as a role model. I saw him as the big brother that always picked on his little brother!

'After growing up, I've looked back on the lessons that he taught me, or inflicted on me, rather, and realised that they were timely lessons for me in my rugby career and in my life as well.'

The role of the All Black captain does not come with a handbook. If it did, it would probably be thrown out as there is no course you can do to prepare. Like the majority of leadership positions, you learn as you go and hope like hell that you have the natural ability to keep your head above water.

Tana doesn't appear to be a captain who would rant or rave. He would say his piece, sure enough, but he wouldn't blow his top at his team. Being a centre, he isn't a Martin Johnson lead-from-the-front sort of captain. Yet for all of that, Tana has personal charisma that inspires teams and makes men follow him.

'I'm not too sure,' he says when I ask him what makes a great All Black captain. 'Obviously you will always be judged on the outcome of games. A great All Black captain is one who wins all the time, so I guess that is the ultimate gauge.'

It would be wrong to compare Tana with previous All Black captains, as he is operating in the professional age, where the pressure of outside demands has increased significantly.

It is a cop-out to suggest that, because players are getting paid and it is their job, handling media and sponsors alike is made any easier.

'It's just something that you have to get used to,' Tana says. 'I have a lot of close friends that I talk to, including especially my wife, and in this group here [the All Blacks] we have a lot of leaders and we try and spread the load. It's something that will never go away and the more you fight it the worse it will get.'

For Tana, the Lions are on the horizon. Outside the World Cup, they present the biggest challenge for a New Zealand rugby player, as they only tour here once every 12 years.

'Some great All Blacks have never had the opportunity to play against the Lions. If you look at it in that way, it is very important and it will be a very special occasion.'

Like most of the current All Blacks, Tana remembers little from previous Lions tours. Of the 1993 tour, he recalls enjoying how Jeremy Guscott played.

'He was very silky and he had all the skills, and I remember thinking that that was how a centre should play.'

The Lions series would likely see Tana up against Irishman Brian O'Driscoll, a player who we both agree is the benchmark for international centres.

'He is the measure for all midfielders,' Tana says. 'It would be great to play against him and it would be a good challenge for me and my midfield partner.'

I put my theory to Tana that his life is like the New Zealand Dream. He's come from relatively humble beginnings to forge a better life for himself and his family. Unlike so many American professional athletes and British footballers, he looks well balanced as a person.

'I feel very fortunate to have ended up where I have. I said that to my wife just the other day. If you compare where we started to where we are now, we are much better off. The plus side for me is that I've never forgotten where I've come from and where I started. I think if I did, I wouldn't be true to myself and the people I love.'

The All Blacks beat England 36–12 in Auckland and Tana displayed all the fine individual traits that he'd shown me when we spoke. He was inspirational all right and unlike so much in professional rugby, I found the hype surrounding him was justified.

MATESHIP AND RUGBY

Saturday, 10 July 2004

I can see the lights of North Harbour Stadium from a distance. They look like giant monsters in the Albany night sky and for a moment I feel as apprehensive as a small child.

'There we are.' My friend James confirms the presence of our destination in the distance. My excitement builds. There have been traffic jams on the motorway to Albany this evening and yet our run was clear.

The odyssey that is the All Blacks' season is continuing tonight against the relatively unknown quality that is the Pacific Island Barbarians.

The Barbarians are an interesting, if fundamentally commercial, concept. Realising that the power of three is better than the power of one, the nations of Fiji, Samoa and Tonga have joined forces and are taking on the Australians, New Zealanders and South Africans in Test matches.

The Pacific unions are going to receive a cut from the gate-take at each of the games, while the players selected for the Barbarians will still be eligible for the All Blacks or the Wallabies at a later date.

The aims of the organisers are not only to raise the coffers of the Pacific unions but also to highlight the more prominent Pacific Island players on display.

It has been a difficult time for the Pacific unions. They had rightly regarded the entry of a team representing them into an expanded Super 14 competition as being a natural progression. But it was obvious that the two extra teams would be Australian and South African.

It was also clear that while Pacific Islanders were making their mark at Super 12, NPC and European Club competition levels, there were not enough television viewers on the islands to put the Pacific Island unions on a sound financial footing.

I have mixed feelings about the dilemma of the Pacific Islands. While I appreciate the magnificence of their players' athleticism and I understand the commercial restrictions on their making progress, I also believe that they owed New Zealand and Australia plenty.

Not only were New Zealand and Australia providing arenas for their best and brightest to shine in but for years both nations had nurtured, tutored and schooled players of Pacific Island background.

Michael Jones, Mose Tuiali'i, Jerry Collins and Kevin Mealamu were all of Samoan descent and all had brought a Pacific flavour to the All Blacks but they were Pacific Island New Zealanders and not natives of Samoa. A mistake of many northern hemisphere rugby writers was to suggest that New Zealand had plundered Island ranks.

Tonight, those issues are not obvious to the thousands of rugby fans making their way to the ground. We park our car on wasteland

and trudge through the mud to the stadium entrance like fans at a weekend music festival in the middle of England.

James and I have been friends since university in Christchurch. Unlike me, he is an Aucklander and comfortable in these surroundings. He understands the mentality of his city folk, the lack of intimacy so common in a big city, the cultural diversity.

James and I are close, although not in a ring-you-every-day sort of way. Tonight is not only about rugby but about spending time together and catching up on how his life is progressing. He got married in April and I want to know how he's finding it.

The Pacific feel to the night is obvious well before the game kicks off. Many Pacific Island fans are dressed in the red, white and blue of their side, while Pacific drums boom across the stadium like a call to arms.

Brown faces are in the majority throughout the ground and I'm not immediately sure whether this is because of who is playing or whether this is simply just Albany. I can't recall seeing so many New Zealand Pacific Islanders earlier in the season at Eden Park.

The mood of the night is festive, partly because of the Barbarian-like occasion but also because the New Zealand Pacific Islanders know how to have a good time. I feel like we are at one big rugby party.

Before we know it, the two teams have taken the field, Inoke Afeaki leading the Islanders and Tana Umaga the All Blacks. Tana could easily have been playing for the opposition.

The game is immediately frantic and, before we know it, the All Blacks have scored almost right under our noses. Befitting their favouritism, the crowd is silenced.

Eventually, the game moves into a set pattern: the Barbarians throw everything at the All Blacks, the home side withstands and almost inevitably pulls through.

We sit back and talk, our feet sloppily perched on the leanings, both of us enjoying the atmosphere, talking, connecting. I tell him about my problems, he tells me what it's like to be married. We reminisce about university days, a period of freedom and promise. The rugby for a time becomes merely a sideshow.

We tune in and out of the match, the Islanders throwing everything at the home side and actually managing to come close at certain points. Yet the All Blacks always seem to have an extra gear and in the end run out 41–26 winners. Ironically, five of their six try-scorers are either of Maori or Island descent.

We get up, stretch and, as we leave, witness the same number of smiles that we saw earlier. It has been a festival of rugby, yet it didn't feel like a Test. Nobody seemed to care: it had been good entertainment and, perhaps as a result to some, good value for money.

As we trudge back across the empty fields, trying to get a gauge on where we left the car, I can remember hardly a thing about the night's rugby. It's not that it's been bad but just that it hasn't been the most important thing. James suggests that we get some food and then go drinking. I agree, smile and realise that this night is far from over.

THE SPORTSWRITER

Sunday, 11 July 2004

I'm driving through the streets of Devenport on Auckland's North Shore and it feels a lot like Christchurch: it's predominately white and upper-middle-class, and there is more than a whiff of affluence in the air.

There is also a comfortable Sunday feel about the place: lovers walking hand in hand along the shorefront, mothers and daughters window shopping, young urban couples sitting in expensive cafés wanting bigger and better. This is modern New Zealand.

The All Blacks have always reflected the society that they represent. The 1905 side that toured Britain was representative of the settler nation: hard-working, white, culturally homesick perhaps. This continued throughout the twentieth century. Think Colin Meads and you think of the New Zealand of the 1960s. Think John Kirwan and you think of the New Zealand of the 1980s; Jonah Lomu, the New Zealand of the 1990s.

I wonder, if this is still the case, then what do the current All Blacks reflect about modern New Zealand society?

So I'm here in Devenport to visit Warwick Roger, one of New Zealand's best journalists and writers. Warwick wrote a book, entitled *Old Heroes*, about the 1956 Springbok tour of New Zealand and it remains the best sports book ever written in this country. Warwick also has a good take on New Zealand society and Auckland life in general.

After five minutes knocking at Warwick's front door and admiring the large palms that stand tall in his front garden like Roman foot soldiers, I make my way round the back.

Warwick looks Sunday relaxed and I wonder for a moment whether I will have the same feeling of exhilaration writing this book as Warwick felt writing *Old Heroes*:

'I had a bag full of tape recordings, notebooks of impressions that made little sense to me, a mind that wouldn't rest. I didn't go back to work but stayed at home, sleeping like a boxer recovering from concussion, Robyn bringing me strong coffee to wake me up, running long distances in the mornings to clear my head, and writing all day before falling into bed exhausted again until it was all out of me. It was one of the happiest times of my life.'

We begin by talking about the Polynesian influence in New Zealand. Auckland has the biggest Polynesian population in the world and the influence on the modern All Blacks has been dramatic.

Warwick tells me that the migration from the Islands began in the 1950s with the banana boats that used to visit Auckland. The Islanders who settled in Auckland initially stayed in Ponsonby and Freeman's Bay, the men working in the Freezing Works, the women working in the hospital or in the laundry in Newmarket.

Sport was also important: the Polynesians playing for the Ponsonby Rugby Club and the City Newton Rugby League Club. The children meanwhile got a quality education at Auckland Grammar and Auckland Girls' Grammar.

When immigration to New Zealand increased in the 1960s and 1970s, the Polynesians tended to settle in South Auckland, still working in manual and less desirable jobs but providing much needed manpower. Developers and the new rich forced many of those settlers out of the city centre when the area began to be upgraded. But many Polynesian settlers were also joining Auckland's middle class and becoming upwardly mobile in other parts of Auckland.

The Polynesian influence in sport, in Auckland especially, has also been dramatic. Warwick tells me that many Pakeha (European) kids don't play rugby in Auckland because of the early physical development of the Polynesians.

I wonder whether the children and the grandchildren of the Polynesian settlers saw themselves as New Zealanders or as Polynesians living in New Zealand?

'I think they see themselves the same way as immigrants in the United States would see themselves,' Warwick says, 'being American citizens but of Polish extraction for instance.'

This notion, although real, would be foreign to the rest of New Zealand and reflective of the cultural differences between Auckland and the rest of the country. Were the differences as great as between, say, London and the rest of England?

'It's actually real,' Warwick says, 'and it's actually a fear of Auckland. The rest of the country thinks that Auckland's crawling with criminals and racial hatred. It's not true and you can see it for yourself if you spend any time here. Yet it's the same thing as you get in other countries with the capital city, like [the difference between] Buenos Aires and the rest of Argentina.'

It seems that as Auckland has moved away from the rest of New Zealand, so too have the modern All Blacks. No longer do they work in the banks, the post offices and the hardware stores like the rest of us. They are now different and I'm wondering whether they symbolise the New Zealand condition any more.

'They still do but not to the same extent,' Warwick explains. 'It's still a game that all classes and races play but it's not such a beacon in society as it was. There are so many other things for kids to do.

'You can't tell what occupations the All Blacks would have had had they not been professional rugby players. They traditionally tend to represent all types of people. If you go down here to the North Shore Rugby Club, you will see a whole range of people and ethnicities. Professionalism has evened things out.'

I wonder whether the modern All Blacks will end up as well balanced as the 1956 vintage that Warwick has written so passionately about. 'You can't tell because they are rugby players. They are not students, they are not farm workers, they don't work in the railways, they are full-time rugby players.

'There is no way to know where they will end up. Not all of them can end up in television like [former All Blacks] Ian Jones or Stu Wilson and, as they won't start their careers until they are in their 30s, I would suggest that the potential for them to drift around is pretty high.'

Warwick puts forward former All Black captain Wilson Whinerary as an old player who always knew what he wanted when his rugby days were over. Whinerary started his career as a farm appraiser before going on to work for timber giant Carter Holt Harvey.

Whinerary was not alone. Ron Hemi was an accountant, Ron Jarden was a stockbroker, Ponty Reid a schoolteacher. The old players were balanced. Yet, as Warwick points out, the players in those days were not required to spend most of each year playing rugby and touring the world.

With professionalism has come the move to commercialism. Many critics suggested that the All Blacks had become too commercial.

'They certainly did under John Hart and John Mitchell,' Warwick says. 'I think Graham Henry will pull them back from that. It's already happening. It's easier to get to the All Blacks now. As a journalist, you can ring Graham Henry and he'll talk to you.'

Warwick maintains that New Zealand's love affair with rugby has always been strong because of the mere fact that as a nation we are good at it. That somehow rugby represents all the best qualities of the national character. That, in other words, New Zealand may be marginally obsessed with the sport but it pulls the nation together.

'New Zealanders are very good at sports that people don't play,' Warwick says reflectively. 'We are good at netball but not many people play netball in the world. It would be interesting to see what society would be like if we were good at soccer.'

I wonder whether the Kiwis take the All Blacks too seriously. Last night they hadn't played well and yet, as Warwick wisely points out, today there is not a cloud in the sky. 'It's an entertainment industry now. When I was growing up in the 1950s, it was sport and a national crusade. Now, it's national entertainment.'

Still, the All Blacks, we concur, remain one of the more obvious symbols of New Zealand throughout the world – a reflection perhaps of patriotism in a not outwardly patriotic country.

'We are rather arrogant people. We inflate ourselves in matters like rugby because we are good at it. We beat our chests and say to the world, "Look how good we are." The world doesn't care because rugby is a minority sport. We make ourselves look ridiculous. We paint aeroplanes with the All Black front row and fly into Los Angeles Airport and people wonder where on earth that came from? We did the same with *Lord of the Rings*. We are quaint, strange people in many ways.'

We are also, it would seem to me, becoming more multicultural and, as a result, the number of kids playing soccer in New Zealand is growing faster than gorse. Is it inevitable that soccer will take over from rugby as New Zealand's national sport?

'It might happen in 50 years' time but it won't happen in my lifetime,' Warwick says. 'A good example is around this area on a Saturday morning. It's full of kids playing soccer, while there is one junior game going on at the rugby ground. In the afternoon, it's the rugby fields and not the soccer fields that are full. The problem in soccer is that they don't go on.'

Warwick had seen more changes in the national game than I had. He'd also seen the game change in national importance. Importantly, he'd seen the changes from a sociological rather than merely a sporting angle. Given all that, did Warwick feel it was a better game now?

'Probably not. I've just been watching *Heartland Rugby* on television. There was a local derby in Te Aroha and there are only two teams in Te Aroha now where there used to be four. The Thames Valley competition has only got 11 [senior] teams in the whole of their competition now. At that level, the game is very weak.

'At Super 12 level, you've got crowds of 20,000 going along and paying large amounts of money. So rugby at a professional level is doing well but at an amateur level it's struggling.'

We then move to Warwick's career in journalism and the researching and writing of *Old Heroes*. I'm like a pig in mud. I could sit here all day and pick Warwick's brains. But I've got to fly back to Christchurch and Warwick has a Sunday to enjoy. As he sees me out and we gaze across the barren sports fields across the road, I appreciate that as important as the All Blacks are, being a New Zealander is about far more. I am not sure that was the case in 1950.

* * *

WINNERS OFF THE FIELD

The 1950 Lions were winners everywhere but on the field. Coming five years after the end of the Second World War, the Lions reflected all that was great about the Empire and the Commonwealth. The squad was generally well educated, talented, happy and fun-loving.

On paper, they were an exceptional side: Ken Jones was a dynamic wing with electrifying pace, vice-captain Bleddyn Williams was a magnificent centre, Welsh forwards Ray John and Bob Evans were terrific, while perhaps the best of them was the dynamic Ulsterman Jackie Kyle.

Captained by the genial Irishman Karl Mullen, the Lions were the last British and Irish representatives to travel to New Zealand by passenger boat. They came out via the Panama Canal and went home through the Suez Canal. Despite physical training on board and running around the decks, most of the players put on a stone during the journey.

The Lions' style of play was immediately adventurous and they played an open brand of rugby that best utilised their outstanding backs. At the forefront was Jack Kyle, a 24-year-old medical student from Belfast.

THE IMMORTAL JACKIE KYLE

It's a cold October afternoon in Belfast, Northern Ireland, in 2004 and I can smell winter. I arrive at the Europa Hotel slightly early. Before I know it, a distinguished silver-haired gentleman greets me. It's Jack Kyle. I notice immediately that he's got that poise possessed by all great men. Unfortunately, he's also got a cold and so we quickly go inside.

'We were strictly amateurs and rugby was a very small part of our lives,' Jack tells me when I ask him whether making the Lions was the pinnacle of his career.

'It was a recreation, something that we did at school, helped the university we had chosen. We normally had one official training session and a game a week.

98

'Occasionally, we had a colours match against another university on a Wednesday but that was all. Our main objective of being at the university, as our parents let us know, was to get a degree and while our rugby was all very well, we were not going to earn our living playing rugby and so you had to get your head down.'

As a result, rugby took up about 10 per cent of Jack's time. It was therefore not totally surprising that in September or October 1949 he wasn't too concerned when he was asked whether he would be available to tour New Zealand the following year.

'I didn't say anything to my father,' Jack recalls, 'and said that I would go. When the team came out in December, I can recall that my father read it in the Belfast Telegraph.

'I wasn't informed and when he read it in the paper that I had been selected for the British and Irish Lions to tour New Zealand and Australia for a period of six months, my brother was with him and I think he bore the brunt of my father's dissatisfaction. I think he said something along the lines of, "Does that young lad ever intend to qualify as a doctor?"'

Luckily, Jack was able to postpone his finals and much of the tour was over the summer holidays, pacifying his father to some degree.

'I think keeping the value of things, keeping perspective, was very important,' Jack recalls. 'Great you are able to do this but . . . I think that was very important.'

Jack brought some books with him to study while on tour. He admits, sheepishly, that they weren't opened too often. 'I recall Karl Mullen, who was a qualified doctor by then, going though some midwifery gynaecology with me but that was only once!'

The excitement in touring New Zealand was understandable for a group of young men on the journey of a lifetime. 'I can remember the excitement of getting books on New Zealand before I left and finding out that there were two islands!'

The touring experience was a novelty. Jack recalls he'd never read anything about rugby until then, never studied it. Afternoons on the boat on the way out were, however, often spent talking rugby. It was a revelation and to some degree covered up the homesickness that some of the squad were experiencing.

'We arrived in Wellington and had a civic reception. The following day we headed to Nelson and I remember walking around with my brother-in-law Noel Henderson on this beautiful, sunny morning and leaning over the bridge and seeing this kingfisher.'

Early wins against Nelson, Buller and the West Coast were an easy entry into the tour for the tourists. A harsher reality was against Otago and Southland in the next matches, both lost. The Lions were not surprisingly written off before the first Test against the All Blacks.

'We had a great old game in Dunedin in the first Test,' Jack recalls. 'We were leading 9–6 and I think Bob Scott then kicked a penalty and it was a draw. That was a great boost to our morale because George Norton – our top full-back and kicker – had been injured, we'd lost two games and we went into this Test match as total underdogs.'

By this stage of the tour, Jack was getting plenty of attention and was the undoubted star.

'I didn't even realise it at the time,' he says of the attention. 'You see, I hardly ever read any paper reports. I tried to keep away from the reports. Also, when you are with a crowd of guys, if you started acting like a prima donna they would bring you into line again. I didn't even know that people were considering that I was playing good rugby.'

A FULL-BACK TO BEAT ALL FULL-BACKS

Bob Scott, by his own admission, had a tough upbringing. His father had been wounded during the Gallipoli campaign and suffered from ill health for the rest of his life. For a time, his parents broke up, meaning that Bob and his siblings lived in a Salvation Army children's home and an orphanage for a period.

Bob fills in the gaps when we talk on the phone in early 2005. In his 80s now but sharp as a tack, he lives on the Coromandel in the north-east of New Zealand. These days he spends his time bowling, being with family and answering questions from people like me. Life seems much better than it was.

'It was the only time that I played before the New Zealand public,' Bob recalls of the 1950 tour. 'I supposedly retired from rugby after that tour and, so, yes, it was a special tour for me.

'We would get together on the Thursday before the Test and practise on the Friday. That was about it. I don't know how these guys feel about it today but we had tremendous pride and togetherness, especially amongst the players that had already played for New Zealand. A few of the guys from '49 had retired but there was still a nucleus there, guys like Kevin Skinner and Johnny Simpson.'

Bob was one of the standouts for the All Blacks in the first Test in Dunedin. Yet the history books suggest that he was beaten by Jack. Nine minutes into the second half, the Ulsterman picked up the loose ball and flashed past the New Zealand backs. Racing diagonally towards the goal line between Bob and 'Brownie' Cherrington, Jack went on to score one of the best tries ever scored at Carisbrook.

'*I don't remember that,*' Bob says, '*but it appears that he was supposed to have beaten me. The one I remember was when he went inside of [George] Beatty on the left-hand side of the field and cross-kicked to the corner.*

'*They said that I fumbled the ball. Well, I didn't really fumble the ball. I went to grab it with my hand. I had this manoeuvre where I acted as though I would continue on with the movement and I came back quickly. In the meantime, my knee had bumped the ball and dear old Ken Jones just dived over the top and scored. My hands didn't really get to the ball.*'

The only person who saw what happened, according to Bob, was his wife. '*She was English and I'm not sure whether she was backing the Lions at that stage. She was in Dunedin to meet her relations for the second time and they had passed her the glasses to watch me and anyhow [she was watching] when I bumped the ball. It wasn't a particularly great moment, really.*'

Bob recalls that in that Test and in subsequent Tests on that tour, Jack was '*incredibly outstanding. He was one of the most gifted players I played against. He was also a nice bloke off the field. He seemed to be too nice.*'

Going into the second Test, the All Blacks had not had a win in seven internationals. The New Zealand public demanded results, despite their team now being underdogs. Playing in Christchurch, the home side had, however, a decided advantage, especially in the forwards.

The All Blacks won 8–0, Bob giving an accomplished display and yet failing with the boot. Jack, it was said, gave another polished display '*and looked the complete footballer*'.

That aside, the match was described as '*stodgy*' and '*boring*', with the All Blacks obviously determined to keep the ball away from the talented Lions backs. The win clearly gave the All Blacks the psychological advantage in the series.

THE RETURN OF THE WOUNDED CAPTAIN

The third Test was '*do or die*' for the tourists. A win would set up an exciting finale in Auckland. A loss would seal the series for the All Blacks. The Lions were not helped when captain Mullen pulled a leg muscle on the Monday and Ken Jones suffered an ankle injury; both were forced to withdraw.

The Wellington weather was windy as usual, resulting in grandstand tickets on the black market selling for three times their original value of one pound. The Test was the first to be filmed by the National Film Unit in New Zealand, while fans from throughout the country flocked to the capital for the match.

101

Perhaps the keenest fan was one A. Bousted of Eketahuna, who made the trip over the Rimutakas (the hills separating Wellington from the rest of the North Island) in his motor-driven wheelchair. Travelling in wet and windy conditions, the journey took him three hours and he must have been freezing watching the international afterwards.

Befitting what was riding on the result, the rugby was intense. The All Blacks' hopes seemed dashed when captain Ron Elvidge had to retire injured seven minutes from half-time. A collision with Jack Matthews had resulted in a gashed head and an injured collarbone.

Ahead 3–0 at the break, the Lions got quite a shock when Elvidge returned one minute after the start of the second half, his right eye covered with sticking plaster and his right arm obviously troubling him. The psychological impact must have been significant for both teams. Elvidge acted as a rover, standing back, while Bob went on the wing.

When Elvidge roamed outside the All Black backs, took the final pass and scored on the outside during the second half, it was like a fairy tale for the captain. That try, scored by their injured warrior, inspired the home side to a 6–3 win.

'I remember it clearly,' Bob says. 'He'd taken a pretty bad knock from a front-on tackle from Jackie Matthews and he'd obviously broken something.

'The atmosphere was incredible. We were playing with 14 men and there was nothing in the game. The Lions had developed tremendously, certainly in their forwards. It could have gone either way but I think Ron Elvidge coming back on made a tremendous impact, on the crowd especially. It didn't alter our back line a great deal or the limitations of what we could do but then it was a day when backs weren't meant to shine.'

ONE OF THE BEST INTERNATIONALS AT EDEN PARK

Losing the third Test was a bitter pill for the Lions to swallow. Their improvement had been marked, although it was obvious the All Blacks were the better side up front. Still, the spirit within the Lions squad remained high. Perhaps because of their even mix of nationalities, the leadership of Mullen and the fact that the memories of war were still fresh, this side remained positive despite the results on the field.

Elvidge was still recovering from the injuries that he'd suffered in Wellington and was not named in the All Black squad for the fourth Test. The Lions made eight changes, the return of Ken Jones being the most prominent. Mullen had injured himself again against Auckland and had to withdraw.

By his own admission, Bob hadn't had the best series with the boot. Something was just not quite right and it might have been that the disappointment of his missed kicks in South Africa in 1949 was having an impact psychologically. Yet on his home turf in front of an adoring crowd on a beautiful day, Bob came to play in the fourth Test.

Otago prop Hector Wilson got the home side off to a great start with a try before Bob and Lewis Jones swapped penalties in the ideal conditions.

A few minutes before half-time, the Lions failed to find touch. Bob fielded the ball 10 yards in from the left touchline and 45 yards from the visitors' posts. With a magnificent drop kick, Bob sent the ball between the posts and just over the bar.

'I can remember the kick very clearly,' Bob recalls. 'I thought it was a tremendous kick, really. I am pretty sure it was Kininmonth that took the mark right on the Lions' goal line and he kicked for the line. I took it between the ten-yard mark and the halfway line on the old grandstand side and I just swung infield and let go. It was a beautiful day, there was not a great deal of wind and so it set sail towards the goalposts and went over, fortunately.

'The thing that I remember mainly was that [full-back] Lewis Jones went and forced it [the ball] down! The referee had agreed that it had gone over. Secondly, I remember the reaction of the crowd. I turned away as it's pretty exciting at that moment and I didn't know which way to turn, really. There was a big impact of emotion at that moment.'

Ahead 8–3 at the break, it looked as though the All Blacks would romp away in the second half. They had chances early on, although Lewis Jones was having a terrific match in defence, denying New Zealand with some magnificent tackling.

Eventually, Peter Henderson scored for the All Blacks after following up a neat grubber kick. The try was a just reward for New Zealand, as for most of the match they had looked the better side. The Lions were, however, far from finished.

With five minutes to go, the Lions threw caution to the wind and counter-attacked. Lewis Jones took the ball on his own goal line and shot through a gap with Ken Jones in support. As Lewis approached Bob at the halfway line, he drew the man and threw a long pass over Henderson's head to Ken Jones, who set off on a 50-yard run to score. The sight of Jones being chased by four All Blacks was one of the most memorable of the whole series.

'How that try started,' says Jack, 'was that we had a lineout right inside our 25. We had a signal to occasionally throw the ball long. It was thrown out to me and I gave it to Lewis Jones, who burst through the

middle and then gave it to Ken Jones. It was a gorgeous day and you can imagine the reaction when Ken sprinted away.'

The try was reflective of the way the Lions played the game, according to Bob. 'They had such a magnificent back line, which is not decrying our back line. They had a little more brilliance, especially with a guy like Jackie Kyle at the helm. Lewis Jones was also outstanding but it was more the likes of Kyle, Williams and Matthews in the midfield and Ken Jones on the wing. They were an outstanding side and probably did not have the success they deserved.'

The gap had been narrowed to 11–8. A despairing dive by Henderson on Williams saved a try. Then Jack, using his artistic footwork, dodged through the home backs and punted over Bob's head. Ken Jones chased the ball but it bounced badly for him.

Right on full-time, Williams dived across from a ruck and, unfortunately for the visitors, struck the corner flag.

As clichéd as it sounds, no team deserved to lose. It had been one of the best internationals at Eden Park, full of drama and skill. The Lions had lost the Test and the series but had presented the strongest argument possible that sometimes the result is less important than how you play the game.

MORE THAN RUGBY

Following the fourth Test, the Lions beat the New Zealand Maori 14–9 in Wellington. When the final whistle went, the spectators swarmed onto the field, swamping players of both teams. The band struck up 'Auld Lang Syne' and 'Now is the Hour', and the crowd gave what were described as lusty renditions.

After the players reached the dressing-rooms and had showered, they attended an informal function in the main stand, where tributes were paid to both teams. The president of the Wellington Rugby Union then presented each member of the touring squad with a set of paua cufflinks. The Lions were later that evening presented with travelling rugs by the NZRFU.

When they left New Zealand for Australia, the Lions were farewelled with yet more music, this time from the Hutt Valley High School band. In poor conditions, the Lions stood along the rail of the ship appreciating the waves of scarves, handkerchiefs and hats. The locals had warmed to the Lions.

'We went out to play open rugby,' Jack admits, 'and although we may not have won the Tests, we played open rugby and that is what the New Zealanders liked. Chaps like Williams and Matthews were tremendously *stabilising. We had Ken Jones and Billy Cleaver and there were some terrific players.'*

The fact that the Lions were prepared to run the ball and take the game to the opposition was well received in New Zealand. Jones's try towards the end of the fourth Test reflected that. The brilliance of the Lions backs also added to the impression that what the visitors did best was attack.

For the Lions, however, when the game was over, the game was over. 'They were great socialisers and very socially inclined,' Bob recalls. 'When the game was over, that was the end of it. We chew it all over.'

With 13 Welshmen in the squad, the Lions had their own choir and would regularly be asked to sing wherever they went. They would sing as a means of thanking the ladies for the tea. They would sing after the match. The singing reflected their team's unity.

'Cliff Davies, who was a front-rower in our team, was our conductor,' Jack says. 'Of course, we all learnt how to sing Welsh songs and I remember that dear old Cliff would get up and say, "Breathing boys, breathing" . . . '

Undoubtedly, their success off the field was partly due to the Lions' attitude to touring. They did mix with the locals, they went out to schools, they went to see sheep shearing and they became engrained in the local culture. It was telling that two of the Lions later emigrated to New Zealand.

'We were a happy side and Karl Mullen was an exceptionally good captain,' Jack recalls. 'He was able to blend all the guys together. He was only 23 at the time but he was very good. Because we had no coach and we had the four captains from the home unions, those guys picked the sides and did the training. There was never anything too strenuous.'

New Zealand treated the Lions well. If the boys arrived in a town and wanted to do something, the manager would link up with the liaison officer and something would be arranged. Jack recalls going to movies and being greeted when they arrived and being looked after with ice creams at the interval. 'They were wonderful times,' Jack says, 'and without question amongst the best times of my life.'

THEN AND NOW

Jack went on to have an outstanding career. He played forty-six internationals for Ireland between 1947 and 1958, together with the six internationals on the 1950 Lions tour. He was in the Irish side that beat Australia in Dublin in 1958 and had the amazing record of playing against Scotland 11 times and never losing. When he retired, he was the world's most-capped player.

While Jack had plenty of rugby ahead of him in 1950, Bob thought that he was coming to the end of his career. Like George Nepia in 1930, Bob figured that a series win against the Lions was a good way to bow out of international rugby.

Yet it was not to be. Bob came out of retirement and was selected for the 1953–54 All Black tour of Britain aged 33. Bob showed on that tour that he had lost none of his ability and confirmed that his decision to make himself available for the tour had been the right one.

Bob was asked to make himself available for the All Blacks for the 1956 visit of South Africa but he politely declined.

After finishing with Test rugby, Bob continued to play club rugby in Wellington. For a number of years, he ran a successful menswear store in Petone with All Black captain Andy Leslie, while he took great pleasure in raising two children with his wife.

'I was in business in Petone for 25 years,' Bob recalls. 'We had a son, who was born in 1947, and a daughter born in 1949. My wife likes to tell me that I was always away when that happened! She's right, too – she had a pretty tough life in lots of ways.

'Our children grew up in Petone. We moved up here to the Coromandel in 1978. Apart from the All Blacks, I'm not sure whom I support. These days I'm a bit like the bloke who walks into the ground not knowing either of the teams and instead supports the team with the nicest colour of jersey.

'I feel very proud of what I did in rugby and how I did it,' Bob says, 'and even today I meet people who say they saw me play and I say that I hope they enjoyed it. If they say they did, I reply that so did I.'

Bob believes that there is no realistic comparison between the game in his day and today's game. Modern rugby bores him because of the requirement to retain possession. Allowing more space, especially in the backs, would allow the game to open up, he feels. He is pleased to have played the game in the era he did but he would have enjoyed the money in today's game.

Despite being known for his achievements on the rugby field, Bob's life is now much deeper, much richer. He says he recently gave a talk to a group of women and he didn't speak on rugby at all. Instead, he spoke about his life and the fact that he had met his wife in England after the war, how she had come out to New Zealand with him and how she was unable to believe the passion that New Zealanders felt for the game.

A LIFE IN MEDICINE

After his rugby career finished, Jack's medical career continued to flourish. He left Ireland to live in Indonesia for two years. After a spell back in

Belfast, he emigrated to Zambia to continue his work as a surgeon and to make a difference.

'When I came back home, I had to make up my mind to stay or go abroad. This job turned up in Africa, I got it and I thought that a few years there would be good. Thirty-four and a half years later, I felt I had to make a move. The time I spent in Africa was a wonderful experience.'

Jack tells me the story of being introduced to one of the senior hospital staff on his arrival in Africa. Someone had informed them that Jack had played for Ireland. 'I remember them saying to that person that they were interested not in how many times I had played for Ireland but what sort of surgeon I was!'

When he eventually retired, Jack says his children didn't know what he would do with himself. He says, however, that he hasn't had a spare moment since returning to Belfast. Not surprising as he is without question rugby royalty in Ireland.

He's not been back to New Zealand since 1950, although he's often thought about returning. He wondered whether he should come down for the 2005 tour. Yet I get the feeling that with all those memories from over half a century ago, coming to modern New Zealand would be a disappointment.

Jack is philosophical about the changes that have taken place in rugby. 'We would have accepted it [the changes]. People say to me that it was a pity that I played in the amateur era. I say, "Thank goodness that I'm not playing today." The game has developed into a very, very hard game and the defence is outstanding . . . in the television era, there is so much money that professionalism had to happen.'

Rugby, he tells me emotionally, enriched his life greatly. Doors opened for him because of rugby, invitations were offered. People wanted to talk rugby with him. Lifetime friends were made. Yet time passes on and today's greats will one day be yesterday's heroes. With that in mind, Jack appears as balanced off the field as he once was on it.

'You know, there was a French philosopher who once said that nature gives the ability and chance calls it into play. Those of us who played rugby at a certain level have got to remember that.'

As we shake hands leaving the Europa, Jack says he's enjoyed reminiscing. Heading back into central Belfast I feel sad, as I cannot imagine the players of today being as balanced as Jack Kyle. Hero is an overused word but Jack Kyle is one of mine.

PART THREE
The Tri-Nations

An All Black side doesn't have star players individually;
there's just one star out there for them and that's the
team itself.

Graham Price (former Wales prop)

DOES RUPERT LOVE RUGBY?

July 2004

I was once taught economics by John Mills, who played two matches for the All Blacks on their 1984 tour of Fiji. Mills taught me the fundamentals of supply and demand: a producer supplies the demand in the marketplace in order to maximise profit.

Pure economic theory is devoid of emotion. Its fundamental rationale is about dollars and cents, not history and philosophy. It rarely takes into consideration the social good. It is brutal and insincere but in many ways it is honest.

It's been said that rugby lost its innocence on 27 August 1995, when at a meeting of the International Rugby Board in Paris it was declared that amateurism was no more and that professionalism had arrived.

In truth, rugby had been semi-professional long before the inevitable announcement came. Players of all shapes and sizes of sterling ability from around the world were now being encouraged to turn out for various clubs and professional sides.

The end of amateurism was as inevitable as the end of any player's career. Few administrators, however, appeared to have the foresight to plan for what professionalism would mean and what effect it would have on the fundamental ethos of the sport.

This was seen in England, where the clubs and the national body would scrap for years over who controlled the players. In New Zealand, problems arose because of the failure of the administrators to accept that, despite the end of amateurism, the vast majority of players would remain unpaid for play.

To fund the wage bill, television revenue was crucial. In 1995, the rugby unions of New Zealand, Australia and South Africa signed a ten-year US$550 million deal with Rupert Murdoch's News

Corporation. The deal guaranteed that there would be Super 12 and Tri-Nations competitions for the next ten years. New Zealand committed to playing seven Tests, five at home and two away.

This deal not only 'saved' rugby from the vultures of rugby league but it changed the look of international rugby for ever. In the southern hemisphere, it meant that the concept of the traditional tour would become as rare as hen's teeth and that the top players would become commercial servants to the almighty television dollar.

The Tri-Nations competition was central to the package as regular top-class competition could be transferred into large television audiences and vast sponsorship dollars.

Looking at the concept ten years on, it is unfair to criticise the southern hemisphere unions for developing the concept that became the Tri-Nations. After all, it is only with hindsight that the competition can be objectively critiqued. However, when the ink dried on the paper in 1995, the unions were fixed in providing News Corporation with product for the next ten years.

What the administrators can be criticised for is not heeding the warning signs and making the necessary adjustments when the News Corporation deal was to be renegotiated in 2004. It became clear early on in the history of the Tri-Nations that the competition would become stale and that players and spectators alike would eventually tune out.

The Tri-Nations was also fundamentally flawed as a competition. Not having a grand final was a mistake, while not connecting the competition with some worthwhile prize was also a sign of bad planning. The Tests quickly became ho-hum, more like one-off games rather than part of a meaningful competition.

While the New Zealanders and the Australians had the Bledisloe Cup to fight over, the South Africans had nothing. It was not surprising, therefore, that in 2003 there were suggestions that the South Africans were seriously considering severing their ties with New Zealand and Australia and joining forces with the northern hemisphere superpowers.

The competition also bred contempt amongst the players, as they played each other up to four times every season, whether it was in the Super 12 or the Tri-Nations. It also encouraged burnout amongst internationals and has been one of the main reasons mentioned by several players departing for the north why club rugby in Europe is more attractive.

While some rugby administrators and players have suggested making the Tri-Nationals biennial, such a prospect has never been seriously considered. Simply, News Corporation, as the major financier of rugby in the southern hemisphere, now called the tune.

While the Tri-Nations rates well in New Zealand and South Africa, ratings figures are relatively low in Australia. This was one of the sticking points as the unions sought to negotiate a new deal with News Corporation in 2004.

The prospect of a renegotiated deal must have scared the living daylights out of the administrators in the NZRFU, along with their SANZAR partners. Given that around half of the NZRFU's income comes from News Corporation, it is not difficult to gauge their dependency.

The difference, of course, in negotiating positions was that in 1995, News Corporation had a competitor in the World Rugby Corporation. In 2004, News Corporation was virtually on its own. This reality ensured that the southern hemisphere unions were bargaining from anything but a position of strength.

The result of any deal that was substantially less in relative terms than that agreed to in 1995 would have been a significant blow to New Zealand rugby. The player drain to the bigger markets in Europe and Japan would increase markedly, while it would become inevitable in the short term that the All Blacks would have to be chosen from playing stock around the world. It would change the rugby landscape in New Zealand for ever.

News Corporation undoubtedly appreciated the strength of their bargaining position. Yet although this was the case, they realised that rugby had on the whole been good for them. It had ensured their presence in the sporting television arena and given them credibility in previously untapped markets.

As negotiations took place throughout 2004, it became clear that SANZAR would not obtain a deal with News Corporation that in financial terms had appreciated in value from 1995. Simply, the product had not increased in value in the way that had been anticipated.

SANZAR administrators had heard the predictions of impending gloom. They were aware of their weak bargaining position and the fact that anything but an honourable result would see huge changes in the game in the southern hemisphere.

As a result of the economic realities, News Corporation had consistently told SANZAR to expect as much as 30 per cent less in

TV rights income. It was not entirely surprising, therefore, when the new five-year US$323 million contract was heralded as a great achievement. The chief executive of the NZRFU, Chris Moller, asserted that the deal delivered more money than the last five years of the old US$555 million ten-year deal and was an increase of up to 25 per cent.

'A key principle was established at the outset of the broadcast agreement discussions,' Moller said, 'which simply stated that each of the partners had to "have a win" and that the other parties must help each partner win.'

Yet it soon became apparent that SANZAR's new deal had dropped in dollar value by at least 5 per cent, while SANZAR had also added an extra two teams to the Super 12 and a further round of Tri-Nations rugby to keep News Corporation happy.

'It's fair to look at it year by year and for the second five years of the old contract, we received US$340 million,' Australian Rugby Chief Executive Gary Flowers told a Sydney rugby journalist.

'The new deal is US$323 million but we won't know the final figure until we finalise the sale of rights to other countries such as Japan, the Americas, Asia and France,' Flowers said. 'The estimate is we could get between US$345 million and US$350 million, with France expected to contribute significantly. If you factor in this income, we see about a 5 per cent uplift from the final five years of the old deal.'

Still, Australia was hardest hit by this loss of value, with some estimates suggesting that it would be as much as US$55 million worse off over the next five years, after its percentage share of the SANZAR pie declined from 30.25 per cent under the old deal to 27 per cent in the new contract.

Australia would be forced to provide an extra US$5 million a year to fund a new Super 12 franchise. New Zealand and South Africa would also suffer US$5 million losses annually.

Not surprisingly, the public reaction to the new deal focused not only on the money but also on the introduction of two new Super 12 franchises and an extra round of Tri-Nations from 2006. More rugby was not overwhelmingly welcomed by a public already saturated.

The players, All Blacks Justin Marshall and Carlos Spencer most prominently, voiced concern about the regularity of the competitions. Their points were valid and yet failed to take into consideration the economic realities of securing the deal with News Corporation.

'The fact that we have been able to maintain and increase revenue a bit is testament to the quality of rugby union within SANZAR countries,' Chris Moller said of the deal. 'Secondly, it makes a lie of claims that the general public finds Tri-Nations and Super 12 rugby boring. To those who say the expansion of Tri-Nations and Super 12 rugby is boring, I think they really have got to reflect on the fact that the people who write out the cheques and who have to make money out of it take a fundamentally different view.'

As could be expected in the professional age, the New Zealand Rugby Players' Association saw the economic possibilities for its members, taking the deal into consideration in their negotiation of a new collective bargaining agreement.

Likewise, the Australian Professional Rugby Players' Association demanded increased payments for the greater workload expected of its members.

Such actions were, on the face of it, callous. Yet it made commercial sense for the player unions to look for a pay rise if their members were being asked to perform more. What other profession would expect its main actors to perform more but not be compensated accordingly?

The NZRFU advised its players to be realistic about what the new deal would mean for their pay packets. Still, asking more of the players had to come at a cost and that had to be an increase in salary for Super 12 players and internationals.

Although paying for their new franchises, both the Australians and the South Africans reacted positively to having an extra Super 12 side. For the Australians, it meant developing the game in Perth. For South Africa, it meant probably breaking up the always uneasy partnership between the Free Staters and the traditionalists in the old Transvaal.

For the New Zealanders, it meant keeping a large slice of the broadcasting revenue and that, the administrators argued, was a good result.

'Quite simply, if this agreement was not in the best interests of New Zealand rugby and its constituents, we would not have signed on,' Chris Moller said.

What New Zealand ended up with was 33 per cent of the future broadcasting revenue split, with South Africa obtaining 38 per cent, and the Australians reduced to 29 per cent, a reflection of the popularity of the product amongst broadcasters there. The News

Corporation deal was neither bad nor a huge coup for SANZAR. It was simply an economic reflection of the worth of the product to News Corporation.

The deal may have saved professional rugby in the southern hemisphere as we know it in the short term but it did not guarantee its long-term survival. Sooner or later, SANZAR administrators will appreciate that in the very near future the SANZAR unions will not be able to match the financial clout of northern hemisphere or Japanese clubs.

To retain their place at the head of the rugby ladder, each of the unions is going to have to ensure that their national side is strong. To do that, they need to pick from the best players. If local competitions cannot afford the best, then inevitably national sides will be made up of players playing around the world. As a noted philosopher once said, 'It's all about economics.'

Despite all of this, the News Corporation deal seems a world away from the honest toil that is club rugby. There has never been a clearer example of the fact that there are two games of rugby in New Zealand: the professional and amateur. Still, I never thought that rugby and commerce would ever collide so brutally when I was sitting in John Mills's class all those years ago.

A MAN OF CHARACTER

Friday, 16 July 2004

The old debate about whether great coaches coach great players or whether great coaches make great players is never going to be definitively answered. Yet with coaches, as with players, the cream rises to the top and good coaches tend to have success follow them.

No one knows this better than Wayne Smith, assistant coach of the All Blacks. It's been a roundabout ride for Wayne and yet I get the feeling that he feels most comfortable coaching in New Zealand.

As a player, Wayne starred in the red and black of Canterbury. He played 35 games for the All Blacks (including 17 Tests), although injury and inconsistent selection blighted his career. In the

1983 series against the Lions, for example, he was ruled out of the first and fourth Tests through injury.

But in playing for Canterbury with his mates, Wayne excelled. He was not only a decision maker but also a leader within one of the greatest New Zealand provincial sides in history.

Wayne was also one of the most well-rounded All Blacks and was a deep thinker with a clear understanding of right and wrong.

It was inevitable that Wayne would move into coaching. Stints in Italy, Hawke's Bay (in administration and coaching) and then back in Canterbury were all part of his apprenticeship.

Taking over the Crusaders in 1997 with Peter Sloane, his side won the title in 1998 and 1999. He was therefore a natural appointment as All Black coach in 2000, following in the wake of John Hart.

Wayne's All Black teams were characterised by their attacking style and their strong sense of unity. They loved playing for the national side under Wayne and enjoyed the way he brought his own humility and a sense of basic human values to the institution.

Then came Sydney 2001. In a fairy-tale ending for retiring Australian captain John Eales, the Australians grabbed victory from the jaws of defeat. This after doing exactly the same thing in Wellington in 2000.

Wayne was naturally shattered. Anybody would have been. In his honest way, he questioned whether he was the right man for the job. He wanted the All Blacks to win that much. His indecision cost him his position. John Mitchell was appointed All Black coach after the Tri-Nations.

The saga cost not only Wayne but also New Zealand rugby. He should have taken the All Blacks through to the World Cup in 2003, preferably with Mitchell as his forwards coach. Wayne was hamstrung by his honesty and the fact that the NZRFU had lumbered him with Tony Gilbert, who was clearly not his first choice as a coaching partner.

'I took responsibility for it,' Wayne says looking me in the eye. 'If you realise you are part of the problem, then you can do something about it . . . sometimes you've got to realise that there is no point in looking at the players and that the answer lies in what you are doing.

'What really disappointed me is that we had lost that game in injury time, like we had the year before. I had to be accountable, like the players were, and I thought that the players would understand that. Their selection is always up in the air and dependent on their performance and I felt that we [the coaches] should be the same.

'I didn't think it was a weakness. To me, it was a good thing, as I wanted to have the opportunity to put it right. As it turned out, I wasn't given the chance. That's life.'

Wayne was hurt at the time. But being able to rationalise what happened enabled him to get on with his life.

So Wayne packed his bags and headed to the Northampton club in England. There, he was an unqualified success: the players liked and respected him. His side played entertaining rugby. He enjoyed the environment, rediscovered himself and didn't want to leave.

Still, when Graham Henry came calling in December 2003, the opportunity to return to the All Black environment was too good to turn down. Wayne returned to New Zealand shortly before the English series in 2004.

'If there's a million-to-one outside bet, that would be it,' Wayne says of his reintroduction to the All Black coaching set-up. 'Although I did follow the All Blacks, like any passionate Kiwi, I never thought I would have any involvement again. In fact [when we left New Zealand], we packed everything up. I was in England on an ancestry visa and I was planning to be there until 2007 to qualify for an ancestry passport.

'When Graham rang, I actually thought that he was ringing to get an insight into the job and the pressures. You could have knocked me over with a feather when he asked me to come over and coach with him. I couldn't even assimilate it for a while.'

Wayne tells me that initially it was a difficult decision to make. Although he hankered to return to New Zealand and link up with the All Blacks again, he was also loyal to the Northampton club and the people there.

He spoke to the club, and the club owner Keith Barwell, about the offer. He knew he hadn't quite achieved everything that he'd wanted but after a week of pondering the offer, it became obvious to him and the club that there was only one answer.

If it's a redemption of sorts for Wayne, he appears pretty relaxed about it. As we sit outside his modern townhouse in the trendy Christchurch suburb of Merivale, I feel that Wayne is at ease.

It might be the fact that he was a top sportsman himself. This man knows what he's about. It could also be that, like I was with Robbie Deans, I'm intimidated because he's a boyhood hero.

I figure that after being head coach of the All Blacks, it must have been difficult for Wayne to come back as an assistant. This despite the reality that in modern rugby the individual coaches all have their specific role and can actually have more hands-on power than the head coach.

'It wasn't difficult at all,' he says of the decision. 'If you can make your contribution, you can do that in whatever role. I think I'm actually in the role that I really enjoy, which is coaching out on the field with the boys and being involved primarily in the performance of the team, rather than doing all the promotions and media stuff.'

Such a comment symbolises Wayne's lack of ego. It is an insight into the balance in his life. Rugby is important, yet it is not the be all and end all.

'I would hope [the balance] is what I am aiming towards, although the reality is not always like that. If you ask my family, they would say that the game rules their lives, which it does to an extent. It's something that I have to work really hard at.

'In my reviews, it's always something that's mentioned. As much as anyone, I understand that from a playing point of view, while from a coaching point of view it is important to look after yourself and make sure that you are healthy and well and enthusiastic and vibrant. It's a challenge for me, as my natural tendency is to work and work and that becomes unhealthy after a while.'

It is clear from his surroundings that professional rugby has treated Wayne well. Alex Wyllie, the provincial coach for much of Wayne's playing career, used to come down off the farm to coach on wet Tuesday and Thursday nights. Still, the accountability of a professional coach has become more profound.

It has also led to some staggering twists and turns. While Wayne should have coached the All Blacks at the World Cup in 2003, he was now poised to be part of the coaching staff at the World Cup in 2007.

He laughs as I point out the irony. 'It's amazing. I still have to pinch myself. I'm doing what I love doing, we've got some talented young players and hopefully we'll get an opportunity to go to the World Cup together. That would be fantastic.'

A further irony was that after coaching one of England's top club sides and a number of players in the English set-up, his first assignment back in the All Black fold was coaching against the English side.

The English game is very strong, he tells me. Twelve near-Test-strength teams, made up of internationals from around the world, ensure that there are no easy matches. The programme is heavy (Northampton played 29 games on the trot in Wayne's last season), and that and the weather conditions dictate the style of rugby played.

'The game tends to be a bit slower, more forward-orientated, but they are tough. It's a contest in the tackle and in every single tackle there's a war going on. Teams are often happy to use their forward advantage, kick to the corners and play old-fashioned rugby. It's a necessity, really. It's not a game you can base on fast speeds and movement all the year round.'

The competition teaches mental toughness in an attritional sense and is maybe better preparation for the vigours of Test rugby. It is also good training for coaches in the day-to-day challenges that arise. Graham Henry, Steve Hansen and Wayne all honed their skills in the northern hemisphere.

Like players, coaches develop with experience. English club rugby, Wayne tells me, enables coaches to regularly confront decision-making situations. The more you do it, the better you become. As a result of the number of matches in England, coaches gain the type of experience that they wouldn't get elsewhere.

Having been absent from the All Black set-up for just under three years, I wonder whether things had changed. Was this All Black side attempting to do the same things as the All Blacks did in 2001?

'The intentions are pretty similar,' Wayne says. 'It all means a lot to us. We're trying to ensure that people who play for the All Blacks treasure what it's about. We're after a pretty open and positive environment. Graham's a very positive coach and very bold in the sort of game we're trying to play and very bold in selections. We're trying to create an environment where people can be themselves and not who everyone else wants them to be.

'There's a lot of pressure on players these days and you can't always live up to what old All Blacks want you to be or the public want you to be. That's been an issue in the past. We just want these guys to be themselves, be true to who they are and be proud of what they're doing. If that's the case, then the players will play with heart and that's what makes the difference.'

The All Blacks' demolition of England in June had been the perfect reintroduction to New Zealand rugby for Wayne. Yet he understands that the losses had provided Clive Woodward with the perfect trial run. Wayne has no doubt that the tour had an impact on Sir Clive and had let him know how tough it was going to be in

2005 with the Lions.

'I think they [the English] had a feeling that we were going to be soft up front. That they would be able to wade through us. That wasn't the case and I think they now understand that it's going to be a bit of a battle. That will help their mindset from the start.'

Keeping the players fresh after a long and hard domestic season will be a challenge for Clive, Wayne feels. He's reluctant to give too much away about what he'd do if he were in charge.

'I think he [Clive] is doing a helluva a lot of planning and he's going about it the right way in terms of talking to players and finding out what happened on the last tour.

'If I were in charge of the Lions, I would be looking at some initiatives to get some enthusiasm in their gameplan and get some enjoyment from the tour. I'd be making sure the players enjoy the experience of touring, rather than thinking that they're just out here to do a job.

'It's a bit military-like at the moment, their whole persona. The whole campaign seems so strategically planned that it's like going into war but it's not that. The players need to be enthusiastic and love what they're doing to do it well . . . '

The All Black management will attempt to make the Lions series enjoyable for the players and although it's important that they win it for New Zealand rugby and for themselves, it has to be put in perspective. Getting the balance is the key to success, Wayne says.

Rugby to Wayne is far more than just performing on the field in front of thousands of people. It's about making friends for life, just like he did with his mates in the Canterbury side in the 1980s. Although money has the potential to change things, the professional teams Wayne has coached have been as close as the sides he was involved in as a player.

The common denominator of course is Wayne himself and the values that he brings to the teams that he's involved with. The professional age should not prevent the adoption of traditional values in rugby, values that make the man as much as the player.

BLOSSOMING LOVE

Saturday, 17 July 2004

It's 7.30 p.m. I'm sitting by myself at a trendy wine bar called Le Plonk on Manchester Street in Christchurch. I'm nervous and like a naughty schoolboy I can't sit still. I leaf through a magazine and wonder when she will grace me with her presence. Had I given her the right address, the right time? I can smell the cold each time someone walks through the door and it's unsettling me even more.

Before I know it, she's arrived and she looks fantastic. She's dressed for winter warmth but already I love the way her hair flows down the back of her neck like a long, even-paced French river. She is girlishly pretty and as she takes her coat off and orders a glass of Shiraz, I know it's going to be a good evening.

* * *

It's the type of night that only happens in Wellington. You wouldn't want to be flying tonight but we still expect 30 All Blacks and Wallabies to brave the wind and rain and put on an entertaining spectacle. Somebody should point out the irony to the administrators.

Stephen Larkham sends his kick-off out on the full; it's going to be that kind of night for inside-backs. The All Blacks put early pressure on the Wallabies, although mercurial full-back Chris Latham does well to keep out the searching grubber kicks and the high balls that are sent his way.

As you might expect, most of the time the ball is sent wide a knock-on results. The All Blacks have 80 per cent dominance in territory in the first half yet lead only 3–0 at the break thanks to a penalty by Canterbury's Daniel Carter.

* * *

I love the way she talks. I love what she talks about. We rest in a cosy leather lounge suite, sipping our red wine and talking about anything but rugby. She tells me she's been to Europe twice, that she loves the sights and sounds of Paris and that she speaks French.

After an hour, we reluctantly leave for the Italian restaurant that I've booked for us. As we stroll across the central city, I'm thinking about what's going on in Wellington, although I have no urgency to pop into a sports bar and see what's happening. It's not just because of the good company. But I'm not sure whether it's because I know what's going to happen or whether I don't care as much as I should.

The Italian restaurant is cosy but sparsely patronised. It's a sure sign the rugby is on. As a result, we have more service than we know what to do with. We talk openly, curiously, yet I feel I'm talking to three waiters and two waitresses as well as the attractive young woman sitting opposite.

* * *

The weather has got worse – if that's possible. Irish referee Alain Rolland is penalising both sides off the park and the frustration is growing within both teams.

The hookers – Kevin Mealamu and Brendan Cannon – vent their frustration and are sent to the sin-bin to cool down, if there was any need in such conditions.

Carter doubles New Zealand's lead after 45 minutes with his second penalty. Both teams, though, are keeping it tight, both appearing overly afraid in such conditions to make mistakes.

Still, when Jerry Collins bursts towards the line and Joe Rokocoko and Mils Muliaina shovel the ball left, Doug Howlett scores in the corner. Carter's conversion gives the All Blacks a 13–0 lead.

* * *

For some reason, we talk about taking high school Latin. It's about as far removed from rugby as is possible to be but I'm in seventh heaven.

There is something about taking a date to an Italian restaurant that reeks of romance: is it the food, the cultural atmosphere, the way male waiters wearing too much cologne stand over you suggestively?

She tells me about the books she likes, how she wants to make her mark in law. I listen intently, thriving on every word. This is not date make-believe: I am genuinely interested.

Afterwards, we go to a movie appropriately entitled *Fog of War* –

I could have been watching the rugby after all. The movie is about the changing philosophy of former American secretary of defence Robert McNamara. It's gritty stuff and I'm entranced. As I savour an ice cream with a pretty girl next to me, I feel balanced. And now deeply ashamed that I'm missing the rugby.

* * *

The Australians aren't finished. With 14 minutes to go, the ball bobbles out from beneath Rokocoko as he attempts to cover a punt from Australian second-five Matt Giteau. Centre Sterling Mortlock slides under the posts.

Giteau converts, and at 13–7 the Australians are in with a shot of an unlikely victory.

Both teams increase their intensity but the All Blacks hang on and when Mortlock makes a high tackle on the All Black captain Tana Umaga, Daniel Carter's third penalty settles it: 16–7 to the All Blacks.

* * *

I come out of the cinema dying to know what has happened in Wellington. I want to stop someone in the car park and ask whether they know the result. I dare not. Still, it would give my companion a taste of things to come if we see each other again.

I drive her home and my mind returns to her. It's been a fantastic night and I'm inspired. I turn the car off outside her house, look at her sincerely and move to kiss her on the cheek. She adjusts her angle and we kiss on the lips quietly. I smile. She gets out of the car and as I drive off, I glance at her. She makes my night by glancing back in my direction.

I drive home quicker than I ought: I've got the rugby taped on the video. Had I known the quality of the rugby, I'm not sure I would have bothered.

FROM WALES WITH LOVE

Tuesday, 20 July 2004

The Marist–Albion Rugby Club in Christchurch is typical of most rugby clubs in New Zealand: close-knit, proudly traditional, respectful of the fact that rugby is not just about the game played on the paddock. Fundamental Kiwi values spanning two world wars, a depression and, in 1981, a Springbok tour.

When I was growing up, Marist (as it was known before amalgamation) was the enemy. Many of their players came from St Bede's College, a Catholic school whom we opposed on the sports fields up and down Christchurch. Their senior sides (striped in green and white) seemed to win more titles than they ought. Theirs was camaraderie glued together by conviction.

The Marist lads always seemed so close. Win or lose, it appeared as though the Pope was behind them and that this was giving them holy strength. How could anyone compete with Pope John Paul II? Apparently, he played the sport during his youth. Perhaps he supported Marist literally as well as metaphorically.

Throughout Marist's golden reign in the 1980s, the name Hansen was always prominent. Des, the father of the family, coached the senior side for years. His legacy was not only champion teams but champion men, many of whom would themselves be good coaches later in life.

Sons Steve, Kelly and Darryl all played for the senior Marist side, Kelly playing for Canterbury against the 1993 Lions. Yet it is not surprising that it is Steve, the eldest son, who has had the greatest impact in a sport that itself became almost a religion in the Hansen household.

I've known the assistant All Black coach for a number of years and I've come to admire him. It wasn't always like that. Before I met him, his public persona suggested gruffness and stand-offishness. But when I heard that while he coached the amateur High School Old Boys club side in Christchurch some of his players (including Rueben Thorne) used to raid his home fridge, I knew that he was a player's coach.

Steve's philosophy centres on getting close to his players. While they have to realise that coaches need to make the tough decisions, the more a coach can understand the mental make-up of a player the better chance he has of helping the player perform.

To understand Steve you have to understand the environment in which he grew up. To say that he was born to coach is corny but it takes into account the cold Saturday mornings when Des Hansen would take his eldest son to rugby at Hagley Park in Christchurch. It is suggested in the nights Des and Steve would sit around the kitchen table discussing tactics when Steve was captain of the Christchurch Boys' High School first XV in 1977. It was also reflected in the years when Steve was captain and Des the coach of the crack Marist senior side in the early '80s.

'He would be the key figure in my make-up as a coach,' Steve says of his father. 'I was fortunate that I had a lot of good coaches and you learn from all of them. Dad challenged us to ask questions and not be satisfied when something worked without understanding why something else didn't. I think that's one of the reasons so many coaches have developed from his teams.'

Steve wasn't a bad player himself: he'd played for Canterbury as a midfielder, while he'd also proved to be a quality captain. A Marist Will Carling. Still, his coaching career has exceeded anything he achieved as a player.

Like Graham Henry, he'd come up the hard way: club, province, Super 12 side, northern hemisphere OE (overseas experience), All Blacks. I remember when Steve was assistant Canterbury coach. He was technically a fine forwards coach, while his players loved him like an elder brother.

He'd followed Graham Henry to Wales and taken over when the Welsh public became impatient for success. Whether he had achieved success in Wales depended on whom you spoke to. Yet there was no denying that he'd returned home a better coach.

So here we are in a pleasant Christchurch suburb, talking rugby. I haven't spoken to Steve for the best part of six years and so I subconsciously compare where I was then with where I am now. It immediately strikes me that when it comes to dealing with the media, Steve's now a seasoned professional.

It also appears obvious that this is a man who's pleased to be home. He spent two and a half challenging years in Wales but the cost had been being away from two of his children, Whitney and Jessie.

'That was the hardest thing about the whole thing, separating the family. It got difficult when you had to say goodbye at the airport but it was always great when you went to pick them [the kids] up. We knew that as a family we had to go through that yet there were benefits as well. The girls got to travel to the other side of the world and they had to learn to do that on their own.'

Returning to New Zealand hadn't been a difficult decision to make for the man known to some as 'Shag'. He'd wanted to return home because of his children but he needed a new goal. Then Graham Henry came calling.

Going from the head coach to an assistant's role wasn't difficult. 'As long as you are in a coaching environment where you have an ability to do your job and have a say in all the things that go with the team.

'With the set-up we have at the moment, that's what's happening. Obviously, Graham is the leader and driving the bus but for any team to be any good, you need a lot of other people helping.'

Being an All Black coach comes with many perks. But it also comes with responsibilities. A truism but a reality when you've got to tell one of your prodigies that he's surplus to requirements.

Steve and Rueben Thorne are close. On one famous occasion on the way to Ashburton in Mid Canterbury, Steve and the former All Black captain Todd Blackadder had a conversation. Todd suggested that if he and Rueben swapped positions (from lock to flanker) Rueben would become an All Black. As it turned out, that's exactly what happened.

I could imagine the emotion within all of the parties when Rueben was told that he wasn't in the first All Black squad for 2004. There may have been tears, as these are, after all, not passionless individuals.

'I've got a lot of respect and admiration for Rueben and we've travelled a lot of roads together,' Steve says thoughtfully. 'We enjoy each other's company and we're good mates. At the end of the day, Ruebey wasn't playing the type of game that we were looking for. I think he's capable of doing that and I think given some support he'll play that type of game and he'll make his way back into the All Blacks.'

Steve's specific role has been that of a mentor to the All Black forwards. The media had had a field day in the first half of the international season suggesting that the fire had returned to the All Black pack.

Such fighting words had evolved through the introduction of

hard men like Carl Hayman and Keith Robinson into the All Black engine room. I wondered whether this philosophy was media hype.

'There is no doubt that we've had to go back to the basics because Super 12 has snowed over the fact that we're not good at it [forward play]. Super 12 is a hit-and-run game. Test rugby is more of a physical contest, it's a closer contest, more dour than Super 12 and played in different conditions.

'Through that we've allowed some of our basic skills to slip away. We've been guilty in the past of thinking that we've got all the answers. When you go up to the UK, you actually find that there's some really good stuff there, especially in their forward play, which is hugely contested.'

Steve is starting to sound like journalist Steve Jones but what he is saying makes sense. New Zealanders often tend to have blinkers on when it comes to evaluating their own rugby. Tradition counts for a lot but it cannot override common sense in the professional age.

FATHER AND SON

Saturday, 24 July 2004

The Springboks are in town but no one in Christchurch seems to give a rat's arse. Blunt as that is, it's the truth. Millions, perhaps, will be tuning in to watch the All Blacks play the Springboks at Jade Stadium tonight but the atmosphere in the week preceding is sterile.

It saddens me that this is the case. First, because the rich and often political history between the two nations deserves reverence. Second, because Dad and I have tickets and we want to feel the atmosphere and the passion of an All Blacks v. Springboks clash.

For years, Dad had bought the tickets to the rugby and taken my brothers and me along. I'm not sure I was always grateful but he was a bloody good father in that regard. On this occasion, I've bought the tickets and told Dad that we would be going together like we did when I was a kid.

ABOVE: Days when rugby was just a game played on Saturdays for fun – the author (second winning Lincoln Under-14 club side, 1984. (Author's collection)

INSET: A hero, then and now – Ulster and Ireland's Jack Kyle, one of the great men of rugby.

BELOW: A gentleman, the writer's hero and a pretty decent player to boot – Ireland and the Lions' Ollie Campbell. (*Irish News*)

RIGHT: 'Rugby is a bit like a circus. You pack up, you go to another game, you pack up . . . you don't know who you are after a while.' – All Black Anton Oliver, the epitome of the modern rugby player.
(Otago Rugby Union)

BELOW: For the love of rugby, times gone by and a sense of belonging – Lincoln Rugby Club president Russell Watkins outside the place that he calls home.
(Author's collection)

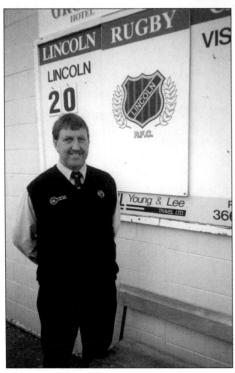

A father-and-son Test – Justin Marshall and All Black captain Tana
Umaga attack the Springboks in Christchurch 2004, a match the home
side almost lost in the merry-go-round that is Tri Nations rugby.
(Geoff Sloan)

RIGHT: When rugby was a game where you swapped jerseys, enjoyed each other's company after the match and made lifelong friends – Canterbury and the All Blacks' Dennis Young at his home in Rangiora, just north of Christchurch. (Author's collection)

BELOW: The iconic Colin Meads makes another strong break against the 1966 Lions. Sadly for the visitors, they lost the series 4–0. (*Christchurch Star*)

ABOVE: When Barry was King – Barry John launches another attack against the All Blacks in the second Test at Christchurch in 1971, the only Test the Lions lost in that series.
(*Christchurch Star*)

LEFT: One of the true stalwarts of New Zealand rugby – former All Black captain Tane Norton relaxes at the new bar he co-owns, the Speights Ale House, in Christchurch.
(Author's collection)

ABOVE: Where have all the good players gone in Scottish rugby?
Utility Chris Paterson is one of a handful of truly outstanding current
Scottish internationals. (Gordon Fraser, Haddington)

BELOW: The soul of Irish rugby – Blackrock players clap off players
from the home club, Shannon, in Limerick in October 2004.
(Author's collection)

ABOVE: Announcing the generals – chief executive John Feehan (left), manager Bill Beaumont and coach Sir Clive Woodward unveil their coaching staff in October 2004 in Cardiff for the Lions tour of New Zealand. (Author's collection)

BELOW: A club's pride – the Lions jerseys belonging to Colm Tucker, Gerry McLoughlin (left) and Mick Galway (right) that are proudly displayed at the Shannon Rugby Club in Limerick. (Author's collection)

ABOVE: The meaning of rugby – the author (far left), Sean Wallace (second from left), Sean's mate, the lad from Limerick and the bloke from Donegal who blew a loan that was earmarked for a new kitchen to come to New Zealand to watch the Lions, enjoy a memorable afternoon in Christchurch before the first Test, 25 June 2005. (Author's collection)

BELOW: Lions supporters invade the centre of Christchurch on the morning of the first Test. They brought with them plenty of fun, spirit and a fair amount of disposable cash. (Author's collection)

I'm feeling embarrassed: although I reckoned it was a good idea to buy tickets, maybe it was too much too soon. Dad is proud. Maybe the changing of the guard should have been more gradual, more sensitively handled.

So Dad and I drive into town, much the same way as we did when I was a kid. Dad doesn't like Tana Umaga: as a player, not as a person, for I don't think Tana and Dad have ever met.

'He's no captain,' Dad says. I wonder whether, like me, he hasn't got over Rueben Thorne being dropped.

'What do you mean?' I ask.

'I mean, centre's no place to captain the All Blacks from. I'm not sure whether he's even the best centre in the country.'

'Come on, Dad,' I say, in my normal non-diplomatic fashion. 'He's world class, anyone will tell you that!' I feel like a teenager doing my best to explain why I've missed curfew on a Saturday night out.

We park behind the railway storage sheds that used to fascinate me as a child. They are red and as big as barns. I used to wonder how many rats and other unsavoury animals called the place home. I had nightmares of being locked in one of them.

We put on our winter woollies and grab the thermos of warm coffee that Mum has packed for us. It's difficult to know who's taking the lead: Dad because he drove us here and, well, because he's Dad, or me because I bought the tickets and now feel as close to rugby as a lover feels to his mistress.

Dad and I stride uncomfortably towards Jade Stadium. I don't know what to say and yet the route to the ground is strangely familiar: it is the same route that we used to take all those years ago.

When we go through the tunnel that used to scare the hell out of me, we can actually hear ourselves talk and it is frighteningly reassuring. It's not packed and for once in my life I feel like an adult of mature standing.

Dad's tiredness is becoming more apparent to me each stride we take towards Jade Stadium. I feel for him: no man of his age should have to work so hard. I feel guilty and an overwhelming urge to take up the slack, to do that work my father does and pay my dues.

When we get inside the ground, we notice the atmosphere is building. It is far from electric and somewhat staid, as Test match atmospheres can often be. It's as if the notion of the nation is that much more difficult for a rugby fan to grasp. The All Blacks are, well, New Zealand's team but the 'us' is bigger than when the

Crusaders are playing and perhaps harder to identify with.

Still, in the professional era, the atmosphere is more corporate. I get the feeling that the true blue rugby fan, the bloke who works in the clubrooms each Saturday behind the bar, is not here tonight. I feel an overwhelming sense of sadness as I contemplate this, a real sense of loss that the average fan has to some degree been left behind in the move to professional rugby.

Dad and I are still not talking much. I really don't know what to say. So we talk about the basics: the way the ground is filling up, where we used to sit when I was growing up. I reflect on the fact that I've got much to thank Dad for in encouraging my love of rugby.

The pre-match antics do not inspire Dad; he wants rugby, real rugby. Eventually the sound of the haka is blasted across the ground and finally I feel a sense of national emotion within the crowd. I am a New Zealander and I am deeply proud.

As we take our seats and await the kick-off, it occurs to me how difficult it must be for Dad's generation to relate to an All Black side of such cultural diversification.

Tonight, there are Fijian New Zealanders, Samoan New Zealanders, Tongan New Zealanders, Maori New Zealanders and European New Zealanders representing their country. All that's needed is for there to be an Asian New Zealander for the side to be a true reflection of cosmopolitan New Zealand.

The Springboks come out firing. They are still clearly a proud rugby nation. They score tries. New Zealand make mistakes. In his tired state, Dad's pretty negative about what's happening. He's probably right but I don't like hearing such cultural blasphemy.

The All Blacks claw themselves back into the match. The Springboks are now giving away penalties. The All Blacks are showing grit and determination. Dad doesn't think we deserve to win. I can sense that in his words. I don't care: I want us to win at all costs.

The tension mounts and we are on the edge of our seats as the crowd realises the All Blacks can claw victory from the jaws of defeat.

I have the feeling the All Blacks will pull through: that somehow the apparent good mood within the camp will ensure that New Zealand will win.

The ball moves through All Black hands, the home side retaining possession and, like a good rugby league side, keeping control of the ball. I don't know how but a gap emerges on the outside. Auckland winger Doug Howlett takes the pass and like lightning scorches over to score in our corner.

The crowd go crazy as Howlett is smothered by his teammates. Many of the South Africans slump to their knees, trudging their way back to behind the goalposts. I pump the air.

The All Blacks are going to win! I do now feel a degree of sympathy for the South Africans: they have played well and, as Dad has continually told me, probably deserved to win this evening.

The high does not go away immediately. The Test has been a drama and although there have been plenty of mistakes, the All Blacks have come though. Despite the over-commercialism and the made-for-TV timing, the contest has prevailed like in an old-fashioned boxing duel.

I look at Dad and I know that he's enjoyed it. It's been worth the money. One part of me wants to say 'I told you so' but it's tempered by the fact that this man loves rugby as much as I do. Despite his tiredness and my restlessness, I've enjoyed the experience.

I've had reinforced tonight the fact that the era of my childhood is a thing of the past. That the days of 15 European men representing New Zealand are over. New Zealand is multicultural and the All Blacks reflect this, as they should.

I've also had reinforced the fact that going to the rugby with my Dad can still be an enjoyable experience. I now realise that this is a man who, whether I like it or not, encouraged and developed my love of the game. He can be cranky right enough. Yet his heart is good and I'm proud to be his son.

As we walk back to the car, I reflect on the night's rugby. I think about Spencer's tactical kicking, Howlett's last-minute try. Yet I'm also thinking about one day taking any future son that I might have along to Jade Stadium to continue the family ritual. It won't be a bad way for the youngster to grow up, I'm sure.

CONTROLLING THE ALL BLACKS

Tuesday, 27 July 2004

Six wins from six Tests. Although the All Blacks were scratchy the previous Saturday against the Springboks, they remain undefeated. The talkback callers are reasonably positive. A fair proportion of them will head to work on Monday morning happy campers.

The real challenges for the All Blacks will come in the away Tests in the Tri-Nations. As with Super 12, there is no underestimating the benefit of home-ground advantage. It is becoming as important as it is in club rugby in France. The New Zealand rugby public is, as usual, getting carried away with the short term.

The All Blacks aren't. If anything, there is a degree of reality within the camp. I detected that from talking with Steve Hansen. I know that the deeply analytical Graham Henry is a realist. The All Blacks talk about the next game being the most important. It is, but it is obvious that they also see the bigger picture.

I like the way this All Black team combines professionalism with old-fashioned values. They appear well balanced. Somehow they have managed to get the balance right between the tradition that they follow and the practicalities of being one of the world's most obvious sporting brands.

Some previous All Black managements have focused too much on professionalism or ignored the responsibilities to media and sponsors. Henry, Smith, Hansen and co. are, however, putting in place an environment that caters for everyone.

The coaching trio's planning and vast experience is obviously a major reason why the 2004 All Blacks are operating like a well-oiled machine. Yet the role of a quietly spoken, young-looking manager should not be underestimated.

You know a person is important when you ring them and only their partner's name is on the answer-machine message. Darren Shand laughs when I mention this to him, before suggesting that it's the role that's important and not the man who fills it.

The All Black manager's job has taken on various degrees of importance down the years. In the past, it was an unofficial name for the coach, as in the role of an honorary manager.

At times in recent years, the All Black manager has been in charge of the overall planning. Under Andrew Martin, for example, the manager was responsible for the whole set-up and, ultimately, was accountable.

That all changed under John Mitchell's reign. He got rid of Martin's style and felt that if he was ultimately accountable for the success on the field, he should be in charge of the whole ship. On the face of it, this was entirely reasonable. The problem was: what happened if the coach neglected certain areas of performance?

When Graham Henry ousted Mitchell at the end of 2003, the role changed slightly again. Now the roles would be clearly defined so that each of the management knew what their responsibilities were.

Ultimately, the on-field buck stopped with Graham but his reign would clearly not be the dictatorial era of that of his predecessor.

'I think we've got a good balance,' Darren Shand tells me. 'It's a difficult balance to maintain. There are demands from all areas and at the end of the day you've got to remember that Saturday at 7.35 p.m. is the critical thing and all roads lead to that.

'It's just about being up front and open and talking to the other parties and seeing where we can fit things in. I've had a basic philosophy [and it relates well to the All Blacks] which is that a lot of people will ask the world of you but if you can give them Fiji, often they will be happy. At the end of the day, it's about delivering something.'

Before we met at a coffee shop in Christchurch, I'd never encountered Darren. I knew that he'd been successful as manager of the Crusaders and that the players liked him. There is no hint of ego in the man, though he appears to enjoy the trappings of his job. New Zealand television viewers know him: he gives the changing-shed reports at half-time during the Tests.

Darren beat two high-profile former All Blacks, Andy Dalton and Andy Haden, to become manager. It says a lot about the man that he felt he had the qualities to do the job and wasn't interested in nor intimidated by his competition.

The job description of All Black manager is a 'monster document', Darren tells me. Following on from the Mitchell reign, the NZRFU wanted emphasis on different things, with the manager having last say.

'Strategic leadership was a key feature for them,' Darren says, 'alongside all the normal duties that you would associate with managing a rugby team like logistics and discipline. It's probably a more wide-ranging role than what it was and it allows the coaches freedom to coach and the manager to manage.'

Being the manager involves far more than just ensuring that the players make the bus on time. As well as strategic direction, the manager plays an important part in developing a team culture, while standards and discipline also come within his wide-ranging brief. A closer link with the NZRFU was also stressed as being very important.

Although he'd been involved in eight professional campaigns and felt he was well prepared for the post, Darren tells me that he wasn't prepared for the demands on the All Blacks, nor the short preparation time.

'One thing I've found fundamentally different [from a Super 12 campaign] is the time that you have with the players to make a difference. In a Super 12 campaign, you may have two or three months before you actually play rugby to develop as a group of people.

'In an international campaign, you are thrust together on a Sunday and you have to play the following Saturday, and there is a whole myriad of things that you have to do outside of preparing for the Test match itself. We might only see the players for around 12 weeks during a season.'

What did not surprise Darren was the support the All Blacks get throughout New Zealand. Wherever they go, the players are fêted like gods. Darren says society has changed but the All Blacks remain sporting royalty in New Zealand. I wonder whether the public, including demanding writers like me, place too much pressure on the All Blacks to win.

'I think the professional game's changed things a bit,' Darren says before sipping on his flash coffee. 'We probably do. The difference between a win and a loss is often small and it's becoming a hell of a lot harder to produce the results that New Zealand expects. Still, I don't think it's unfair to demand that we perform to a really high level and I think that's still a motivation for the staff involved with the All Blacks.'

The role of manager can be enormously frustrating. You feel the losses almost as deeply as the players but you have limited control on the field. 'You are kind of powerless,' Darren admits. 'You certainly feel like you do a lot to ensure things go well but a lot of the things that you do aren't measurable in terms of how the team performs. It's a weird feeling. Straight after the game there's a lot of stuff that needs to be done but you don't get the chance to sit in the shed and reflect on a poor performance. Certainly when you read the papers the next day you feel a sense of loss.'

There's a fine line between being close to the All Blacks and keeping a professional distance. Discipline may need to be administered. The role must be akin to being a friendly schoolmaster. 'I've always kept myself a little removed,' Darren admits. 'It's interesting now that some of the players who were around when I first started are no longer playing, at least in New Zealand. 'For example, I caught up with [former All Black] Darryl Gibson when I was in the UK last year and he welcomed me into his home like a long-lost brother. As a player and a manager we got on fine but we weren't close. That's one of the cool things about rugby.'

Within the All Blacks, they talk about their jobs as professional sportsmen. The management tell them that 20 per cent of their job they may enjoy, 60 per cent of the job they do because they have to, while 20 per cent they do but don't like doing. The challenge for the management is to keep the players motivated and focused on the bigger picture for the All Blacks.

For most of the All Blacks, the enjoyable 20 per cent is usually the playing.

'Don't think for one minute the players don't give their very best when they play for the All Blacks,' Darren says. 'I've been in the changing-sheds after the game and it's often like a train smash. I know that there were hard men in the past but the game's different now. It's not comparing apples with apples.'

Justin Marshall was but one All Black to lampoon the expansion of the Super 12 and the Tri-Nations. Too much of the same was his opinion. Darren is not a player but he disagrees with the criticisms, as you might expect from an employee of the NZRFU.

'I don't really agree. Why did Michael Schumacher, the world champion, try so hard when he was 18th after his crash last week to win the race? Does Andre Agassi get sick of going to Flushing Meadow every year to play in the US Open? It's the environment.

'The thing we have to look at is what is the right amount of rugby for them to play and to lose some of the emotion about them [the All Blacks] not playing NPC, as it is simply not realistic for an athlete to play 12 months a year.

'We are asking them to play in three different competitions

under three different coaches and that's tough work. If we are going to add more Tests, we are going to have to take something else away at the other end.'

Twelve months out from the Lions tour, the All Blacks' planning has begun. You get the feeling that it's the mid-term goal for this management team, with the ultimate aim being the World Cup in 2007.

The players, Darren says, will be eyeing the opportunity to play the Lions like a jaguar his prey. The momentum will build and the scale of what is about to happen in New Zealand will not be lost on the players.

'There is a whole lot extra associated with it [the Lions tour] with someone of Sir Clive Woodward's personality attached to the team and I imagine there will be a fair amount of banter going on at the start of next year.'

Darren has been preparing: the pressure on the infrastructure in the main cities during Test weekend requires it. It means organising hotels, flights, buses and all the essentials required by an international rugby team: being as prepared as possible.

'The Lions manager has been out three times already and so we don't want them to be a step ahead of us in our own backyard,' Darren laughs.

ADVANCE AUSTRALIA FAIR

Thursday, 5 August 2004

When I was growing up, Australia was the poor rugby cousin and nobody in New Zealand took the Wallabies seriously. The Australians felt the same way about our cricket side until the early 1980s.

We'd thrashed the Wallabies 3–0 in 1972, while there was a minor crisis when they beat us in 1979. I recall Dad coming back from the pub in a rage when we'd lost the decider against the Aussies in 1980.

It was only in the 1980s that we started to take the Australians seriously. South Africa's partial isolation had something to do with it, as did the move from amateurism to semi-professionalism. While the Australians traditionally lost their best and fairest to rugby league, it was only a matter of time before the Australian Rugby Union stopped the flow.

Apart from their girlie gold jumpers and their ability to produce amazingly hairy back-rowers, I'd always admired the Wallabies. David Campese, Mark Ella and the immortal John Eales were a few of the greatest of all rugby players.

So I'm standing on a pleasant beach on Sydney's eastern coast and thinking about Wallabies past and present. It's a beautiful day and, if the truth be told, too nice a day to be thinking rugby. After finishing my ice cream, I head to where the Wallabies are based.

I quickly find where the press conference is going to be and wait like a dutiful child. Some of the Wallabies are doing some sort of promotion that involves them signing a giant inflated rugby ball. In New Zealand-speak, it looks daggy, but the photographers love it and click away like their lives depend on it.

The whole thing could not be more staged and I wonder for a moment what legendary All Black Colin Meads would make of this. Eventually, however, we go back inside to the press room and the press officer says, 'If you take your seats, I'll bring Eddie down,' doing his best to get the media's attention.

Eddie Jones strikes me as being one of the most articulate coaches in world rugby. The Australians always seem to produce intellectual coaches, an indication perhaps of the traditional standing of rugby in their community.

A press conference with Jones is like going to a philosophy lecture. It is not necessarily what he says but it's the way he says it. It all makes perfect sense and as such it's difficult not to admire the man.

'It's exciting,' he says of the Test match on Saturday against the All Blacks. 'It's exciting for the players. They know there's going to be a good crowd out at the stadium. The emotion runs pretty high at these games and it's a very important game for the Tri-Nations.'

After what seems like a thousand questions that have obvious answers, I meet Spiro Zavos. I'd long admired Spiro. He's obviously got a passion for rugby, a passion that comes through in his writing.

Spiro's is an interesting story. A New Zealander with Greek parents, he'd fallen in love with rugby at an early age. He's written about it ever since, having a varied professional career before ending up in journalism. His career led him to a job as an editorial writer with the *Sydney Morning Herald*. He later became their esteemed rugby columnist.

What I like about Spiro's writing is that (like Ron Palenski) he elevates rugby to a higher, almost intellectual, art form. He's proved that the sport isn't just for buffoons who don't read. Through his column writing he's also developed a delightful insight into the game and its trends. I want to pick his brains.

He's an intellectual-looking man: the greying moustache, the bookish eyes. He is warm in his welcome and after we meet up with his wife Judy, we set about strolling.

We walk along the seafront, talking casually and looking out to the blue yonder. The day is still warm and in no time I've worked up a decent sweat. The Zavoses are interesting people: articulate, informed and passionate about the world. I like them a lot.

Spiro and I are both thinking about Saturday's Test. In some ways, we rugby lovers prepare as much as the players, except we prepare to watch and analyse and they prepare to play.

We pass a memorial to the victims of the Bali bombing in 2002. It stands overlooking the Tasman Sea and it is a moving tribute. The memorial sobers us, makes us remember that at the end of the day rugby is just a game played by mortal men in the prime of their lives.

Our walk takes us to a small café. Judy wants a swim. I want to discuss rugby with Spiro. It seems odd to think that two days out I'm starting to get excited about a Test match between Australia and New Zealand. It's probably because I'm away from home. It could also be because, when it comes to professional sport, few countries do it better than Australia.

Spiro saw his first Test at Athletic Park in Wellington in 1949. Appropriately, it was between New Zealand and Australia. You wouldn't think that Spiro would have fallen in love with rugby: as he was Greek, he didn't speak English when he went to primary school. Not exactly the background of a regular Kiwi kid growing up in the 1950s.

'So when I went to school I was very anxious to be a Kiwi, to be a New Zealander. Rugby was a way to do it. We'd often only have 12 or 13 guys in our rugby team at Star of the Sea school in Wellington. I was a half-back and a natural player. One of our coaches was Charlie Oliver, a double All Black in the 1930s. He taught us cricket and rugby.'

When he got older, Spiro would go to the parks in Wellington and watch rugby. He was the slowest half-back in the city, although he kept playing social rugby until he was 30. He also played social rugby in England. He went to every Test he could. Rugby was part of his life and he needed it like air.

'New Zealanders of my generation have this rugby need. This sort of national ability to understand and play the game, like the Brazilians have with soccer.

'When I was working on the *Sydney Morning Herald*, people would ring me up and ask me, "Mate, why aren't you writing about soccer?" and I would reply, "Mate, because I was born in New Zealand, mate." Although my parents were Greek, I had no idea how to play soccer; but living in New Zealand, I instinctively knew how to play rugby.'

New Zealand's identification with rugby was almost as strong as the Australians' identification with Gallipoli, Spiro believes.

He says New Zealanders took great joy in beating the British at the game they invented and that this had a huge impact on the way New Zealanders viewed themselves.

Ernest Rutherford could, for example, go to Britain and split the atom, while other New Zealanders could make their mark in a range of different fields, knowing they were as good as anyone.

'I think New Zealand's love affair with rugby has been a very powerful influence on the self-image of New Zealand and the notion that we can compete in so many different areas,' Spiro tells me.

I agree with Spiro. When I lived in Ireland for three and a half years, people regularly connected my New Zealandness with rugby. In my case, it was spot on but I would have hated to have been a non-sporty Kiwi. It was as if the All Blacks defined New Zealand.

Spiro goes further: 'I've read all the papers, books and magazines of the era and I'm certain that New Zealand applied to rugby the pragmatic values of the model society.

'They [the New Zealanders] applied that to rugby and they developed systems and methods before anyone else and that was just an expression of New Zealand's culture.

'[Former All Black] Chris Laidlaw talks about the relationship between New Zealand culture and rugby as like that between Siamese twins. I would go further than that and consider it to be the DNA of New Zealand life. Rugby has created a New Zealand type in my view, male and female. At a deep level, I consider that rugby created New Zealand and that New Zealand created rugby.'

I listen intently, agreeing. Rugby reflected the colonial heritage of the New Zealand settlers and the tribal culture of the Maori. It defined New Zealand as a nation.

While New Zealand had been good for rugby, rugby had been good for New Zealand. As well as being symbolic of the nation, it was also one of the best marketing tools for the country. Whether it is the Australians, the French or the Irish, everyone loves the brutal beauty of the haka, despite it only being performed in New Zealand by the All Blacks since 1987.

'Regardless of where you go in the world as a New Zealander, they know the All Blacks,' Spiro says. 'I believe that has given New Zealanders a confidence to do anything, anywhere. It's the one New Zealand artifact that is world class.'

While New Zealanders understood rugby, they were taking time to come to grips with professionalism. They could not understand, nor perhaps accept, that the All Blacks would never again dominate against the Australians like they once did. A Test win against the Australians needed to be savoured and not taken for granted. History can often breed contempt.

'I do find that New Zealanders are natural pessimists,' Spiro says. 'It's easy to get a New Zealander to talk about doom and gloom. Australians on the other hand are natural optimists and I put that down to the way the countries were settled.

'Australia was essentially settled by people who had nothing to lose and had to get on with it. New Zealand was settled by people looking for security and the settlers from Europe tended to be safe people, like the English or Dutch, rather than southern Europeans. New Zealand has this pessimistic, security-conscious, fearful aspect to its psyche [as a result].'

From what I'd seen on this trip and on previous journeys across the ditch, I think Spiro is right. Yet a further difference was that the Australians didn't hang their national identity on the Wallabies. As a result, it didn't matter so much if they lost.

What I do believe from spending time overseas is that the Australians do have a much greater sense of their place in the world than the New Zealanders. Buoyed by hosting the Sydney Olympics in 2000, they bow to no one. New Zealanders often appear almost apologetic in so much of what they do and polite to the point of nearly being walked on. The Australians appeared brash but it was mighty refreshing.

There was a flow-on effect to their rugby. At the start of this century, the Wallabies seemed to have the advantage over the All

Blacks. In the tight Tests, they managed to pull through and to have a greater sense of self-belief. It seemed to me that this outward view, this ability to back themselves and this growing international maturity, was part of the reason. No longer did the Wallabies fear the All Blacks.

It's not difficult to sense this national maturity as we sit at a pleasant café drinking expensive coffee and talking rugby. It fits nicely with the rugby culture in Australia, a culture marked by private schools, professional careers and society's more exclusive echelons.

Professionalism has ensured that the best rugby players have not automatically transferred across to league, sure enough, but you can still smell the money in Australian rugby. You can see it in the standard of dress at Tests, the coverage rugby gets in the newspapers, the feel in the streets of downtown Sydney. As a result, rugby union will never reflect Australian life the way the All Blacks symbolised the New Zealand condition.

After finishing our coffee, Spiro, Judy and I walk back to their car. We still talk rugby and somewhere amongst our words and our views, I feel at the heart of rugby's epicentre.

Back at the Zavoses' we drink tea and talk about the books Spiro has written, his columns. Their house is book-lined and appears to accurately reflect their personalities. I feel right at home. He gives me a copy of a book of his and I clutch it like gold.

After tea, we go to an art gallery and embrace Sydney's rich culture. As I leave my new friends and head back into town, it occurs to me that without rugby I would never have met these wonderfully interesting people.

LOOKING OUT FOR YOUR BROTHER

Saturday, 7 August 2004

My brother's done well for himself: he's been in Sydney for four years. He's got a good job and a girlfriend. He lives a lavish lifestyle. I wonder whether he will return home one day. I've never visited him in Sydney until now and, as a birthday present, he's shouted me to the Bledisloe Cup Test tonight.

I don't like the waiting to go to the rugby; it frustrates me. I want to be there, to savour the atmosphere and to feel the nerves that the players must be feeling.

Tonight, I'm waiting for my brother and two of his friends, and I'm wishing that it was just him and me. I would love to be going to the rugby with my brother, like we did when we were kids. Yet I get the feeling that for my brother and his friends, it's more about entertainment than the rugby itself.

That view is cemented as we catch the train into Sydney City and then out to Homebush Stadium. The trains are packed with scarf-wearing, flag-waving Kiwis and it's clear that most are using the rugby to display their nationalism like sporting soldiers.

There are a lot of Kiwis in Sydney and they all seem to be at the ground tonight, full of bravado. Well, as full of bravado as normally reserved Kiwis can be.

The stadium is overtly modern, combining, it is said in the match programme, the best of functional architecture with outstanding surroundings. It's a bit like Disneyland: people everywhere going somewhere in search of entertainment and fulfilment.

My brother has paid well over AUS$100 for each of our tickets. That gets us a seat behind the goalposts. I'm excited to be at this giant, all-encompassing stadium and I can't help but appreciate the price that my brother's paid for the privilege.

Fifteen minutes after we've been seated, my brother and one of his mates go out and buy beer. I don't like drinking at the rugby. In fact, the only thing I do like at the rugby is nervous anticipation and all-out exhilaration. Rugby to me isn't about entertainment. It's about the battle, the gladiatorial contest.

When my brother comes back, a beer in each hand, I wonder for a moment whether we are related. He seems to be enjoying himself, and that's important for him and for me, but who said that rugby was ever about mere enjoyment? One of his mates, an Australian of all people, is also getting stuck into the drink. I know that it's going to be a long night.

We've got to the ground remarkably early. There is nothing to do but watch the crowd fill the stadium. There's no doubt they're passionate about their sport in Sydney, yet the size of the venue and the number of people make the atmosphere somewhat distant.

Still, in front of us a happy band of Kiwis wear black proudly. They hope there will be no mourning tonight. They are in good spirits, waving their flags, shouting the national anthem, celebrating their nationhood as if they were the Kiwi descendants of William Wallace.

'How you going, Toddy?' my brother asks, noticing that I'm soaking up the atmosphere but not saying much.

'Good, mate,' I reply politely, sharply.

My lack of communication is obvious but my brother understands me, thankfully. My brother's phone rings. Who would ring before the rugby starts, I wonder? It's Mum and Dad back in Lincoln. They know that my brother and I are here together.

My brother makes small talk before handing the phone over to me. 'Yes, Mum, we are having a good time. Yes, Mum, we are looking forward to the rugby.' After reassuring my folks that I'm having a good time in Sydney, we focus back on the rugby. The teams are about to come on the field and the atmosphere is as electric as a power station in a lightning storm.

As suggested earlier, you are never prouder of your nationhood than when you are not in your own country. I'm sure of that, although that reality frustrates me. I want to be a proud New Zealander regardless of where I am. We New Zealanders are an apathetic nation and it is in some ways remarkably immature.

Still, at least we have a national colour that is big and bold. Surprisingly, for such a proud nation the Australians have namby-pamby yellow and tonight it's fluttering throughout the stadium like a constant Mexican wave. I recall former New Zealand Prime Minister Robert Muldoon saying on one occasion that canary yellow was an appropriate colour for the Australians to wear. Harsh as that comment was, he had a point.

George Gregan and Tana Umaga lead their sides out and the crowd is now in a frenzy. It's as if these matches don't happen twice a year. If you didn't know the rugby history of the nations and the fact that the teams are evenly matched, you would have thought that it was big brother versus little brother.

Not surprisingly, the Australian supporters outnumber their New Zealand counterparts and, rightly or wrongly, they appear worldlier. I'm not sure why this is, although I think that Spiro might have hit on something on Thursday when he talked about the experience the Australians have in hosting big sporting events.

After the slush of Wellington earlier in the season, the Australians appear to relish playing on the hard, fast home track. It's an intimidating place for the New Zealanders to play and you get the feeling that playing at home must be worth at least ten points to the Australians.

The All Blacks lead 9–0 after 20 minutes thanks to three Daniel Carter penalties. We sit back in our seats and enjoy the occasion. It looks as though it's going to be a good night. I look around and smirk at the Australian supporters. 'We are the chosen rugby race,' my smirk says. Forget Australia's maturity and the fact that they've hosted the Olympics, when it comes to rugby there is only one home.

Replacement Matt Burke and Carter swap penalties. The All Blacks now lead 12–3. Yet the tide has turned, Australia have been let back into the match. That's another thing I like about the Australians: they've an ability to back themselves and unbelievable confidence. They are rugby's equivalent of Bill Clinton.

Three Matt Giteau penalties tie the scores. It's 12–12 at half-time. My brother needs more beer. I'm shaking like a leaf! You might say that these states of anxiety reflect our personalities but you would be wrong, as we are both high-strung individuals. I get the feeling that the Wallabies will pull through. We're well known for choking when it comes to playing Australia. I feel we need to be ahead at the break.

As the second half begins, something strange is happening to my brother. An outsider might call it drunkenness, while I call it losing focus. He is becoming as talkative as Ronnie Corbett and, if we were not at the rugby, he would have been mildly entertaining.

Still, we go behind when Giteau kicks his fourth penalty and the night is becoming as painful as ongoing root canal work. Carlos Spencer squares the scores with a penalty. I look at my brother and neither of us is convinced that we will pull through.

The game turns when Lote Tuqiri scores for the Wallabies. Tuqiri's a magnificent athlete, all muscle and poise. Someone once said that grace is the combination of athleticism and poise. When I see Tuqiri, I always think of that description. Next to Mat Rogers, he's undoubtedly Australia's most gifted rugby player.

I squirm in my seat and feel sick. I know that try will win the Wallabies the match. I feel that someone is spitting on me from an almighty height and it's likely to be an Australian.

There is a point in every match when the side that is down has to step up to stay in the game. I get the feeling that that point has arrived when Andrew Mehrtens comes onto the field. If anyone can change things, it's Mehrts. It's been his year. Yet tonight, I still think victory's going to be Australia's.

Mehrtens kicks a penalty – New Zealand's sixth of the evening by the third different kicker of the night. The All Blacks are now down by only two points. Yet I (and probably most of the New Zealand supporters in the crowd who are realists) know that sooner or later the All Black set piece will start to crack. It does.

It's the lineout. It hasn't been the best all night. A lost lineout gives the ball back to Stephen Larkham. Tana Umaga stops fullback Chris Latham and saves a try. A Wallaby knock-on brings relief for the All Blacks before the visitors are again offside. Burke kicks another penalty. We are down 23–18.

The All Blacks continue to push. The Wallabies continue to defend. There is a ring of familiarity about it. I know what's going to happen before it does. All New Zealanders have been here before. It's telling that it's George Gregan who kicks the ball out to end the match. He seems to reflect the confidence that the All Blacks often lack.

My brother takes the All Blacks' loss well considering he has to live in this country. I'm flying home tomorrow and yet it feels to me like a death in the family. We head to the bar under the stand and the corporate hospitality and I know that I can't drink: someone is going to have to get us home.

A drink or two would have eased my pain and made the night more bearable. After my brother and his friends have had a couple more drinks we head into town. There is no big night out, just a greasy burger and chips at a dodgy takeaway. As we sit scoffing our fast food, I want this night to end.

My brother insists we take a taxi. This is his city and I take his request seriously. Yet I'm still his big brother and, as I'm sober, I decide for the both of us that taking the train is the most cost-effective option.

We walk to the station and the train takes an unusually long time to arrive. Rugby fans mill around the station like flies in the summer air. I make no attempt to hide my All Black scarf, but I'm still feeling the loss as if it were a slap in the face.

Eventually, the train arrives. My brother has gone quiet. We travel across the Sydney Harbour Bridge in silence, the lights of the city twinkling in the distance like wild dandelions. The harbour's a beautiful sight and my pain is eased by the magnificence of the setting. Is there a more beautiful city in this part of the world than Sydney?

When we reach our stop, we take the ten-minute walk home

slowly, as if we are walking it for the first time. My brother awakens when we get home, as if the familiar surroundings have brought him back to life like Frankenstein's creature. He decides he wants sandwiches. Fried sandwiches. I'm horrified but kind of impressed by his culinary skills at this time of night. Thankfully, there is no smell.

My brother's girlfriend comes out of the bedroom, having obviously heard us come home. She looks sleepy but not surprised to see my brother in this state. To be honest, I am. I've never seen him drunk but in some strange way I've never felt closer to him. At that moment, deeply sober, I can't give a hoot as to who won the rugby tonight. It seems as immaterial as the passing seasons.

THE NUMBER 9 FROM MATURA

Saturday, 14 August 2004

Losing to the Wallabies in Australia and then having to jump on a plane to South Africa for a Test the following weekend is tough for the All Blacks.

The New Zealanders and Australians hate travelling to Africa after a loss. It's as if the journey is twice as long and twice as reflective. That feeling must be even worse when it's an international that's been lost.

All Black half-back Justin Marshall knows that feeling better than most. He's played against South Africa 22 times, more than any other player in the history of the game.

'The time that I came in was basically the time that we started the Tri-Nations,' he tells me reflectively. 'If you look at the personnel that we had in 1996, a lot of those guys have either moved overseas or retired, or in Mehrts' and Jonah's case, had their ups and downs.'

Justin loves playing Tests. He brings out that cliché that playing for your country in a Test is the ultimate for any rugby player. Yet I can detect disappointment in his voice when he says that he hasn't played against the likes of Canada and Japan, for instance.

'I don't get bored of the Test matches but I do think that it's a bit monotonous because it's the same scenario every year.

'As a player, you like to be challenged and South Africa and

Australia are challenges, so once you get to the Test match and play it, it's a Test match for your country and it's a great honour to be involved with it.

'But it wouldn't hurt to have some variety. I have been an advocate, from when I started playing with Southland in 1993, for sides to play against touring teams.

'The best memory I have of this season is the English series, as England hadn't been to New Zealand for a while and it was something different. I think the whole country bought into it as well. That sort of thing inspires me and motivates me, rather than the same old, same old.'

The situation is made worse by the fact that the players from the Tri-Nations countries meet each other at least once each year in the Super 12 as well.

'The biggest challenge with the Tri-Nations at the moment is coming up with ways of manipulating the opposition, as we all know each other so well. We play each other through the Super 12 and then we have six weeks where we don't play each other before playing each other again in the Tri-Nations.

'So we have got to come up with ways of being original. You know, for example, that De Wet Barry and Marias Jourbert are going to rush up out of line. So all you are doing is coming up with variety and something new. Whereas [with] teams that are new you don't know the players as well and so you can go out and just play and enjoy the challenge.'

Justin feels the public is likewise crying out for some variety and that shows in the interest in the English tour this year and the Lions tour.

'Who really cares who wins the Tri-Nations each year? It's important at the time, don't get me wrong, and always will be important but the Rugby Union has a good fall-back when they say that the public can't be that unhappy as the television ratings are fantastic for Tri-Nations and they fill the stadiums.

'My argument is that you are always going to fill the stadiums and people are going to watch the All Blacks play regardless of who it is. So, it's a pretty weak way of saying that it's working.'

Justin has never been scared to do things his way. When he first arrived in Christchurch in 1995, the legend goes that he handed out his résumé to local journalists. It has made him decidedly refreshing and, ultimately, a favourite with the public.

Part of Justin's appeal has been his down-on-the-farm approach to rugby and life. He may be earning far more money than the majority of New Zealanders but, thanks to his approach, he has remained one of them.

It seemed to me that the All Blacks who were the most popular – the Andrew Mehrtenses, the Richard McCaws and the Justin Marshalls – were the professionals with old-fashioned values who said things the way they were.

Justin, like most of his teammates, recalls the 1993 Lions in New Zealand and he did watch the series in South Africa in 1997 and in Australia in 2001. He feels the 2005 tour will provide some of the variety that he's been craving.

'It's not the be all and end all for me,' Justin admits, though. 'I would love to play in the series but I'm not sure whether I'll be picked, so that's how comfortable I am about the series. There will always be things that I haven't done – winning a World Cup for example.'

Justin's never been one for recognition and statistics. If he leaves New Zealand for opportunities elsewhere, he will still have achieved far more than he could have dreamed of when he was growing up in Matura, a small town in the depths of Southland.

'For me, working in the Freezing Works in Matura gave me the background to get where I am because it's hard work and you don't get anywhere without putting in the effort. It's also about going through a big learning period and when you get something, not taking it for granted.

'I'm talented but I'm not somebody who can go out onto the field and do things [automatically]. I have to work hard behind the scenes at my game and make sure I approach it in the right frame of mind.'

In many ways, it's appropriate that no one has played more Tests against South Africa than Justin, as he shares many of the characteristics of traditional Boks sides: hard, uncompromising, mentally tough.

As a player, Justin's been priceless to Canterbury, the Crusaders and New Zealand. His value as a player and as an individual cannot be underestimated and yet I wonder whether he will only be fully appreciated once he's no longer playing.

Back on the field, the All Blacks lose to South Africa 26–40 in Johannesburg and finish the Tri-Nations with a 50 per cent winning record. I don't feel any sense of mourning or any great regret at what has occurred. I know I will feel differently if the All Blacks lose to the Lions next season. The players may in the short term care who wins the Tri-Nations but the majority of the rest of us don't. A long way from 1959 in fact, when rugby was all the rage in New Zealand and when the Lions toured.

* * *

ENTERTAINERS ON AND OFF THE FIELD

Like their predecessors in 1950, the 1959 Lions squad contained a relatively even spread of nationalities. Of the 30 originally selected, 9 were from Wales, 9 from Ireland, 7 from England and 5 from Scotland.

Another similarity with the 1950 side was that this Lions squad was also captained by an Irish hooker, this time Ronnie Dawson. An outstanding man in many respects, Dawson was pressured for his place throughout the tour by Welsh hooker Bryn Meredith but in the end justified his selection as tour captain.

As Australia were not strong enough to justify a Lions tour of their own, the Lions played six matches there before coming to New Zealand. Although the Lions won both Tests against Australia, they were beaten by New South Wales. The tourists then flew to Auckland, staying the night there before flying down to Napier the next day.

When the Lions arrived in Napier, they were greeted by a huge crowd. They were then escorted to an enclosure on Marine Parade in the city, where thousands of people offered resounding cheers. In the presence of noted former All Blacks George Nepia and Bob Scott, each Lion moved up to the microphone to announce his name, club and country.

The Lions back line was star-studded. Along with the charismatic Tony O'Reilly (a star in South Africa in 1955 for the Lions) were talented Englishman Bev Risman, highly rated English midfielder Jeff Butterfield, the outstanding Ulster midfielder Dave Hewitt and the strong-running Scottish utility Ken Scotland.

The Lions forwards did not have as many big names. Still, Rhys Williams, who had toured South Africa with the 1955 Lions, was a hard, rugged lock. He came to New Zealand with a fine reputation and, if anything, left the country with that enhanced.

149

THE TRIP OF A LIFETIME

It's a pleasant autumn day in Edinburgh in October 2004 and yet I'm in immense pain. I've got gout in my left foot and I can hardly walk. The last thing I need is a talkative taxi driver. Yet he natters away like his life depends on it and I grimace as we drive through the pretty suburbs of Scotland's capital.

After a 15-minute drive (in which I've extolled New Zealand's virtues, explained what I'm doing in this part of the world and dissected Scottish rugby) we arrive at a quiet, comfortable enclave. I struggle to get out of the car and when I do, hobble 20 or so painful metres. Sadly, I need a doctor and not a chat about rugby.

Ken Scotland's wife greets me. My accent has given away my identity. She ushers me upstairs to a large comfortable apartment. Ken welcomes me and I'm amazed by how young he looks. He could pass for 45, yet I know that he was born in 1937.

Scotland had a terrific tour of New Zealand. He captained the Lions from full-back against the New Zealand Universities and Otago, played the first and third Tests in the same position and then appeared at centre in the fourth Test. He scored 45 points, including 7 tries. He was described as a 'speedy and elusive player' who 'was also a fearless tackler in spite of weighing just over 11 stone'.

'More or less they took two players for each position, so theoretically you had a 50/50 chance of selection,' Ken tells me. 'Occasionally, they would select someone who had not been playing for their country. One of the stars of our team was Dickie Jeeps, who had not been capped by England that year.

'That year Ireland did not have a regular full-back. They used Noel Henderson, who was a centre and a veteran at that stage. So effectively the full-back position came down to two out of three.'

Going into the 1959 season, Ken's ambition was to win back his place in the Scotland side. He'd first been capped in 1957 but had been dropped in 1958. Timing, he tells me, was vital in his selection.

'It would have been very difficult for me to go in 1958 because by then I was studying at Cambridge and I would have been missing my first-year exams. It would have been very difficult for me to go in 1960 because I would have missed my final exams. [In 1959] I was in my middle year and did not have exams and so again the timing was perfect for me.'

Ken knew little about New Zealand. As a ten year old, he'd watched the 1945–46 Kiwis go down to Scotland. That had fired his ambition to play for his country. He'd seen the 1953–54 All Blacks play at Murrayfield and watched the immortal Bob Scott in action.

'I was well aware of the power of New Zealand rugby,' Ken says *thoughtfully, 'but I actually knew very little about the country itself. I knew that it was on the other side of the world but that was about it!'*

It took the Lions 48 hours to fly to Australia – Zurich, Beirut, Karachi, Singapore, Darwin and finally Sydney. 'It was quite an epic journey,' Ken recalls, 'even by aeroplane in those days.'

When the tourists eventually arrived in New Zealand, the locals embraced them immediately. 'We probably saw more of New Zealand than what most New Zealanders ever see,' Ken recalls. 'We were there for three and a half months and we criss-crossed New Zealand. We played four games in Auckland and three games each in Wellington and Christchurch, so we were back and forward all the time.'

The New Zealanders were incredibly enthusiastic about the Lions. The players were recognised wherever they went, something that surprised the Lions, who were normally anonymous back home.

'It was an obsession with New Zealanders,' Ken says, 'and we could not believe how important it was. Every little place that we went to there was a civic reception. The mayor would be there and there would be a few speeches of welcome. It was very genuine.

'We travelled through the North Island on a rail car and every now and then we would stop at some remote place and there would be mobs of children there just to wave more or less as the train went past. It was amazing.'

On the field, the Lions won their first four matches of the tour, including the Auckland match. Ken captained the Lions in their first loss of the tour, 26–8 against Otago in Dunedin.

'Losing to Otago wasn't fun but it wasn't like losing a Test match,' Ken says. 'That day we had two back-row forwards playing in the centres, while we had a prop hooking. Otago played well and we made too many mistakes.'

The Lions won their next two matches in the South Island but still went into the first Test in Dunedin as underdogs.

The first Test will always be remembered as the Test in which All Black full-back Don Clarke kicked six penalties and the Lions scored four tries and lost.

'It still kind of leaves a scar,' Ken chuckles. 'You never like to lose any game and you certainly don't like to lose games where you've been ahead and go behind right at the end of the game. The feeling in the dressing-room after that game was nothing that I ever experienced before or after. Everybody was just so deflated. I don't think anyone was blaming the referee, it was just how the defeat had come about. It knocked all the stuffing out of us, I think.'

A MAN OF FORCE

It's just after midday on a midsummer Sunday in early 2005. It's not particularly hot, although it's pleasant, like a Dublin evening in spring. I'm only about 14 kilometres from home yet I'm embarrassingly lost. When I find the right driveway and cautiously turn off my car engine, I notice Tiny Hill sitting at the front of his apartment watching me carefully like the soldier he once was.

Tiny is one of the legends of New Zealand rugby. If you believe his press, he was one of the hard men of the game and the bloke who taught Colin Meads how to be a man on the rugby field. Yet his record suggests much more: 19 matches (11 Tests) for the All Blacks, a championship-winning Canterbury coach, an All Black selector between 1981 and 1986.

Tiny has also played a substantial role in the development of rugby at the grass-roots level in Canterbury, including initiating a camp for secondary school players in the South Island. Tiny, it could be said, is a rugby man through and through.

Tiny was 32 in 1959 and his career was winding down. He felt his family had had enough of rugby and he knew the time was fast coming when he needed to do his own thing. The lure of the Lions, whom he had not played before, provided the last hooray. Tiny, though, came across the Lions sooner than he had expected.

'The Lions played Auckland and then they came to Christchurch on the way south. At that stage, I was injured and so I went to the hospital and lo and behold about six of their guys came in and sat down.

'They didn't know who I was, because I was in my soldier's uniform! I didn't let on, even though I was in the Test team! All they could do was grizzle about what had happened in Auckland and how they got kicked and punched. I started to grin and they must have found out who I was in the first Test.'

During the tour, the Lions were great socialisers. The New Zealanders found this refreshing after the dour experience of hosting the more conservative Springboks in 1956. Friendships developed as a result. For example, Tiny became good mates with lock Rhys Williams.

'Rhys, in fact, died a couple of years ago. His son and daughter wrote to me wanting to know more about Rhys when he was touring here and so I wrote back and said that we became great friends off the field.

'I remember asking him what he thought of New Zealand. He replied, "New Zealand's OK, Tiny, but there is one place in the world where I'd never go back to in New Zealand." I asked him where that was and he said it was Greymouth on the West Coast, where it rained non-stop. "What a place," he said.'

The All Black selectors made eight changes for the second Test, which was surprising after the victory in Dunedin. Still, the new selections included Colin Meads and Kel Tremain, two players who would become All Black legends.

The Lions had injury problems, with four of their backs – Ken, Hewitt, Jackson and Risman – not available. There were also three changes to the Lions pack, confirming that this Test would be significantly different from the first.

Queues began to form outside Athletic Park on the Friday morning and by the time the gates opened on the Saturday, thousands of people had assembled. In a nice touch, Lions Jeff Butterfield and Malcolm Thomas visited the fans on the Friday night.

By the time the ground was full, there were still thousands wanting to get in. In a scene that would make public safety officials squirm, gates were lifted off their hinges and fences pulled down by the frustrated fans who poured into the ground. Although the official crowd was 53,000, that was almost certainly a conservative estimate.

Playing in his first match for the All Blacks, winger Ralph Caulton scored two tries in the first half to give the home side a significant advantage. Terry Davies kicked a penalty for the Lions before a dummy scissors move saw Malcolm Price (playing in the unfamiliar position of first-five) flash through. He threw a high pass to John Young, who went over for the try, which Davies converted.

Ahead 8–6, the Lions looked as though they would win. The atmosphere was electric, the All Blacks doing everything they could to claw back the lead. With a minute to go, the All Black forwards stormed ahead. From a ruck, John McCullough ran the blind side with Caulton in support and only Young to beat. Don Clarke, like a Ferrari, suddenly appeared between McCullough and Caulton and spectacularly scored with a huge dive. His conversion gave the All Blacks the win, 11–8.

'We were lucky to pull that bugger out,' Tiny says. 'You could see it [the Clarke try] coming though. Although our backs didn't always function as well as they should have, Clarke just came around the blind side and in the end scored with ease.'

The Lions had been unlucky and they could have won either of the first two Tests. There were no such doubts in the third Test, being beaten 22–8 by a rampant All Black side in Christchurch.

The Lions had Ken, Jackson and Hewitt back for the Test, although this game was won up front. Playing on a beautiful Christchurch afternoon, Hewitt scored a magnificent try for the visitors but Caulton scored twice for the All Blacks.

Although Caulton was again outstanding, it was as clear as the blue sky

*overhead that while the Lions had the better back line, the All Blacks had
the better forwards.*

'Everything seemed to fall into place for us that day,' Tiny recalls. 'We
played bloody well, we kept it up front and tried to keep the ball away from
their backs. It was the same against South Africa. The other thing was if
you look at rugby these days no one is frightened of the forwards. They [the
Lions] were bloody scared of our forwards, I reckon.'

DOWN BUT NOT OUT

*Although the Lions had already lost the series, the New Zealand public
was still keen to see the visitors. Crowds poured into Auckland, special
planes were put on and crowds began to form outside Eden Park early on
the Friday morning, as had been the case in Wellington. When dawn
broke on the day of the Test, the lines extended for some way outside each
of the gates like unmoving caterpillars.*

*Ken was moved from full-back to centre for the match, his place being
taken at the back by Welshman Davies. He was happy to play anywhere
and, he says, lucky to have played a lot of rugby on the tour. Risman was
back at first-five, while the entertaining Andy Mulligan came in for Jeeps
at half-back.*

*Clarke kicked a penalty for the home side after nine minutes before the
Lions backs scored another classy try after twenty minutes: O'Reilly came
into the back line and made a break, offloading to Ken, who passed to
Jackson, who left the defence in tatters to score. The score remained 3–3 at
half-time.*

*The Lions struck first in the second half: Mulligan fed O'Reilly on the
blind side and the Irish winger beat one defender to score in the corner.
Clarke evened the scores with his second penalty of the match soon after.*

*The Lions scored again after 20 minutes in the second half when
Risman ran the blind side and beat the defence to score a magnificent try.*

*With the visitors ahead 9–6, the pressure was mounting, the crowd in
a frenzy. Some Kiwis subconsciously wanted the Lions to win: the series
had been won, the Lions had played attacking rugby and they felt they
deserved some success.*

*With five minutes to go, a Lions player was ruled offside. Clarke had
the opportunity to draw the match but his kick passed across the front of
the posts.*

'I think to win the fourth Test showed great character in the side,' says
Ken. 'It certainly meant a lot to me to actually beat New Zealand. There
are actually very few Scotsmen who have played in a winning side against
New Zealand. I'm very happy to have been one of those.'

'I think it was probably just reward at the end of the day. It was a pretty miserable day, wet, and they weren't conditions that particularly suited us. We scored three tries to none in adverse conditions and I think probably the best thing that came out of it was the forwards got the recognition they deserved. We could never have scored the tries we did if the forwards had not been so outstandingly good.'

The tour was over and the Lions had received reward for their efforts. They deserved nothing less. The tour had not been a success on the field yet it had not been a failure either. The style of rugby the Lions had played had won them many friends and had been true to the rugby ethos.

After the players arrived back home, most were sent a scrapbook of the tour by schoolchildren in New Zealand. 'It was actually quite touching,' Ken says. 'The kids had cut photographs and news reports out of the newspapers and stuck them in. I think they were given some encouragement to select one of the Lions to support during the tour.'

For Ken, becoming a Lion is something that he still cherishes. 'There is nothing more that you can achieve in rugby terms in the UK [and Ireland]. It was great at the time and it's something that's great to look back on. It's something that can never be taken away, so I suppose you're part of history really.'

A BALANCED LIFE

After the Lions tour finished, Ken resumed his university career, graduating a year and a half later. He then went and worked in the Midlands of England, played for Leicester, Ballymena and London Scottish along the way and got married soon after leaving university.

The Scotlands raised their children in Aberdeen, Ken playing for Aberdeenshire. The family later moved to Edinburgh for business reasons, Ken working in the construction industry.

With three boys, Ken got sucked back into rugby, refereeing and doing all those things that parents do. He ended up president of his club, Heriot's, a few years ago and now, he says proudly, he's back as a spectator.

'Sad, really,' Ken says when I point out that the Lions would be taking 44 players to New Zealand in 2005. 'It's like preparing for World War Three now. For us, it was an odyssey, a chance of a lifetime to go and play rugby in very much the top place. We got the opportunity to express ourselves and bond as a team.

'There was no coach. There was the manager and an assistant manager, who acted as a kind of secretary and did all the administrative stuff. It was down to the players to do any coaching or training. To me, it seemed much *more worthwhile doing that than doing what they do now, where the players are being limited in what they are being asked to do.'*

Ken has minimal involvement with rugby these days. He has a bit to do with his club but not a lot else. He doesn't particularly enjoy the razzmatazz of professional rugby and watches less rugby in Scotland these days, although he feels the game is cleaner than it was.

There is no bitterness about missing out on the professional era, no sense of frustration at having to study or to work and earn a living while he played.

'Virtually everyone of my generation who I speak to is happy to have played in the era we did,' Ken says thoughtfully. 'I think that having rugby as a full-time career is pretty limiting. My generation had to do national service and then some of us went on to university. I wouldn't have missed these things for anything: they were part and parcel of your life.'

Ken has never been back to New Zealand since the tour. He figures that it would be an anticlimax. Having enjoyed virtually every minute of the 1959 tour, he knows that it would be a hard act to follow. For the moment, he's happy to have the memories of one of the most enjoyable adventures of his life.

A MAN OF MANA

The 1959 series was the best Tiny ever played in. The rugby was close, evenly fought and often attractive. He was sad to leave the guys after the series, although he was being posted with the army to Papakura, south of Auckland. It was time to move on. The 1960 tour of South Africa had no attraction, not only because Tiny had Maori blood but because South Africa simply didn't interest him.

He retired. Briefly. The Counties coach naturally came calling. He resisted at first but ended up playing 20 games for the union before being posted to Waiouru in the middle of the North Island. He eventually served around 12 months in Vietnam.

Tiny came back to Burnham in Canterbury before being transferred back to Waiouru for two years. It was during that spell that a motor accident nearly killed him. 'I didn't think I would walk again,' he says thoughtfully. 'It was a wonder I didn't cut my neck off. I must have a neck on me like iron!' he laughs. 'The walk back was bloody sore.'

It was after coming back to Canterbury that Tiny was offered the coaching job of his old province. He'd had enough and said no. The union kept at him, nominated him from the floor at the selection meeting. Sure enough, he made himself available and he was elected.

Tiny's tenure was successful: Alex Wyllie was captain and his side played *a not surprisingly uncompromising style of rugby. He was then made an All Black selector alongside his ex-All Blacks mate Peter Burke and Bryce Rope, another ex-military man.*

'The All Blacks are easy to pick,' Tiny says, 'if you know what you're doing. I never had any problems. You can get wrapped up a bit if you start listening to people and that can become a problem. Before you know it, your mind is like porridge! You've got to make up your own mind about players.'

Rugby administration followed after Tiny stepped down as an All Black selector in 1986. He became president of the Cantabrians, the Canterbury equivalent of the Barbarians, and president of the Canterbury Rugby Football Union. He gave back far more than he ever took out.

These days, modern rugby and the way forwards and backs have almost dual roles confuses him, as it does many ex-All Blacks. 'I like the way the English have brought back the old-fashioned element, where the forwards win the ball and when they are ready for it they give it to the backs and they score the tries.'

Tiny would like to see the current players have jobs. It would, he considers, make them more-balanced individuals. How the coaches would arrange that, he doesn't know, but he is sure that it would make the players better footballers. 'In what job do you have to focus on your work seven days a week? It leads to burnout, regardless of what you do.'

He laments the passing of the All Black mystique and feels international sides play each other too much these days for that to be retained. And then there's the commercialism.

'If you look round, every bugger's wearing an All Black jersey. You can go downtown and buy one for NZ$190 or whatever it is. So the silver fern doesn't mean as much as it used to. When I played, that bloody fern meant everything to me, same as when I put the Canterbury jersey on. That was something.'

One of the things that I like most about Tiny is that throughout our conversation we talk about the amateur as much as the professional game. There is no doubt that amateur rugby matters to Tiny as much as the All Blacks and the Lions. Perspective, that's it. Tiny has perspective. I wonder whether the professional age will produce men of the mana and perspective of Tiny.

HEARTLAND NEW ZEALAND

August–October 2004

In the professional age and with a Lions tour looming, it is easy to forget that rugby for the vast majority in New Zealand is something to be fitted in around school, study and personal life.

The National Provincial Championship (NPC) has traditionally been the toughest domestic competition in the world. Since the advent of professionalism that may not still be the case but it remains the lifeblood of the game in New Zealand.

It's been argued that the NPC is where the game's heart rests in New Zealand. It's also been said that the NPC is where you can experience the real spirit of New Zealand rugby. It's also perhaps a barometer to the cultural and national soul.

The NPC began in 1976 after national rugby administrators realised that some form of national competition was required. Ironically, soccer was the catalyst, as a club competition had been initiated in that sport in the early 1970s.

It's amazing to think that before 1976 there was no national competition in New Zealand. What existed was essentially a round of friendlies. The real prize was the Ranfurly Shield, although that worked – and continues to work – on a challenger basis.

I've seen a lot of NPC rugby down the years. Seeing Canterbury win the first division in 1983 and 1997 were certainly highlights. Yet in recent times I've got most satisfaction from seeing the smaller provinces – the Nelson Bays, the Mid Canterburys – do well.

I may be wrong but I believe that winning an NPC title means more to a smaller union. Their local communities get behind their players and winning a title can put them on the national rugby map for a short time.

Yet there are changes on the horizon. An NZRFU competitions' review has recommended significant changes for the NPC. From 2006 there will be two and not three divisions. Amalgamation is on the cards for some provinces and I want to know what the players think about this.

On a personal level, I want to obtain some of the brute

enthusiasm that is such a part of amateur rugby. I want to hear a player's excitement at playing a rugby match not for money but for the pure satisfaction of representing his province, his community.

So I've decided through the 2004 NPC to follow the progress of three players, one in each of the divisions. I will talk with them on three occasions over the course of the competition and try to gauge their take on their progress and that of modern rugby.

The three players – George Naoupu from Canterbury, Michael Johnson from Hawke's Bay and Luke O'Donnell from West Coast – are from different-sized unions in different parts of New Zealand.

They have different levels of experience, come from different cultural backgrounds and have, I am predicting, different expectations when it comes to their rugby. What I am sure about is that each individual will have a love of rugby that is as pure as snow.

* * *

A big man is George Naoupu. He's the size of an American basketballer, except George's size is muscular and not vertical. He's all athlete and I cannot imagine how tough it would be to tackle the 22 year old in full flight.

George's résumé is impressive: he's played for New Zealand Under-19s and the New Zealand Colts (Under-21s) in 2004, while he's also a newcomer in the Canterbury NPC squad. He's also played a season in Japan, which was organised by the CRFU. George, it appears, is a player on the up and up.

Canterbury is one of New Zealand's proudest rugby unions. Second only to Auckland in the number of All Blacks produced, the union won first division NPC titles in 1977, 1983, 1997 and 2001. Bob Deans, Fergi McCormick, Robbie Deans, Andrew Mehrtens and Richard McCaw are some of its proudest sons.

Since the advent of the Super 12 and the basing of a side in Christchurch, Canterbury had attracted top players from around the country. Although around half the team was not originally from Canterbury, the locals loved them regardless.

'I'm delighted with the way the team is performing,' George tells me of Canterbury's season so far at Rugby Park in Christchurch, 'but there are a few small things to get right and hopefully we'll do that and make the finals.'

George knows that he has to reach the next level with his rugby. Making the grade teams has been great but he wants to be an All

Black and he's determined to reach his potential. Still, his focus right now is on the NPC and on winning a championship.

'In NPC rugby, you come across players who are bigger, stronger and faster than you are and you come across teams who are just real gutsy and go until the final whistle. It's been a real mixture so far.'

George is different. He played rugby league until he was 15 and attended Christchurch Boys' High School. He made the first XV there in his last two years and looked destined for a professional career.

'I come from a sporty family,' he tells me. 'My father played rugby league here in Christchurch and that was probably why I wanted to play it as well.'

George's father has given his blessing to his son's sporting change of code. His dad doesn't mind what he plays, as long as he's playing something and making the most of his ample athletic abilities.

George is unsure whether he would have made it in rugby league. Growing up, it was for him all about running around and playing with his mates. A professional career was the last thing on his mind.

He doesn't regret his decision to play rugby union and it's now certainly paying dividends. One of the most rewarding aspects has been playing with so many All Blacks in the Canterbury NPC squad.

'It's an incredible feeling having all these really experienced players who have reached the top level nearby. I'm learning from them all the time and seeing how they do things.

'Everybody seems to get along and it's just a really positive place to play. I can't believe I'm here, really.'

The flip side of the coin in playing with so many great players – the Richard McCaws, the Rueben Thornes – is that George hasn't got the sort of game time that players in other provinces might get.

He's philosophical about that, as he is about the amount of attention he's recently received. In Canterbury's successful Ranfurly Shield challenge against Bay of Plenty last weekend (when he came on as a replacement), he stood out because of his athleticism and ball-handling abilities.

Still, he can see that the publicity may help him achieve his main goal this year, which is to make next season's Crusaders squad.

'My first goal, though, is to make the starting NPC team. There are still a lot of games to come this season and so I'm aiming for that. It's a long way before the Super 12 next season, although I would love to be in that squad and be a Crusader.'

Like many sportsmen of Samoan origin, George is a shy man, reserved even. He is guarded in what he tells me yet where it matters most – on the field – he is a dynamic individual who is a natural ballplayer. I wonder what the season will hold for him and whether he will get that elusive start for Canterbury.

* * *

Michael Johnson (26) had at the start of this season played 57 games for Hawke's Bay, a proud union on the East Coast of the North Island. Despite its second division status, the union has produced numerous All Blacks down the years, including Kel Tremain, Ian McRae and Bert Cooke.

'The union has an awesome history and our players are taught what it means to play for the Bay by the past players,' Michael tells me. 'That's one of the great things about this union: the heritage is passed down.'

Michael has the added responsibility of captaining his province this year. He says captaining the Bay is an honour and somewhat daunting but he hopes his actions will speak louder than his words.

Michael is a down-to-earth Kiwi who is a pleasure to talk to. He is not lost for words and he is as sincere a rugby player as I've ever met. He is a man who loves rugby with a passion, who plays it because he enjoys the camaraderie and the sense of belonging.

Like a lot of young Kiwi lads, Michael started playing rugby when he was five in the Hawke's Bay. He played first XV rugby and worked his way up through the colts to senior rugby. Making the Hawke's Bay senior side was a dream come true.

Hawke's Bay has won its first two NPC matches of this season. They've been second division champions since 2001 and are undefeated in 32 competition matches. Michael is wary of the pressure.

'There are certainly two divisions within the division,' he says, 'although like any rugby competition, we know that any team could knock us off on any occasion. As a side, we're just looking to improve.'

Michael works as a builder in a team including plumbers, farmers, winery workers and students. He regards himself as semi-professional, although he admits that balancing work and rugby has its pluses and minuses.

'On the one hand, the variety is good. It's a real change to go off to training after working all day and that keeps me fresh. I'm not sure whether I would like the monotony of training all day.

'On the other hand, it's sometimes a struggle trying to combine work with training. I'm in an industry where making deadlines is important. If I'm not there, the job may take longer and there is certainly pressure in balancing the two.'

Michael's week involves a gym session on Monday and team trainings on Tuesday, Wednesday and Thursday. He leads a captain's run on Friday, followed by the game on Saturday and recovery on Sunday.

'Rugby's become an all-year-round passion,' Michael admits. 'It's a way of life and whether it's the club competition or the NPC, there's always something to do. This year I didn't play for the Hurricanes training squad because I was getting married.'

The average age of players in the NPC is also decreasing, Michael says, suggesting that at the ripe old age of 26 he doesn't like being called 'old man' within the squad.

'It [rugby] does seem to be becoming a young man's game. Blokes aged 19 or 20 are coming out of school and playing NPC rugby. It's great for us older guys, as they provide real enthusiasm.'

Having played both amateur and professional rugby, Michael says the game at second division level is becoming more professional each season.

'It's constantly changing. Teams are now bringing in coaches to coach their attack and their defence. It's definitely more specialised and teams are going the extra mile to get an edge.'

Michael has thought about playing first division rugby but Hawke's Bay is home and it has obvious attractions.

'House prices here are more realistic, the beach is great, it's central to everything and it's home.'

Captaining the Bay was a huge honour. 'I want to be a part of a Bay side playing first division rugby.'

Right now, though, Michael's focus is on Hawke's Bay winning. This week they're taking on North Otago. They've won their two games handsomely. However, Michael knows the real tests are yet to come.

* * *

Luke O'Donnell won't tell me why he's called 'Elvis' by his West Coast teammates. I want to know, I really do. Apparently, it's got something to do with his singing, funnily enough.

West Coast, one of New Zealand's smallest unions, is also one of the country's proudest, having been formed in 1883. It's also one of the most diverse, with players from deep South Westland eligible to play for the union.

The West Coast is better known for rugby league and yet there is a spirit about Coast rugby that is as pure and as true as anywhere else in the country.

Luke came to the Coast in 2001 after playing senior rugby in Christchurch and representative rugby in South Canterbury. At the start of the season, he'd played 13 games in all for the Coast and was looking at retiring.

'The Coast sides normally have small forwards and young backs. That's certainly been the case since I've played for them.'

Luke got into rugby partly because his father was a 'rugby nut'. Educated in Christchurch, he played first XV rugby and eventually played for the Marist–Albion senior side.

He went to South Canterbury to study journalism after doing a BA at Canterbury University. He now works as a journalist on the Coast, a place that to him was something of a culture shock to begin with.

'My mum's from the Coast but it does take a while to get used to. The club rugby here's about the same standard as senior B rugby in Christchurch and middle-of-the-road club stuff in South Canterbury.'

Luke plays for the Marist club. For the first half of the club competition, the five clubs in the Coast union play each other. For the second half, they combine with clubs in the Buller union.

The rugby doesn't get any more intense during the representative season. The Coast squad trains on Tuesdays and Thursdays and plays at the weekend. Because the club competition isn't strong, some players are brought in from Canterbury.

'It means that we only really have one team-training session a week [the Thursday]. I do a bit of road running on top of that but gym work is difficult.'

In all, Luke will probably play around 16 games of club rugby and 7 games of NPC rugby this season.

'Rugby here is very semi-professional,' he tells me. 'We get around NZ$100 a game, a bit of Adidas gear, petrol vouchers and meals. We get a lot of support from the union, though.'

There's no pressure on the players to perform because there's simply not the numbers. 'If you miss training, you're not going to be dropped, because who are they going to replace you with?' Luke tells me.

The beauty of playing rugby on the Coast, however, is the spirit and camaraderie. 'The hospitality here is fantastic. The rugby may not always be of the highest standard but the players always mix and that's cool.'

The Coast has lost its first two NPC games of the season – against South Canterbury in Greymouth and Mid Canterbury in Ashburton. Luke is reflective.

'The 48–10 loss to South Canterbury wasn't a fair reflection of the game. It should have been 25–10. In the end, our fitness and lack of depth showed through but at least it showed us where we were at.'

The Coast side remains positive. 'The spirit is good,' Luke tells me. 'The squad is tight knit and I'm confident that we can upset a team or two before the season's out.'

* * *

George is on tour with the Canterbury Colts when I catch up with him six weeks later. Four matches for the A team (including three as a substitute) had whetted his appetite for NPC rugby.

The highlight for George had remained being part of the Canterbury squad that had travelled to the Bay of Plenty and come home with the Ranfurly Shield.

'I'm happy,' George tells me, 'as I've achieved my goal of starting a game for Canterbury (against Taranaki). After that, I've not been used,' he says with disappointment in his voice. 'With Richie McCaw coming back, there's a lot of competition within the loose forwards. I'm still hanging in there and I'm hoping to get another shot, whether it's with the Bs or the As.'

Another shot would promote George's claim for a Super 12 contract, something that he says he would love to be offered.

'I don't think I've done enough yet. Hopefully, when I came on for the first three matches, I got recognised by the Super 12 coaches but either way I'm still pretty happy to keep playing the way I am.'

George is realistic about being picked up by the Crusaders and fitting into their outstanding mix of loose forwards. If he isn't, he would go into the draft and hopefully be picked up by another franchise. That wouldn't be ideal, he tells me, but it's the reality of the Super 12 in New Zealand.

Starting against Taranaki in his first NPC match was 'great fun', although George says he would have preferred not to have defended as much as he had to.

'To be honest, I was a little bit nervous. It's something special playing against the top team on the table at the time and it was a really good time for me to start. I sort of felt like I'd done as much as I could to secure the number 6 for the following week.

'The speed of the game really hit home to me. The guys are really physical and if you're not really prepared week in, week out to play against guys who are bigger and stronger than you are, then you're not really ready for the step up to Super 12.'

George admits that it was frustrating going back to play for the Colts. 'It's like playing the top national team and then coming back and playing first XV rugby again.'

Keeping his standard high remains a paramount goal. The temptation is to slip back into the old habits, which for George means letting his defence slip.

'I'm not really sure whether I'm a marked man but I guess making the New Zealand Colts this year and making the Canterbury NPC side does put a mark by my name. Yet it doesn't really mean anything if you don't play to your potential.'

While he was now playing with the Colts, he was still training with the NPC squad. He says that in many respects it's as good as playing with the As.

'Training with those guys is actually like being there and playing with them. They are teaching me all the new skills and even though I'm going back down to play with the Colts, I can pass on what I learn to the other boys.'

After having a taste of NPC rugby, George says he desperately wants more. He tells me the only way he can achieve that goal is by working hard and learning as much as he can, as quickly as he can.

* * *

Michael Johnson is excited. I can tell from his voice. Hawke's Bay have continued on their winning ways, now winning six NPC matches this season on the trot, including a 44–12 win over old enemy Manawatu last weekend.

With two games to go, they've already qualified for the semi-finals. 'We've got to play Counties and Nelson Bays, and they will be good challenges for us,' Michael says. 'Therefore, what we're doing is really building up for the semi-final.'

Hawke's Bay has now extended its winning sequence to 35. The pressure, Michael says, is increasing. 'Each week we dread reading in the newspapers about how many games we have won without a loss. That builds pressure but as long as we keep winning I'll be happy.

'What I notice is that each team we play against tends to lift against us and that makes it frustrating in some respects but that's something we've got to get used to. For example, last week East Coast raised their game and played really well.'

The local derby against Manawatu had likewise been tough, despite the score. 'I wasn't happy with the way I played yesterday. I also feel that I've got a bit to work on with regard to my captaincy. I've got some books out from the library and I feel the key for me is not to stop learning.'

With the pressure mounting, Michael tells me that he's learnt to switch on and off from rugby. 'The deadlines that we have at work are pretty strict but at the moment we are winding down on a job and so it's not quite as intense as it would be otherwise and I'm able to concentrate on rugby.'

Michael admits that Bay of Plenty holding the Ranfurly Shield this season buoyed him and his side. It proved to Hawke's Bay that the Shield could be won by one of the less glamorous unions.

'All the support they received was fantastic and I felt they were really unlucky to lose it to Canterbury at the end of the day. It brought the passion for the Shield back and it proved that smaller unions can win the Shield and do well off it.'

Michael says that the issues of the day in rugby – the expansion of the Super 12 and Tri-Nations, the fact that the All Blacks may not play too much NPC rugby in the future – do not affect his boys too much.

Their focus is on winning another title. 'The team culture is great. Last week, we went up the Coast to play. It was a six-hour trip on the way back and it allowed us to bond as a team. We showed plenty of spirit in that match, coming from 24–6 down to win 30–24. There are no big heads in the squad and we all get on really well.

'After the match, the boys like to have a quiet drink together, even though I don't drink myself. A few weeks ago, we had a barbecue at the coach's place, while next week we are having dinner with the partners.

'Before home games, the partners meet at around 1.00 to 1.30 p.m. and have nibbles and drinks. They mingle and get to know one another and so, yeah, there is plenty of spirit throughout the team.'

For Michael, this was almost crunch time in the season. Still, the reason why he played the game was not lost on this modest man.

'You make friends right across the board that you probably wouldn't make otherwise. The captain of the Manawatu side yesterday was a local guy from the same town as I'm from, so we knew each other and had trained together. You never forget those things.'

He says the players these days are more mature when it comes to alcohol. 'Back when I started, a few of the younger guys used to play the game and go a bit silly. These days, guys know that they've got to keep working and improving the next week and that if they want to drink they can do that in the summer.'

Michael's focus is on the next month and finals rugby. I know that the next time we speak he'll have gone through hell to achieve his goals.

'Ultimately, I want Hawke's Bay to be playing a winning style, to be playing positively and showing people why we are winners. That would be fantastic.'

* * *

I've promised Luke that I'll come over and watch West Coast play at home. So my girlfriend and I rent a car one Saturday and head to Greymouth in search of rugby and, maybe, romance.

Falling in love is the strangest thing. It usually involves spending prolonged time together and finding out whether the other person is the one for you.

Somewhere between Christchurch and Greymouth I discover that Stephanie is the one. Ever since our first date in July, we've got on well. It says a lot for a girl that she's prepared to travel across the South Island to watch rugby with me.

When the girl to whom I've dedicated this book and I arrive in Greymouth, it is beginning to rain. When we reach Rugby Park, we don't have any trouble getting a parking space but we dread the wet afternoon ahead.

There are no queues, no great sense of expectation. We walk

through the gates without paying – we tell the gatekeeper we are writing a book – and have no trouble finding a seat at the top of the only stand.

As we battle to keep warm, the West Coast and Buller Under-18 sides play the curtain-raiser. The blue, red and white of their somewhat muddy jerseys contrasts magnificently with the lush green native bush on the hills that surround Greymouth.

With the drizzle giving the ground a closed-in feeling, the scene is like something out of the movie *The Piano*. We are cold but we are close and I know that coming over here was a good decision.

I could probably number the NPC games the West Coast have won in the last decade on one hand. They are not rugby's glory boys. Up against them today are King Country, the home union of Colin Meads but another union that has seen better days.

King Country is expected to win today. They've got a number of players who've played for first division sides and they certainly run onto muddied Rugby Park with the air of winners.

The Coast are a team of battlers. Reputations don't mean much when it comes to battling through the Greymouth mud. The Coast deservedly take a 15–9 lead by the break. An upset may be on the cards.

At the interval, I look across at Steph. She looks absolutely frozen and has a cherry-red nose. But in a strange sort of way she looks as though she's enjoying this taste of New Zealand culture. I know I am.

The highlight of the second half comes after eight minutes when the Coast's lock forward Peter Nicholls (no relation) collects the ball from broken play and runs like a three-quarter to score a great try.

In the wind and the rain, the bearded Nicholls looks like he's just come down from the mountains but I naturally feel an affinity with the Coast's captain.

The Coast and King Country exchange tries. We're waiting for Luke to take the field. He's played every match for the Coast this season but, just our luck, today he's on the bench.

It doesn't matter, as this is the best match I've seen all season. Luke takes the field with the Coast up 27–14. He's playing full-back and makes some strong runs as the Coast run out eventual 27–19 winners.

The hearty souls who have braved the conditions are rewarded with a home win and a cracking game of rugby. I've never seen the

Coast play before but I'm also on a high. Watching grass-roots rugby with the girl I'm falling in love with cannot be beaten.

After the match, Steph and I stride across the sodden turf and find Luke. As he's only played a quarter, he's not exhausted. 'This is certainly a bolt from the blue,' he says of the victory. 'To keep these guys down for the best part of 60 per cent of the game is bloody magic. Although I had a pretty limited role to play, from the kick-off things looked promising.

'You could probably pick out any of the eight individuals in the forwards who shone. They were bloody good and really stood up today.'

Wins like these are made sweeter by the fact that they happen rarely on the Coast. 'You come to expect a difficult season,' Luke says, 'and you measure the benchmark against the bigger teams, and King Country would certainly be regarded as being one of the bigger teams for us.'

I ask Luke whether it's difficult to keep spirits up when a side is losing as often as they do but as quick as a flash he replies, 'Then you get days like this, Todd.' I feel emotional when he says this and I know then and there that writing this book has been a worthwhile exercise.

'Beating Buller is always pleasant,' Luke tells me when I ask him whether this has been a highlight of his rugby career on the Coast, 'but as far as the third division goes this is top notch.'

Luke tells me that the Coast won because they attuned to the weather better and started well in the first half playing into the wind. I get the feeling, though, that the Coast won because they displayed good old-fashioned guts. I'm proud to have been in attendance.

'I've never seen spirit like it in all the rugby I've played,' Luke tells me. 'There was a bit of biffo and while that can't be condoned, it brings a team together.'

Tonight, the Coast will celebrate. Six of their players are heading back to Christchurch for a 30th birthday but they will catch up with their teammates next week.

'What this win gives us is a shining light at the end of the tunnel to perhaps make the top four. As we're Coasters, it doesn't matter where we will be celebrating, but we'll be celebrating tonight.'

With the wind gusting at our ears, we leave it there. Luke needs a hot shower. We need to get some food. As Steph and I walk across Rugby Park, proudly watching the scoreboard attendants take down the day's score, I'm on an amazing high.

Not only am I with a girl for whom I've quickly fallen but I've seen a bunch of Kiwi battlers win a struggle they weren't expected to. What's more, I've met in person one of the nicest people in New Zealand rugby and, perhaps most importantly, I've fallen in love with rugby again. You don't forget days like this.

* * *

When George and I talk for a third time, the NPC is over. Canterbury, laden with All Blacks, have won the first division, beating Wellington in the final.

George played out the season with the Colts but continued to train with the NPC squad and was there in Wellington when the championship was won.

The Canterbury Colts lost only one game (to the Otago Colts) but, according to George, the competition was fierce within the squad, as there is always the promise of professional rugby around the corner for those who make the grade.

'There were pros and cons in playing for the Colts,' George tells me. 'The pros are that I was playing with a bunch of guys who were the same age as me, some of whom I went to secondary school with.

'The cons are that, as we spoke about last time, there is a real risk that I'll drop my standards and let my motivation slip. I guess it's been a real test of my professionalism and I think I've come though it well.'

As George predicted, he didn't make the Crusaders squad. He was named in the back-up training squad and he feels reasonably happy about that.

'I'm on the verge of it [the Crusaders],' he tells me. 'I'm nearly there and if I continue to work hard then hopefully my time will come. I know that I'm part of something that's really big. It would be fantastic to start my professional career with the Crusaders.'

We reflect on George's season and he tells me that the undoubted highlight was playing for the NPC squad. 'Being part of the Canterbury squad and getting on against Bay of Plenty in the Ranfurly Shield match was something that I could only have dreamed of.

'Also, I guess being part of the squad that travelled to Wellington for the NPC final was very special. But the best thing overall was just learning off the boys. When you're training with All Blacks like

Richie McCaw, Rueben Thorne and Dan Carter, you can't help but learn. That's been special and priceless.'

The NPC, George tells me, is where the All Blacks of tomorrow are produced and he does not subscribe to the view that the competition is out of date. Rather, he says, it's the step below Super 12 and any weakening of it would in the long term weaken New Zealand rugby.

'People say that the NPC is weak and redundant. But I can tell you that when I had my photo taken as part of the NPC squad alongside some of the legends of the game, there was no prouder man. That's what it means to me to play for Canterbury.'

George has started training – for next season. His goal remains making a Super 12 side. He would love that to be the Crusaders but he knows that he might have to go elsewhere. His cause has not been helped by former Highlander loose forward Sam Harding joining the Crusaders.

Sevens rugby is also on the cards. George is on the verge of playing for the national squad after starring in the game for a few years. 'Any opportunity you get to put on the black jersey, you take it,' he tells me.

Right now, though, George is enjoying having a lighter load. Having played in Japan and then come back to a season which included playing for the New Zealand Colts and the Canterbury NPC side, his mind as much as his body is crying out for a rest.

George appears more relaxed than on the earlier occasions we've spoken. Undoubtedly, he's got more time to talk and reflect on the season that's been.

George is a quietly spoken, shy bloke. A natural athlete, one of my lasting memories of the 2004 NPC will be of George attacking the Bay of Plenty defence with the ball tucked in one hand. He may play for the All Blacks one day and if he does, then I'll know the hard work and effort that's gone into him getting there.

* * *

In some ways, I wished I hadn't spoken with Michael Johnson again. Since last time, Hawke's Bay's unbeaten run had ended. They had beaten Counties Manukau but had lost 34–32 to Nelson Bays in the last round-robin game.

The loss had meant that they would concede home advantage if they made the final and Nelson won their semi-final. That happened: Hawke's Bay beat Counties Manukau 41–20 while Nelson beat North Otago 32–15.

'We played really well in the semi-final and we had a good win,' Michael tells me. 'The expectations, however, were high in the Bay, although perhaps not as high as they would have been had we still been unbeaten.'

The results meant that Hawke's Bay travelled to Nelson to take on the home side in the final in a match that was going to be as torrid and physical as any first division NPC encounter. Hawke's Bay ended up losing 19–14.

'It would have been great to have that home support and in the end I think that told. People said that we had the better team but we didn't play that well. Nelson shut us down and as soon as their crowd got behind them, they took it away.'

Michael says Hawke's Bay played pretty well in the first half but couldn't capitalise. 'We were really disappointed, especially after winning the last three years. Obviously as captain it was one of the things that I didn't want to do. Perhaps we went into our shell a little bit and were really conscious of not losing. We perhaps should have focused on winning.'

When the final whistle went, the home crowd ran onto the field like they used to do at the bigger grounds in more innocent times. It was testimony to how much the win meant to the local community. 'You don't see that too much these days,' Michael says. 'It [the win] was good for their team and their community.'

The losses to Nelson Bays had been the disappointments of Michael's season. Yet it hadn't been all doom and gloom. He'd been selected again and made captain of the New Zealand Divisional XV that had toured Fiji at the end of the season.

'I got named for the trials and although I was in the squad the year before, you don't take things for granted. I was captain of one of the trial teams and luckily we won both the trials.

'To get into the team was awesome and to be named captain really blew me away. I wasn't expecting to be picked and it was a bonus really. It was such an honour and something I'll never forget.'

The tour was challenging. 'A lot of the guys had never been to Fiji before. We were training in Auckland in beanies and the like to acclimatise but when you hit Fiji the heat really hits you.

'We weren't expected to win the Test matches but we actually managed to win the first Test. We played three games in seven days.

We hit the wall in the last twenty minutes of the third game, and they [the Fijians] ran away with it.'

Back home, Hawke's Bay are one of the leading contenders to go up to an enlarged first division competition starting in 2006. Michael feels that this proud union deserves a spot in the first division.

'It appears that only two teams in the second division can go up but I hope that Hawke's Bay are one of them. Especially as everyone has been pushing the Bay for the last few years. The community would really get behind the union.'

Michael feels the jury is out on whether the two-tier competition will work. He feels there is a real risk that the gap between the stronger unions and the rest will continue to grow and be impossible to bridge.

Michael isn't thinking about rugby right now. He's thinking about taking off with his wife overseas in a week. 'We're heading over to Bristol. We're just going over for seven months at this stage. We really want to get away and see as much as we can while we are still young and before we have kids, I suppose.'

Michael intends to play a little bit of rugby while he is away, club stuff but not professional rugby. 'I'm going halfway through their season and I don't want to be tied down in case we want to do a lot of travelling.'

Michael's job will be left open, while his wife has two terms off from her teaching job. They intend to come back to New Zealand at the start of July in 2005. 'This is not retirement. I'll play a few games over there and keep fit. I would love to play for Hawke's Bay again.'

When they talk about the spirit of New Zealand rugby in future, I'll think about Michael Johnson. I would argue that he's a better role model than most fully professional players as he's more balanced. It is clear that he hasn't lost sight of what rugby's really about or the passion involved in playing for your province. If only there were more Michael Johnsons.

* * *

Beating King Country has been the season highlight for both Luke O'Donnell and the West Coast.

After that match Wairarapa Bush had beaten them 42–7.

They'd followed that up with a 53–24 loss to Poverty Bay at

home in the last game of the season. I'd almost gone across to watch that game rather than the King Country match. Luke didn't have to tell me that I'd made the right choice.

'It was a shame to finish the season with those two losses,' Luke tells me down the line. 'We really should have ended up mid-table. We really needed to do better given the reduction in teams in 2006.'

That reduction could see both West Coast and Buller miss out on NPC rugby. We both agree that would be terrible for the future of rugby in the area and a slap in the face for two proud rugby unions.

'I don't think that a combined West Coast–Buller side would work. Guys would have to travel one and a half hours to training and they still wouldn't be competitive. So the Coast will be left playing Canterbury Country or the Canterbury Under-19s.'

This season had been more successful for the Coast off the field because there had been fewer loan players from Canterbury in the side. 'The guys were committed to what we were doing and that made a world of difference. The spirit was bloody good.'

While the representative side had been struggling for some time, it was an appropriate reflection of the club game on the Coast. Fewer senior players meant that clubs were amalgamating. The future was not rosy and Luke wonders whether the Coast will only have a senior B competition in future.

'We'll get to the stage where the Coast and Buller are just feeding grounds for bigger unions. Players like [All Black] Ben Blair [who came from Westport in the Buller union] are already being offered scholarships to attend schools in Christchurch and further afield.'

Luke sees similar things happening to the club game in Christchurch and Dunedin, albeit to a smaller degree. 'Club rugby remains the heart of rugby in New Zealand and I would like to see the NZRFU do more for not only the clubs but also the smaller unions.

'Although we didn't have a hugely successful season, I would like to think that we played with enough courage and spirit to suggest that there is a place for the Coast in NPC rugby in future.'

Luke was happy enough with his own performances this season and he's appreciated 'playing behind a pack that gave us backs plenty of pill'.

Now 25, Luke says his body is taking longer to recover from matches these days. Still, the passion remains. 'I'll keep playing for as long as I can at this level. I haven't travelled yet and so in the next year or two I'll take off to Ireland or Portugal or somewhere and play a bit of footy and do some journalism if I can.'

Luke probably won't return to the Coast when he returns from overseas: the lure of the press gallery in Wellington will be too strong. He tells me that whatever happens to him in future, he'll probably never be happier than when he was playing rugby in the cheery red and white of the Coast.

'There is something about the people here. They make you feel welcome straight away and that's especially the case when you play rugby. To me, the spirit of rugby is very much alive and kicking here.'

* * *

Each year, rugby journalists in New Zealand talk about the NPC playing second fiddle to the Super 12. They wheel out clichés about how the public is not interested in semi-professional rugby and how the All Blacks not playing in the NPC will ruin the spectacle and intensity of the competition.

I must say that before I took a close look at the competitions I too was somewhat bored with NPC rugby. It wasn't that the competitions were bad, rather that by the time August and September rolled around we had already gone through Super 12 and the Tri-Nations. Simply, I was all rugby-ed out.

Yet after following the progress of my three profiled players, it appears to me that the traditional virtues of rugby – the camaraderie, the pride in playing for your team, the guts and determination in reaching your goals – are never better demonstrated than in the NPC.

Not every individual can play Super 12 rugby, let alone be an All Black. What the NPC does is give players of some ability in New Zealand the opportunity to represent their province with pride in the knowledge that they are part of something bigger, something real. In its own way, it allows more individuals to be part of the New Zealand rugby community.

The NZRFU is fully aware that it has a bigger role than just making sure that the All Blacks win as many games as possible, important as that is. The NZRFU, given the responsibility of promoting the game, must ensure that the sport is developed at all levels throughout New Zealand.

For it appears to me that what makes New Zealand rugby great is not just the Richard McCaws, the Jonah Lomus and the Sean

Fitzpatricks or indeed the famous black jersey itself; it is also the commitment of the players at all levels to the game itself.

It is the George Naoupus striving to get a Super 12 contract, the Michael Johnsons working 40-hour weeks and then having the responsibility of leading their provinces at the weekend, the Luke O'Donnells playing NPC rugby alongside their mates.

The NPC remains part of the eternal soul of New Zealand rugby and the national psyche, much the same as soccer in England and cricket in Australia. The blood in this vein runs much deeper than just the All Blacks and was demonstrated by the three individuals that I followed during the 2004 NPC.

Their stories, rich in diversity, inspired me not only as a lover of rugby but also as a human being. Their love for the sport mirrored mine and left me with the overwhelming feeling that whoever leads the All Blacks out against the 2005 Lions won't have 14 players behind him, he'll have 4,000,000.

* * *

LAND OF MILK AND HONEY

Symbolising the national condition, the All Blacks were by 1966 in the middle of perhaps their most triumphant era. The 1963–64 tour to Europe had been successful, Australia had been beaten in 1964, the Springboks in 1965. With names such as Meads, Gray, Lochore, Tremain and Laidlaw at the helm, this was an All Black side that worked as efficiently as a Rolls-Royce engine.

The Lions selectors, on the other hand, had cast their net in the wind and chosen 32-year-old Scot Michael Campbell-Lamerton to captain their squad. It was argued – perhaps rightly – that Welshman Alun Pask or Irishman Ray McLoughlin should have got the nod instead.

Campbell-Lamerton's credentials were shaky. He had been dropped by Scotland that season, while there was also the suggestion that thanks to severe crushing of the bones in his right foot he was not physically fit. The man himself was surprised to be named.

The Lions squad itself had some talent: Mike Gibson, then at Cambridge University, was perhaps the team's best player, five-eight

David Watkins was a tricky runner, while flanker Ron Lamont, number 8 Pask, prop McLoughlin and lock Willie John McBride were quality individuals in the pack.

The Lions won seven and drew one of their matches in Australia before arriving in New Zealand. After the 1950 and 1959 tours, the Lions were eagerly awaited and were warmly welcomed by a crowd of some 200 when they arrived at Christchurch Airport.

The New Zealand portion of the tour started disastrously with an 8–14 loss to Southland, a scratchy win against a combined South Canterbury side and another loss to a strong Otago side. As if that wasn't bad enough, some journalists were describing the Lions as 'unsociable' and 'aloof'.

THE KING OF BALLYCLARE

Although I lived in Belfast a few years ago, I don't know how far Ballyclare is from the centre of the city. So here I am in October 2004, sitting in a black taxi whizzing my way towards a place I've never been. In Belfast, members of the republican community run the black taxis. I'm heading to a Protestant town. Naturally, we get lost but after more than a few puzzled looks from locals, I arrive at my destination.

I nervously walk up the driveway and knock on the door. Mrs McBride answers and before I know it Willie John is on the doorstep shaking my hand. He's still not a small man but he isn't as big as the bloke we met at Lincoln College in 1983. He is again very friendly and so we go into his lounge and talk.

Willie John tells me the 1966 Lions didn't believe they could win. He'd been to South Africa with the Lions in 1962 but things hadn't improved one iota.

'We had a guy called John Robins, who was assistant to the manager and who tried to do some coaching but he snapped his Achilles tendon. The manager, who was a lovely man who played for Ireland, called Des O'Brien, hadn't been in touch with rugby for years but it was a pat on the back for him. He buggered off to Fiji for a couple of weeks. So we were left with a poor man called Campbell-Lamerton who was a compromise captain.

'Michael Campbell-Lamerton was a very nice guy but, quite honestly, he wasn't the captain of a Lions team and he was put in a difficult situation. The captain on that occasion should either have been Alun Pask of Wales or Ray McLoughlin of Ireland. They went for a compromise in between. It was wrong.'

Willie John says the tour was a joke. 'We had good players. I'm not saying we would have beaten New Zealand if we had done certain things,

177

as New Zealand rugby was very strong and they had a wonderful team at that time, but we could have been so much better. There was no planning, there was no thinking, it was nonsense.'

As an example of the poor planning, the Lions were sent to icy Queenstown to prepare for the first Test in Dunedin. Because of the conditions, the tourists struggled to find somewhere to train and ended up on an airfield.

'We would be trying to do a lineout or something and someone would shout "Aeroplane" and we would all run like hell and hide behind the hangar until it landed! Then we would train again. It was a total joke and unbelievable. We had no mission of beating the All Blacks. We weren't organised.'

Willie John's views are reflected by the fact that the Lions convincingly lost the first Test 20–3. The power of the New Zealand forwards had proved too much and added to this some incisive running from the backs ensured that the New Zealanders had a decisive victory.

Willie John was a reserve in that first Test and got to appreciate the talent within the opposition. 'Those 1966 and 1967 sides were probably the best All Black sides that I saw. Those teams were so much ahead of us in thinking and planning.'

The Lions were undefeated between the first and second Tests, beating amongst others Canterbury and Auckland. The spirit within the Lions squad remained good and hopes were high of a victory in the second Test in Wellington.

The Lions made seven changes for the second Test, with Willie John joining Delme Thomas in a new-look second row. Playing in muddy conditions, the Lions took an early lead with a penalty before Kel Tremain scored a try for the All Blacks, which was converted by full-back Mick Williment.

A drop goal and a penalty gave the Lions back the lead but Williment had his kicking boots on and added a further penalty soon after to narrow the Lions' lead to just one point at the break.

The All Blacks regained the lead in the second half when Colin Meads finished off a strong All Black surge. They scored again near the end when winger Tony Steel crossed and that, combined with another Watkins penalty, completed the scoring. The All Blacks had won again, 16–12, although the Lions had improved on their first Test performance.

'I enjoyed playing with Delme Thomas [in that match]. He wasn't taller than I was but he had a tremendous leap and he was physically strong. He also had a good mind and he never gave in. We could have won the second Test. We could have and should have won it and that would have made for a good series.'

The All Blacks were 2–0 up and once again the Lions did not experience the joy of winning. 'I think we disappointed New Zealand in 1966,' says

Willie John, 'in that we did not take on the All Blacks; in fact, we didn't really take on some of the provinces either. That's sad, because the New Zealanders like a challenge.'

THE GREATEST ALL BLACK

I feel guilty ringing Colin Meads. He's been voted the greatest All Black ever, a living icon, and everyone wants a piece of the man. Now it's my turn.

It's impossible to name the greatest All Black as, Colin himself says, no one remembers the great players from early last century. Yet Colin justifiably rates as the most iconic. It's not just because of his physical prowess that he's ranked above the rest. Nor is it because he was a member of so many great All Black sides. Nor perhaps because he epitomises the New Zealand condition so well: modest, strong, practical.

Trying to define Colin is like trying to define artistic brilliance – you know what it is when you see it but you're not quite sure what it is. The record books say he played 55 Tests for New Zealand, a staggering 113 matches for the All Blacks between 1957 and 1971. He is a legend.

Colin's a generous man – generous with his time, generous with his recollections. He tells me that he likes talking about rugby and that requests such as mine are no bother. If they aren't, the man's got the patience of a saint.

'In our younger days, the major rugby teams were the Springboks and the Lions,' he tells me. 'Those teams were idolised in New Zealand and yet they were also the teams that we kids wanted the All Blacks to beat the most.'

To Colin, beating the Lions was a flow-on effect from the traditions that had been established by the 1945–46 Kiwi team in Britain. They played attractive, winning rugby and, perhaps most importantly, they played with a style that re-energised the public's imagination.

'Growing up, we were really proud of what those guys had achieved,' Colin tells me. 'They had a winning tradition over the Brits and it was something that the All Blacks wanted to continue in 1966.'

Winning for their coach, the immortal Fred Allen, was also motivation. 'Fred was very hurt by what had happened in South Africa in 1949 [the All Blacks lost the series 4–0] and we felt we had let him down when we dropped a Test to the Springboks in 1965. There was a lot of motivation to make it 4–0 in 1966.'

Not surprisingly, the All Black selectors made no changes for the third Test in Christchurch. The Lions made three, though, including the surprising decision to play Thomas at tight-head prop, a position he had never played before. The general consensus was that it allowed Campbell-Lamerton to come into the side and it gave the tourists another lineout option.

179

Before the Test, the Welsh scribe Viv Jenkins had written words to the effect that if the Lions didn't win he would eat his hat. 'That provided plenty of motivation,' Colin recalls, 'and it wound us up a fair bit.'

Playing in cold, overcast weather, the Lions were competitive in the first half, Lamont and Watkins scoring tries to counter two penalty goals by Williment. The teams were locked 6–6 at the break.

Although the Lions had the better of the early stages of the second half, a try by All Black Tony Steel swung the tide. Two tries by flanker Waka Nathan sealed the All Blacks' 19–6 victory.

Although New Zealand's victory had been comprehensive, the Lions backs were always dangerous. The All Black forwards, with Colin at the helm, were the architects of the home victory.

'We knew they had a good back line,' Colin recalls, 'and throughout the series we tried to make sure we kept the ball away from them. Their pack, though, never seemed to click and I felt we had the wood on them throughout the series.'

Playing against Willie John in the second, third and fourth Tests was a different proposition to playing against Campbell-Lamerton in the first Test. The difference was obvious.

'Willie John especially was one of those blokes who never gave you an inch on the field and never gave in,' Colin recalls. 'Straight away, we knew that he was a completely different proposition and that he wasn't going to take a backward step.'

In saying that, Colin had plenty of respect for Campbell-Lamerton – as a person. 'He was if anything too nice. I'd got to know him when we were both members of a World XV tour of South Africa. He was a good bloke all right, but he didn't have the toughness that someone like Willie John had.'

After the third Test, as with all the Tests, the All Blacks and the Lions had dinner together. It was a wonderful way, Colin remembers, of players meeting and getting to know each other.

'It was great to catch up with the likes of Willie John and Ray McLoughlin again. We'd have some good honest fun, a few laughs and they'd say how they were going to deal with us when we came to Ireland.'

Fred Allen didn't ease up on the All Blacks leading into the fourth Test in Auckland. History, in the shape of a 4–0 Test series victory, beckoned.

'Fred told us that if we didn't win we would be wasting all the hard work that we had done. He kept on telling us that we were playing in front of a partisan crowd and that we had to win.'

Whether the All Blacks needed any motivation or not, they ran out comfortable 24–11 winners. Playing in front of 58,000 people, the All Blacks scored four tries, being ahead 10–8 at half-time.

The Lions went down fighting and had the satisfaction of scoring two terrific tries in the first half, although they had again been outplayed by a rampant All Black forward pack. Colin had again been at the helm, although he had blotted his copybook somewhat by felling David Watkins at one stage.

'Looking back now, those sides from 1965 to 1969 were all pretty special,' Colin recalls. 'It was good to be part of that and we were terribly proud of what we'd achieved. At the time, though, I'm not sure we knew what we'd done.'

Although the All Black backs had been solid, had the Lions been that bad? 'I think the Lions have been slated down the years and although we were pretty good in 1966, I don't think they were as bad as people thought they were,' *Colin tells me.*

For Willie John and the Lions, it was, if nothing else, the chance to go away and to lick their wounds. 'In one way it was a development for me and for rugby in these isles,' *he says.* 'We were getting better and better. We ended up believing that we could beat the All Blacks. In that sense, what occurred in 1966 was a great learning experience and a forerunner to what was to occur in 1971.'

LEGENDS NEVER DIE

In 1966, Willie John was in the middle of one of the great rugby careers. He would return to New Zealand and win with the 1971 Lions, while he would captain the unbeaten Lions in South Africa in 1974.

He retired from international rugby in 1975, having played 63 Tests for Ireland and 17 for the Lions. He was to Irish rugby what Colin was to New Zealand rugby – iconic. When his rugby career finished, his involvement in the game, however, was far from over.

Willie John coached Ireland for a time, while he managed the unsuccessful 1983 Lions in New Zealand. It was, he tells me, another disaster, not helped by the fact that the standard in the Five Nations that season was so poor.

Despite the Lions going down 4–0 on that tour, Willie John's reputation within the game remained undiminished. He'd developed character by being on 26 Irish Test sides that lost.

Outside rugby, Willie John brought the same honesty that he applied to his rugby to his life. He remained loyal to his employer (he worked as a bank manager), loyal to his community and loyal to the Ballymena club. He is old school when it comes to the changes in rugby and proud of it.

'I look at the Ulster games and the internationals and I ask how many of those people there are a member of a rugby club? It's [now] about excitement and hype. It's about entertainment now. From a playing point of view, it's about money and greed and anything you can get out of it.

'We have forgotten why we play the game of rugby. When I played rugby, it was a game devised for the development of young men and [to teach them] how to live with their fellow man, to teach him teamwork, to teach him tolerance and all the good things that are associated with life itself. That's gone.'

Willie John sees the changes that have taken place throughout Irish rugby and laments the loss of honesty and collective spirit.

'You've got kids coming out of school going around the clubs and asking, "What have you got for me?" I was brought up [to believe] that if you achieve something you had to earn it. Rugby players aren't earning it nowadays.

'They never sack the rugby players, they sack coaches, and players get their money no matter what happens. When I was a bank manager, I was paid on performance. Rugby players aren't paid on performance. They get their money anyway.'

Willie John tells me there are different pressures and priorities nowadays. As a result, everyone in rugby has got to work harder at keeping the game alive. What's the answer, I wonder?

'I don't know, or whether it's gone too far. The answer to me was at the beginning. It [professional rugby] was never going to work. I believe the individuals who brought in professional rugby should all have been sacked. There was no planning, nothing, and they made it a professional game from top to bottom. In Ireland, anything under province must be totally amateur.

'That's another thing with the professional game – the players don't know each other like we did. I don't know whether they even meet after the match. The game's lost the ethos that we knew. I've been to New Zealand a few times and you meet the old guys and you would go out fishing or whitebaiting. It was great fun. I don't think the guys playing these days will do things like that together in future.'

The changes have manifested themselves in other ways, Willie John believes, such as the way former internationals in Ireland are treated by their home union.

'We had a gentleman's agreement with the union that a former international had the opportunity to purchase two tickets for the home internationals,' Willie John tells me passionately. 'They [the IRFU] wrote to me this year, as I suppose they did to all internationals, and said that if I wanted tickets for the English international I'd have to buy two for the American game [as well]. They've broken the unwritten agreement, so I crumpled it up and threw it into the fire.'

Willie John tells me he simply doesn't understand modern rugby. 'Clive

[Woodward] is taking 44 players and 25 support staff to New Zealand. We took 30 players and maybe one or two support staff. I never go to the games today, I go to the club. Any money I have for rugby football I give to my club.'

Willie John is not bitter, merely passionate about the game that he loves. I like his passion and how, in his own definable way, he demonstrated what the spirit of rugby is all about.

'We have about 15 to 20 guys who meet on a Tuesday morning in Ballymena. Retired men, who meet and have a cup of coffee, have a chat about Saturday's game, moan and groan. They call them the Slavers.

'Those guys go out and paint the windows, replace a broken tile, replace a broken pane of glass, they walk the pitch, they lay a few slabs for a new pathway and they do it all for nothing. They have a lot of fun. That's what the spirit of rugby is all about.'

LIVING ICON

Like Willie John, Colin was also in his prime in 1966. As he implied, in the years between 1965 and 1969 he was at his peak as a player. Whether with ball in hand or in the tight exchanges, he was a magnificent forward.

He toured South Africa in 1970, broke his arm and then came back and played in the later stages of the tour. The following season, he captained the All Blacks against the Lions. Although the All Blacks lost that series, Colin was always inspirational.

In all, Colin played 361 first-class matches, a record for a New Zealander. Included in that were 139 games for his beloved King Country, whom he later coached. He also became president of that union.

Colin also became an All Black selector, a manager for the All Blacks, and a member of the NZRFU board, while he coached the 1986 Cavaliers side in South Africa.

When his rugby finished, Colin continued to farm in the King Country and then, as now, worked tirelessly for the IHC (Intellectually Handicapped Children) and numerous other charities throughout New Zealand.

Then at the turn of the millennium, a whole new wave of Colin hysteria hit New Zealand. In a public poll, he was voted the greatest All Black of all time. He received all the accolades in good spirit.

'It didn't really affect me, to be honest. It was something that was said at the time and it was a silly sort of a title. It was a public poll but who was going to comment on the good players of the 1920s, the 1930s, at the turn of the twentieth century? It's something I've been loaded with but it hasn't been a burden.'

These days, Colin is one of the more accomplished public speakers around. He has his stock stories down to a fine art and he knows how to work an audience. He is a man who now knows the power of profile.

At the same time, he's remained one of the most humble All Blacks. He's universally liked throughout New Zealand and is himself reflective of the Kiwi psyche.

Colin doesn't recognise the game that he and his underrated brother Stan played from the game played these days. Still, he accepts that change in rugby was as inevitable as autumn becoming winter.

What concerns him is amateur rugby in New Zealand. 'The little unions, like King Country, Poverty Bay and South Canterbury, are never going to have another All Black and that's sad.

'These days, if we here in King Country have a promising player he's snapped up by one of the big unions when he's at high school and given a scholarship. That's professionalism but still sad.'

Colin can see few comparisons between the 1959, 1966 and 1971 Lions and the squad brought out to New Zealand by Clive Woodward in 2005.

'I personally think that bringing out so many players and support staff has the potential to make some blokes who aren't getting games disillusioned. When I was playing, we had two support staff and we thought that was enough.'

As a result of changes like this, Colin is happy that he played rugby in his era. 'We had some wonderful times and we were often away for four and a half months. I was lucky enough to play in an era when New Zealand rugby was strong and we had some great players. I wouldn't swap that for the world.'

Although he is iconic in New Zealand and he was recognised as the greatest All Black, there is an honesty about Colin that I like. It could be a big part of the reason why he is so revered.

At heart, Colin is a man whose greatest joy was pulling on the All Black jersey. He regarded the garment as pure gold. When I ask him whether beating the 1966 Lions was a career highlight, his reply is simple.

'Becoming an All Black was the greatest thing for me. When I became an All Black aged 20 in 1957, I wanted to be a great All Black. That was then my next goal.'

There is no doubting that Colin achieved that. He became a great All Black because of, amongst other things, the great thrill he got in representing his nation. Partly as a result of his honesty, his country loved him in return. There wasn't a pay cheque in sight but merely courage, devotion and pride.

PART FOUR
Four-Nation Odyssey

I love what rugby is – brain as well as brawn, and then beer together afterwards. There is no other sport which caters for all shapes and sizes, or where players and spectators mix together so naturally after a match.

Roy Laidlaw (former Scottish half-back)

IN ENGLAND'S PLEASANT FIELDS

Monday, 4 October 2004

It's just after 6.00 a.m. and my bags are taking their time to find me at Heathrow. I'm amazed that so many people look so bright-eyed at this time of the morning – especially since so many have been on my 13-hour flight from Singapore.

I'd had the misfortune to be seated next to the toilet on the Singapore–London leg. Another mystery of life is why people have to relieve themselves at the same time? Why isn't there a steady stream rather than an almighty queue? As a result, I spent plenty of time looking at expressions of exasperation.

Luckily, there was in-flight music, and as embarrassing as it sounds, I have much for which to thank Anastasia, Westlife and Barry Manilow (my eclectic taste must have been due to the lack of sleep from Christchurch).

Eventually, my bags arrive and I find my best friend, who lives in England, waiting in the arrivals hall. He's made the two-hour journey from his home and also looks surprisingly bushy-tailed. It makes me feel more weary but I'm glad to see him.

It's a dark and dreary autumn morning. It feels like rugby season and after a day getting to grips with where I have to be and when, I arrange to go down to London the following day to begin my European odyssey in earnest.

I'm in Britain and Ireland to try and get a feel for the professional game here. I lived in Ireland for three and a half years and have some understanding but professional rugby does not stand still.

I know that in the month I'm here I will only get a taste but at least it will provide me with some context ahead of the Lions tour of New Zealand.

My odyssey begins in England, the country that invented the sport. When I arrive at Heathrow, I'm acutely aware that England are world champions. Being on a rugby journey, I suppose it's natural enough that I feel that way but it is still decidedly uncomfortable.

England is not home to the IRB but it's more or less home to professional rugby and it is here where serious money can be found. I'm thinking about this as I make my way down to the city of London on the train from Suffolk like some bored stockbroker.

Rightly or wrongly, to the outsider English rugby has always appeared stuffy. If you said English rugby in New Zealand when I was growing up, people would most probably laugh and say, 'What a bunch of toffs.'

To us, English rugby was about public school boys who played the game to learn good etiquette and develop social connections.

Although there was probably a degree of truth in this generalisation, English rugby did not help itself. They had beaten the All Blacks at Twickers in 1983 and 1993 but when it counted (i.e. the World Cups in 1991, 1995 and 1999), England came up short against New Zealand, despite making the final in 1991.

Perhaps most relevantly, New Zealanders did not have a lot of respect for English players because they appeared soft and, it must be said, decidedly arrogant. They were, if you like, the epitome of the 'born to rule' mentality that we colonials hated.

There is a story told that accurately reflects this view, pathetic as it is. During a semi-final of the 1995 World Cup between New Zealand and England, the All Black centre Frank Bunce tackled English captain Will Carling. After he did so, he squashed Carling's face in the ground and said something as profound as 'and that's from all of New Zealand'. Carling, you see, was the stereotype of this perceived English mentality.

Then came Johnson. If ever a man was going to break the English stereotype it was Martin Johnson. Tough, rugged, no-nonsense, with little arrogance, he appeared more All Black than English. New Zealanders took some credit for him: he did play in the King Country for a time and he did marry a New Zealand girl after all.

When England beat the All Blacks in Wellington in 2003, it finally dawned on New Zealanders that England were now a force in world rugby. When England won the World Cup later that season, it proved that the future of world rugby dominance quite possibly lay north of the Equator.

It was also becoming apparent that the English club competition was regularly drawing talented players and coaches from the southern hemisphere. Some were using it as a retirement plan, sure enough, but others were honing their skills and developing their talents in a completely different environment.

THE WEST LONDON GEZZER

Tuesday, 5 October 2004

'I believe you want a word,' he says, walking over like the quasi-typical west London geezer. Lawrence Nero Dallaglio is so big that even if I didn't, I would.

He may be getting on in professional rugby terms (he's 32) but he's still in magnificent shape and I would rather have him on my side than not.

Lawrence looks relaxed, like a boxer the day before a fight. He's just finished weight training at the Wasps' training facility at Acton in west London and I can almost smell the salt of the sweat on his brow.

I'm used to interviewing rugby players but I can't get over how big he is. He's what I imagine Goliath would have looked like – all arms, chest and muscle.

He's no longer an England international, having retired from the arena between the time I'd asked for the interview and today, but he acts like one. It looks as though retirement has done wonders for his stress levels, as he is friendly and forthcoming and not short of a word.

Lawrence remains rugby royalty in this part of the world. He was there in Sydney in November 2003, sure enough. Yet the respect from his peers goes deeper. He appears a man of maturity and obviously has a clear view of the world.

He speaks easily, fluidly, proudly. I like the fact that I can ask a question and then sit back and listen as the tape recorder runs like the Thames. He answers my questions firmly, as if there could be no other answer.

Nearly a year on, Lawrence appears to be still basking in the glory of England's World Cup win (and Chelsea's great start to the Premiership). He keeps referring to it like it's a favourite child.

'If you'd said to me at the start of 2003 that you're going to win the World Cup, the Heineken Cup and the Premiership, then I'd be pretty happy with that,' he tells me.

Not surprisingly, Lawrence is less keen to recall England's New

Zealand tour earlier this year and the drubbing they received. To him, it must be like an open sore that won't heal.

'I was really excited about that tour. Because the club was successful, we were playing right through to the end of May. From the point of view of the Wasps players, we were on a huge high. You don't feel invincible but you're battle-hardened.

'We knew that it would be a tough tour with a lot of guys injured or retired but I was still optimistic and excited to go to New Zealand to play the All Blacks. That was shared by some members of the team but, unfortunately, the structure of the game meant that a few of the guys hadn't played for four or five weeks.

'But no excuses, we were beaten by an incredibly well-motivated team who played exceptionally well. I wouldn't say that it was a hiding to nothing, because in a sick sort of way I really quite enjoyed the tour. I don't like being beaten by 30 points, because that's not what international rugby is all about, but I still enjoyed the adversity that the tour created.'

'Will the lessons learnt on that tour have a bearing on the Lions' tour of New Zealand in 2005?' I ask.

'You learn a great deal from any tour, whether it's positive or negative, or both, and there were obviously lessons to take out of this tour.

'But as I said on the tour, I don't think the New Zealand public has seen the best of most of the England players, as physically and mentally we weren't at the races in any way.'

The jury is out on whether Lawrence will be in New Zealand with the Lions. It's the question he knows I've been waiting to ask. The water has been made murkier since his retirement from international rugby. If he were playing for England, he would be a shoe-in.

Clive Woodward had given mixed signals. On the one hand, he had said that he would need to have a good reason to look outside the players playing international rugby. On the other, he was stipulating that no one was out of the equation. If I was confused, I couldn't imagine how Lawrence was feeling.

'It would be nice but it's not something that I'm in any way guaranteed of, to be honest. I've retired from international rugby and I'm not sure what the criteria for selection are.

'It's not for me to pick and choose whom I'm going to play for. All I can do is play as well as I can for Wasps and if they need someone to go on the tour [like me], then I'd love to go.'

I get the feeling that lurking beneath that cool answer is an ambition that burns brightly. Of course Lawrence would be foolish to announce his desires. His destiny would rest with the form of the loose forwards during the 2004–05 Six Nations. Yet I couldn't imagine Clive leaving him behind. As Lawrence told me earlier, you can't buy experience.

Lawrence would certainly be fresh if Clive came calling. In the last 24 months, he'd played 71 games of rugby, which equates to one every 10 days. Take his English commitments out of the equation and you get a more rested player.

Retiring from international rugby was not an easy decision to make. Yet I get the feeling that for Lawrence it was a relief of sorts. He's no stereotypical blockhead.

I don't know Lawrence but from what I've read the death of his elder sister Francesca had a dramatic impact on his perspective on life. She was killed in the *Marchioness* disaster, a young life taken alongside so many others. It would have affected any sibling.

Rugby needed to be put in perspective. Life for Lawrence involved far more. Retiring meant owning his time to a greater degree, having more control over decisions that affected his life and obtaining that essential balance often missing in professional sport.

He's not saying so directly but I detect that Lawrence has become somewhat disillusioned with some of the game's traditions that have been lost. He'd started his career as an amateur. He knows no amount of money can buy or replace what makes the game great.

It's telling that a man who's seen so much rugby, both at amateur and professional levels, fears that some of the essentials of the sport are being lost.

'I do worry that some of the players coming through forget the fundamentals of why they play the game, which is essentially to have fun. I worry that some of the friendships, some of the core values of rugby in the amateur days are [being] lost.

'I don't necessarily think they have to be lost. They can be retained, although obviously not to the same degree, as it's a serious business and it's now not a race to the bar after you've had your shower.

'It concerns me that rugby continually looks ahead, to the next game, the next fixture, rather than taking time to enjoy what you're celebrating, which is the game of rugby.'

The opponents that Lawrence has become friends with are almost exclusively from the amateur days. He says he misses the characters in the amateur era, a time when blokes from different walks of life could come together and play the sport.

'Life experiences off the pitch can enhance you as a player on the pitch both physically and mentally,' he tells me, 'and sometimes I wonder whether the young players coming through have that life experience.'

Whether or not Lawrence makes it onto the plane with the Lions, his career has panned out beyond what even he expected.

Like Martin Johnson, he's redefined the English rugby stereotype. He's matched the rugged, dogged toughness that used to be exclusively New Zealand's or South Africa's and become one of world rugby's most interesting characters.

RUGBY'S PREMIERSHIP

Tuesday, 5 October 2004

It seems to me that English rugby has got a lot to thank Premiership soccer for. Before rugby went professional, the soccer fraternity had created the model. Of course English rugby struggled to get the club/country balance right in the early days. When they did, however, the rest of the world knew that it was only a matter of time before they flexed their collective muscle.

I've only been in England a few days but it seems apparent that the dominance of soccer in this country has had a significant impact on rugby. So much of what occurs in rugby mirrors what happens in soccer. They appear professional cousins.

Take coaching for example. Club coaches are now almost like football managers, leading a team of highly skilled professionals in an attempt to create a winning squad. They obviously need to have technical skills but management skills appear just as important.

The format is also similar: club and country. In this country, a soccer environment prevails and whereas in New Zealand a Saturday afternoon used to be all about rugby, in England it's about soccer. How could the rugby community here not be influenced?

I'm sitting here at the Wasps' training ground in west London and the parallels appear even more obvious. It could be because Wasps share this facility with the QPR soccer club, who are currently doing pretty well in the Coca-Cola Championship this season. As a result, memorabilia from both clubs is scattered on the walls.

Warren Gatland is in a better position to comment on the similarities than most. A former All Black, he'd had success with Connacht in Ireland before spending four years at the helm of the Irish national side.

They'd also tasted some success, although the IRFU had eventually decided they wanted an Irish coach, so Warren had packed his bags.

He'd come to Wasps with the club at the bottom of the Premiership. He'd led them to English and European glory and had, if the commentators were correct, been their saviour.

Warren had tried to put in place at Wasps the structure of an international team without the resources. That included hiring quality staff, getting back to the basics and ensuring the players were honest to themselves and each other. It was that old chestnut again of implementing traditional values within a professional environment.

Warren had also proven that he was more than prepared to call a spade, well, a shovel. He'd proved that when England had been in New Zealand in 2004.

He'd been back home during the tour and had given an interview to a journalist from his local newspaper in Hamilton. After he thought the interview was over, the journalist had asked him whether he'd caught up with the Wasps players on tour.

'I said I'd had a barbecue with them. I said they were pretty disappointed after the first Test and then I made a couple of comments that they may have been training a bit too hard and as there were 19 coaches out here, probably it was too many and perhaps there were a few too many meetings. That was about it. Of course the headline in the *Waikato Times* the next day was that England was an unhappy camp.'

Clive Woodward was none too happy. Warren got hold of him, apologised, said that he had been caught badly. There appeared to be no bad feelings: Clive sent Warren a copy of his book, thanking him for his support. As a club coach, Warren had assisted Clive in the build-up to the 2003 World Cup.

Rugby should be enjoyable. It's now a serious affair but the players who perform are normally the ones enjoying their rugby. Warren tells me that England wing Josh Lewsey returned from New Zealand after the one-off Test in 2003 disillusioned. The reception the English had received from the New Zealand public had been far from positive.

Warren fears that even if they win the rugby, the Lions will lose the war. What he means is that the 2005 Lions won't have the same type of experience that the players in the 1950, 1959 or 1971 teams had for example. Wouldn't it be nice, he says, to hear the crowd sing 'Now is the Hour' after the third Test in Auckland.

To be fair, Clive's been saying the right things about the importance of players walking around the hotels with a smile on their faces during the tour. The point is well made. A successful Lions tour is a happy Lions tour.

Having coached Wasps to the top of English and European rugby, Warren is rightly proud of what he's achieved. Still, he's under no illusions about the standard of club rugby in England.

'In the last four or five years, this competition [the Zurich Premiership] has become very strong. When [All Blacks] Craig Dowd and Ian Jones came here straight out of Super 12, they felt that the top four or five sides would comfortably beat a Premiership team. That's changed. As a competition, it's got stronger from year to year.'

It frustrates him that other rugby countries don't have or haven't had respect for the English game: that they are not aware of how the Premiership is becoming the centre of world club rugby.

'The few times I've been home I've been frustrated by many of the comments of ignorant New Zealanders who have no idea about what's actually happening over here, or about the players.

'They just talk because they are arrogant enough to believe the All Blacks are the best in the world. We should be learning from the rest of the world and tapping into their methods.'

Unlike the NPC in New Zealand, there are no easy games in the Premiership. The competition, Warren feels, prepares players for international rugby and it ensures that they compete at a very high level, week in, week out. It also prepares English players to grind out victories in tight situations.

'In the five games we've played so far this season, we've got 99 points for and 90 against. We've won three and lost the other two by one and three points. It's a great experience for the players on the big stage, having been in those situations lots and lots of times.'

If an improvement is to be made, it may be in the standard of refereeing. Warren would like to see the best referees, regardless of where they're from, taking charge of Premiership matches. Referee accountability – just like that of players and coaches – is vital.

England's World Cup win in 2003 has presented a viable sporting alternative to the English public, Warren tells me. Soccer has harmed itself with the inflated salaries of players and the constant trouble that footballers seem to get themselves into. In that sense, the sports have had less in common.

He does not see a time in the foreseeable future when the Zurich Premiership, solely, will play host to the world's best rugby players. The salary cap and the limit on foreign players will prevent that. The restrictions on the capacity of stadiums and the finite amount of television pounds will also ensure that there is not a mass exodus of players from the southern hemisphere.

What will grow in the short term, Warren says, is the concept of Europe. The French have now bought into it and each year clubs savour the competition. With the crowds growing and becoming more partisan, the Heineken Cup has become central to the game in England and its most defining shop window.

It seems to me that Warren's time in the northern hemisphere – with Ireland and with Wasps – has been positive for all parties. In this global age, the market prevails and English clubs will continue to strive to get the best coaches, regardless of where they are from. Not a million miles removed from the Premiership in soccer in fact.

THE OVERSEAS PROFESSIONAL

Tuesday, 5 October 2004

We can be an inward-looking bunch in New Zealand rugby. This is at odds with the general outward-looking approach of most New Zealanders and in many ways it's a sign of arrogance.

For a large part of New Zealand's history, New Zealanders tended to look to Britain (England especially) for identity and understanding.

That's never applied to rugby. In New Zealand rugby, once someone leaves the inner circle they tend to be forgotten as quickly as you can say 'Take me to Heathrow, squire'.

That applies to both players and coaches alike and is incredibly short-sighted as there will come a time when a vast proportion of New Zealand's rugby resources will be plying their trade overseas.

Craig Dowd played 67 games (60 Tests) for New Zealand between 1993 and 2000. As a prop, he formed with Sean Fitzpatrick and Olo Brown a front row that was as solid as the Rock of Gibraltar and which was crucial in New Zealand's golden 1995–97 period.

I've never met Craig before. When I'd seen him play back home, I'd thought of him as some big bear-like front-rower that grunted and snarled when he spoke. What I found was an articulate New Zealander who was appreciating a different culture and growing as a rugby player and as a person.

He'd come to England to play because he was stale and because he needed new challenges. He'd been to two World Cups, won Super 12 titles with the Blues, and NPC titles with Auckland. He'd even won club titles with his club, Suburbs. Wasps was a challenge.

'I could earn good money over here [as well],' he tells me honestly. 'The money was one of the motivating factors but when I got here I found the lifestyle and the environment which I'm playing in really refreshing and I'm really enjoying it. It's rekindled my career and I'm excited about the game again.'

Now aged 35, Craig has been something of a revelation in the English game. He's been labelled the best prop in the Zurich Premiership and his impact on Wasps is best illustrated by the success his club has had since he has been with them.

Playing in England has also allowed him to spend more time at home and to have a more rounded life. He still feels somewhat bitter about the fact that in 2000, when in camp with the All Blacks, he had to obtain permission to attend the birth of his second child. Playing for Wasps has put his rugby–life balance into its proper equilibrium.

'You know, we play Saturdays over here and although we might spend a night away before the game, we're always home on Saturday night. That's something I really enjoy.'

Craig knew the standard of rugby was good in the northern hemisphere before he came here in 2001. The standard has continued to improve in the subsequent years and he oozes with enthusiasm about the talents the Lions' selectors will have to choose from.

'These guys love to work hard. That's not a vision New Zealanders have of English players. New Zealanders probably look at the English players as being a bit lazy, a bit girlie.

'These guys will spend hours in the gym. We say we'll do fitness and conditioning and they'll front up, they'll be there. They love the contact, they love smashing each other and it's not something they shy away from.

'They do work very hard and it's almost like the military compared to in New Zealand where we're a bit freer with our style of play and training.'

Although there are obvious differences between rugby in New Zealand and the northern hemisphere, to Craig the fundamentals remain the same.

'At the end of the day, a rugby player is just a guy who turns up, puts his boots on at the weekend and plays a wonderful game. We're all similar, regardless of where we come from. One thing about rugby is that it teaches you to get on with other people, regardless of where you're from.'

As an example, Craig hated Lawrence Dallaglio with a vengeance before he came to Wasps. He'd played against him, smashed him in a tackle and held no love for the guy. Now they are good mates and go into battle together. 'It's been eye-opening,' Craig laughs.

The Dowds have enjoyed London, and London, Craig admits, has been good to them. Their two children are well established in schools, while Craig's wife is teaching. The family is settled. 'We have a good lifestyle and we enjoy London. We have good friends in our area and life couldn't be better, really.'

Craig wants to get involved in coaching once his playing days are over. This season he's coaching the Wasps second XV, while he's also been involved with the English Academy. Long term, he would love to be involved in some level of coaching full time. He sees the irony in a New Zealander assisting England's young talent.

Playing for a major club in England does have plenty of benefits, it appears. For a start, the money is good. There are no two-week hikes to South Africa if you're an Australian or New Zealander, no month-long adventures to Australasia if you're South African.

A good player, unlike in New Zealand, can be anonymous in London, Manchester or Edinburgh. Playing for a prominent club can also be a shop window for potential internationals and allow them to compete against some of the best players in the world.

The standard of rugby is good, while your teammates are likely to be internationals of some sort. What's more, both the Zurich Premiership and the Heineken Cup are fast becoming the most prominent club competitions in world rugby.

* * *

BARRY'S GRACE

The 1971 Lions coach, Carwyn James, must have come away from New Zealand after the 1969 Welsh tour with mixed feelings. His side had been thrashed in two Tests, yet subconsciously he might have known that this All Black team was not going to get any better.

His troops, on the other hand, were sure to grow and mature over the next two years. By the time many of them toured New Zealand they would be ready for the greatest challenge in rugby. His boys would have become men.

One of those was Barry John. If one man characterised the 1971 tour it was Barry. Terry McLean has written, for example, that in bingo halls up and down New Zealand during 1971 they were shouting, 'Number 10, Barry John.'

My European trip in October 2004 would not have been complete had I not interviewed Barry John in Cardiff. Being the year I was born, the '71 tour had always been symbolic to me. Barry symbolised that and more.

I'd struggled to find a number for Barry. When I finally reached him, it was like talking to rugby royalty. We agreed to meet at the Cardiff Rugby Club one Wednesday morning when I was in town.

When the morning came, I received a jumbled message from Barry saying that he might not make it as he had a cold. Disappointed, I tried calling him to reschedule. When I didn't manage to touch base, I figured my chances of seeing Barry were remote.

Yet right on the time that we had arranged, Barry arrived with his umbrella close by. I was surprised but you could not wipe the smile off my face for I would have given my right arm for this interview.

There is a large painting of Barry on the wall of the Cardiff Rugby Club. It hangs alongside similar paintings of Gareth Edwards and Gerald Davies and is testimony to the impact that Barry and his mates have had on rugby in this part of the world. I ask Barry about what it feels like to be so honoured.

'Obviously it's a great privilege. But it's like you going to your local pub in downtown Christchurch. Initially, it was fine but after all these years you are part of the scene and it's like looking at the carpet. You get reminded now and then when you bring new people to the club. My *children used to take the mick out of me when they used to visit.'*

The Lions lost their first match in Australia against Queensland. A win against New South Wales in the next match did not silence the critics. Some suggested this would be the weakest Lions team ever to tour New Zealand.

Despite the shaky start, Barry thought the squad was looking good. When he rang his wife back home, he pointed out that there was experience in the forwards, while Carwyn James's coaching was top notch.

'The New Zealanders weren't quite certain,' Barry recalls, 'about what we were going to do. They'd seen Lions teams come and promise, and cometh the big day they'd come and fallen over. Yet we looked strong up front and they noticed that straight away and maybe started to think that we wouldn't be so bad after all.'

The Lions started the tour positively with four wins in their first four matches. Included in these were wins against Waikato and the New Zealand Maori. Yet it was in the fifth game of the New Zealand section, against Wellington, that the Lions really shone, beating the home side 47–9. Barry was the star.

'We had, injury allowing, as good a side as we could [put out]. Wellington were strong and we slammed them. That game defined the tour and that's when the journalists started sharpening their pencils and they realised that they had to take us seriously.'

Five further wins (including a 14–3 victory against Canterbury in one of the most violent Lions games ever) ensured the Lions were well prepared for the first Test against the All Blacks in Dunedin.

Barry, sitting on the sidelines next to Carwyn James, had watched All Black full-back Fergi McCormick in the Canterbury match the week before, studying his positional play closely.

'We were geared up for the Test,' Barry recalls, 'and we knew that it was going to be tough. The weather had been poor and so I remember looking at the pitch on the game time on the Friday and just looking at the little things. I'd studied Fergi the week before. Carwyn had said to me "Interesting" in Welsh and I'd replied the same. We were ready.'

Ian McLauchlan appropriately scored the only try of the Test after he charged down a clearing kick by All Black number 8 Alan Sutherland. After having both their first-choice props injured against Canterbury, it was fitting that one of their replacements had crossed for the decider.

Barry kicked two penalties, McCormick one. The Lions had deservedly won the first Test 9–3 and were now one up in the series. Barry was surprised that the All Black selectors reacted by dropping Fergi for the second Test.

'*I must confess that we found it amazing that they dropped Fergi, because he was playing in his own backyard in the next Test and if anyone was going to be fired up, it was going to be Fergi.*'

The All Black selectors replaced Fergi with future All Black coach Laurie Mains. Three further wins and the Lions were clear favourites going into the second Test in Christchurch, a game the All Blacks had to win. As it turned out, they did, thanks to one of the great tries in international rugby.

ONE OF THE GREAT TRIES

I meet Ian Kirkpatrick ('Kirky') for breakfast one cold Thursday morning in July 2004. He's in Christchurch to provide sideline comments for a television station at the All Blacks–Springboks Test at Jade Stadium. He's running late this morning and as I wait for him, I ponder what an amazing career he's had in rugby.

He played 39 Tests for the All Blacks between 1967 and 1977 and 113 matches in all for his country. He'd captained New Zealand in 1972 and 1973, including on their tour of Britain and France, while he was a stalwart of his Poverty Bay union.

He is a rugby man through and through and when we meet I can see why: a lean, athletic body, the rough man-of-the-land features that mark his generation, a rural sensibility that is an essential part of his character. He appears a real New Zealander.

The All Black jersey, Kirky tells me, was never his to own. He was merely wearing it until the next contender came along. It is a way, he says, of ensuring that the tradition is greater than the individual.

In 1971, Kirky was at the peak of his powers. With a tour of South Africa behind him, he was perhaps the star of the All Black forward pack. He was also by definition a natural leader of men and one of few certainties in the squad.

A fired-up All Black side had the better of the early stages of the second Test in Christchurch. First five-eight Bob Burgess scored for the home side after three minutes when he ran an angle and crossed five yards from the corner flag.

The Lions responded after 21 minutes when J.P.R. Williams fielded the ball on his own 25 and made ground before unloading to Mike Gibson. The Ulsterman drew Laurie Mains and sent Gerald Davies away to score midway between the posts and the corner.

The All Blacks struck back almost immediately when half-back Sid Going burst around the blind side to score close to the corner. Mains converted, although Barry reduced the lead to 8–6 with a penalty.

The second half belonged to the All Blacks. A penalty try was awarded to the home side ten minutes after the resumption of play when Bryan Williams was taken out by Gerald Davies, preventing a certain try. The conversion made it 13–6.

Burgess scored his second try midway through the second half with Mains adding a penalty with ten minutes remaining to extend the All Blacks' lead.

Then it was Kirky's moment. From a maul near the halfway line, he burst through with the ball in hand and fended off several would-be tacklers, including J.P.R. Williams, in a thrilling run to the scoreboard corner. With the crowd willing him on, it was one of the great individual All Black tries.

'Scoring tries wasn't necessarily a goal of mine,' Kirky says, 'but if it came along, you took it. It was really for the team. I don't think anyone wants to go out there and score tries for themselves if their team loses.

'That one [the try] just evolved from the ruck. It rolled a bit and before I knew it I was out in the clear and the thing to do was to run. All of a sudden, I could see the try-line and I just kept going. I guess a couple of their guys didn't tackle that well, or I pushed them off and then the corner flag came up very quickly.'

Kirky didn't realise what he'd done. Even walking back after scoring, it hadn't dawned on him what a great try he'd just scored. 'It was a bit embarrassing in some ways, really,' he says modestly. 'In those days, you just walked back to your own half and got on with it.'

Yet if it wasn't the greatest individual try an All Black has scored, it was in the best handful. It was a dramatic score, symbolised by its power, athleticism and speed. Most importantly, it also ensured that the All Blacks would win the Test.

'When women talk about having a facemask when they plaster themselves with mud, I now know what they mean,' Barry says. 'Kirky did that for me.

'Afterwards, the boys said to me, "You ran with him for ten yards, why didn't you bring him down?" Remarkable player, remarkable try. That was a brilliant athlete who seized the opportunity, saw the situation and who fancied his chances.'

A Gerald Davies try and a Barry drop goal reduced the deficit to 22–12 but the All Blacks deserved their victory. Their forwards had been outstanding, while Going and Burgess had stood out in the backs.

'I'LL BE BACK ON SUNDAY, PAM'

With the series locked at 1–1, the third Test in Wellington promised to be a torrid affair. Before the Test, the All Blacks dropped a bombshell by calling up the previously retired Brian Lochore to replace the injured lock Peter Whiting.

The story goes that Lochore left a note to his wife Pam on his kitchen table on the Friday informing her that he was going to Wellington to play in the Test and that he would be home on Sunday. What she must have thought when she returned home!

A drop goal by Barry and a converted try by Gerald Davies gave the visitors an early 8–0 lead. Then, after 17 minutes, Gareth Edwards ran strongly from a lineout, fended off two All Blacks and then fed Barry, who went over near the posts. With the conversion added, the Lions led 13–0.

Although Mains scored a try for the home side in the second half, the Lions had the match won in the first quarter. Barry had been the star for the visitors, although Edwards, Gibson, Davies and J.P.R. Williams had also excelled.

'After Christchurch, I think it may have come back to the psycho part of the coaching,' Kirky tells me. 'We were allowed to think that maybe we were better than what we really were. Maybe we should have been brought back to square one, not that we were overconfident.

'After a win like we had in Christchurch, we needed to be sat down and told, "Hey, this is only one win. We haven't won the series." We probably had too much confidence. Brian was talked into it and he'd probably say that it was the worst thing he did, but as far as we were concerned as players, it was a really good decision.

'It was one of those games where we didn't really get out of first gear and for me personally if I'd have had my way I would never have played. Poverty Bay/East Coast had played the Lions between the Tests and in the game I'd popped my ribs. It was bloody uncomfortable and you can't rush it. I thought I'd got over it before the Test but then I was thrown off a horse at home. I hurt it again.'

Kirky rang the selectors and told them that he didn't think he could play. They told him to get a doctor's certificate. His regular doctor was away and so he went to see Dr Bill McKay, the 1950 Lion who had settled in Gisborne, and told him that he didn't think he could play. McKay said that he would be OK to play.

'It was the stupidest thing that I'd ever done. Players know how bad they are, doctors don't. You know what it feels like and what you can't do. So I went down and struggled through training.'

Kirky had a jab before the match, although it didn't work. 'It was no *excuse. You go out there and if you've got an injury that's your bloody problem. If you don't play well, that's your hard luck.'*

Barry tells me that as the Lions had created more chances in the second Test than the first, they were actually confident going into the third Test.

'The series was hanging. It was a fortnight before we went home. We went to the Bay of Islands and had two full days of messing around. We got down to it then and prepared for the Test.'

MAKING HISTORY

With the Lions 2–1 up, an All Blacks victory in the fourth Test in Auckland was required if the home side were going to square the series. Playing in front of a crowd of 55,000, New Zealand took first use of the south-west breeze.

A Wayne Cottrell try and a Laurie Mains conversion gave the home side an early 5–0 lead. A Mains penalty increased the lead, before Barry kicked his first penalty of the match.

Just on half-time, the Lions won a lineout close to the New Zealand line. Gareth Edwards was tackled just short but from the ensuing play, Peter Dixon picked up the ball and crossed for a try. With Barry's conversion, the teams went into the break at 8–8.

The second half was just as close, Barry kicking a penalty, before Tom Lister scored for the All Blacks. Then, after 15 minutes, J.P.R. Williams fielded a ball near halfway and kicked a remarkable drop goal. The joke was that Williams never kicked droppies, hence the crude smiles on the faces of his teammates after the kick went over.

With the Lions ahead 14–11, the atmosphere was electric. The All Blacks threw everything at the visitors and finally, with eight minutes remaining, Peter Dixon was lured offside. Mains kicked the penalty and the scores were tied 14–14.

The match finished with the score unchanged and the draw was a fair result all things considered. The Lions had become the first side from the British Isles and Ireland to win a series in New Zealand. They had created history and they deserved it.

'We were disappointed not to win the Test,' Barry recalls. 'There were moments there where we would have liked to have finished on a big high and scored one or two lovely tries to have left a legacy and to have finished painting the picture completely.'

Barry felt the Lions marginally deserved to win the series and that the 2–1 result was a fair indication of the way the series had gone. It had been a tremendous series, one marked by the Lions backs.

'*As a unit, I don't think I would want to swap them,*' Barry says. '*They were amazing. From J.P.R. at the back to Gareth at half, they were outstanding. John Dawes was a levelling force and had some magnificent touches. The nice thing was that we all played to each other's strengths. It was like a dream.*'

When the Lions arrived home, the squad received a thunderous reception at Heathrow. They were on the front pages of many of the national newspapers. '*When those sorts of things happened, we realised that we had taken the sport to a different level in the UK.*'

Barry loved New Zealand. '*If the Welsh people had a gutful of me, I would probably end up in New Zealand. Not just because of the rugby but because of the people. I liked the lifestyle, the more laid-back attitude. I loved the beauty of the country and the Maori music.*'

Barry's success was his worst enemy. The demands on him significantly increased. He was now attending numerous functions, civil receptions, visiting the prime minister at 10 Downing Street. It all became, he tells me, too much for a shy lad from west Wales.

STILL WE ARE HEROES

Not surprisingly, Barry never again attained the same heights as he had reached in New Zealand. How could he be that good or that dominant? He'd starred in New Zealand, been part of a Lions side that was one of the best ever.

He played in the 1971–72 northern season, assisting Wales to an unbeaten record and scoring 35 points in 3 Tests. Then he retired. Aged only 27, he hung up his boots and moved into rugby folklore. He was encouraged to carry on but chose not to. The pressure, partly, had been too much.

After finishing playing, Barry went into journalism, writing articles for the Daily Express and appearing on radio and television. He and his wife Jan had a second daughter, Lucy, and he quickly became a highly sought-after figure on the after-dinner speaking circuit. He became Welsh rugby royalty.

Barry sees no comparison between the squads that he played with and the current Lions set-up. As far as is he is concerned, they have the same blazer and tie but that's about it. The trips he was on were brilliant fun.

'*I am more than happy to be a Golden Oldie now. They are modern Lions now. Our tours were educational and we enjoyed the people and I hope they enjoyed us. There was more balance in our day. Today, people are being paid and things have changed. If the things that happened on our trips happened now, we would have been home in two days!*'

Barry's a likeable man. He's got that wonderful Celtic ability to tell a story and make it funny. He's obviously used to attention, as he's relaxed with my compliments. But although seemingly extroverted, he also appears amazingly shy. As if the people of Cefneithin, where he's from, wouldn't approve of some lad getting too big for his boots, even if those boots were pretty huge.

LOSING IS NEVER FUN

While Barry was in the twilight of his international career, Kirky was in the middle of his. As mentioned, he went on to captain the All Blacks in 1972–73 and played for his country up until 1977. His last series was against the 1977 Lions.

Throughout his career, he continued to play outstandingly and never let his country or himself down. When he finished his career, he'd scored 16 Test tries, which at the time was a record for a New Zealander.

'Losing to the Lions was the end of the world as an All Black,' Kirky recalls. 'You always think about it as a lost series and you don't remember it fondly. That try in Christchurch went out the back door and didn't mean anything, as we lost the series.*

'Lions tours were the main series we had, as South Africa were not allowed to come in 1973. At that stage in the early 1970s, British and Irish rugby had some terrific players, some terrific teams. They'd moved on from the disappointments of 1966 and had learned.'

Kirky's since seen many of the Lions he opposed in 1971. They reflect on the series from time to time but they talk as much about how their lives have unfolded since then and how the game of rugby has changed.

'It's a different sort of thing now. I mean, the Lions are bringing 44 players and that's just totally different to our day. That's the way it has evolved. It's the way the game is going with professionalism and the way that sport in general is heading. It's a fact of life.'

Rugby remains part of Kirky's routine. He likes what he sees with the All Blacks and what they've done under Graham Henry. He laments, however, the changes that have occurred in Poverty Bay and the problems that are occurring at an amateur level in the sport in New Zealand.

'Young guys don't have to play rugby to have a social life like we used to,' Kirky says. 'There are so many other things that they can do. Young guys don't have to do the hard yards like we used to.'

Society in New Zealand has changed. Clubs in Poverty Bay are regularly amalgamating, while there are fewer teams in the clubs that remain. 'It's a bit sad. The population hasn't dropped. There are the same number of young guys around but they are just not playing rugby and that saddens me greatly.'

In professional rugby, what concerns Kirky is the number of New Zealand's second-tier players heading overseas to play. Not the All Blacks but guys on the fringes whose job it is to push the top players.

'We've lost a number of those sorts of players who would be playing NPC or Super 12,' Kirky says. 'I think we've still got enough quality to produce a top All Black team but I wonder whether we have the depth in New Zealand rugby that we once had.'

I get the impression that Kirky hankers for the old amateur days. He's not saying so directly but I feel he laments the end of the era when rugby, and not money, marketing and commercial contracts, was everything. That fits Kirky's psyche and his approach to life. Honesty personified.

SCOTLAND THE BRAVE

Wednesday, 6 October 2004

New Zealanders have an affinity with all things Scottish, particularly the further south you go. Dunedin, for example, was established as a Scottish Free Church settlement in 1848 and remains the most Scottish of cities outside of Scotland.

New Zealanders have down the years respected Scottish rugby and admired the talents of the likes of Andy Irvine, David Sole, Finlay Calder, Ian McLauchlan, Gavin Hastings and John Rutherford.

For some reason, the Scots (unlike England) have toured New Zealand regularly and in my lifetime have visited in 1975, 1981 (when they played in the World Cup), 1987, 1990, 1996 and 2000.

Scotland have always been competitive in New Zealand. They'd played terrifically at the World Cup in '87, drawn with the outstanding French and arguably given the All Blacks (the eventual winners) their most difficult game.

In 1990, they'd come very close to toppling the All Blacks at Eden Park, only the boot of Grant Fox getting the New Zealanders home. Hastings, Chalmers, Armstrong, Jeffrey, Calder, Milne and Sole . . . ah, the Scottish names. They deserved to win that day and half of New Zealand wouldn't have begrudged them.

Yet it had become clear that Scottish rugby was now struggling to keep pace with the top nations. Not only were England, the All

Blacks, Australia and the Springboks handing out regular beatings but so too were France and Ireland.

Scotland had dropped into the bottom tier of the Six Nations and the prospects of a revival did not look good. Despite contributing so many great players to Lions squads down the years, it appeared that the standard of Scottish rugby had significantly slipped.

So I've travelled to Edinburgh to find some perspective. My bed and breakfast is newly decorated, extraordinarily comfortable and close to Murrayfield. The proprietor, Maggie McKenzie, is, as they might say in this part of the world, one in a million. She looks after me so well that I want her to adopt me and bake me cookies.

I've been to Edinburgh before but this time I'm particularly impressed. The city has a spirit about it that I can feel in the autumn leaves that float like free spirits. There is a richness in the character of the people, an identity that we sometimes lack in New Zealand. I could live here, I think.

Despite suffering from gout and being hardly able to walk, I make it to Murrayfield. Edinburgh Rugby's franchise is based here and I've an appointment to see their CEO, Jim McKenzie. My objective is to discover whether professionalism is the root of all of the problems within Scottish rugby.

Jim tells me that the Scottish union is in the process of a strategic review for next season. One of the key recommendations will be that the professional clubs (there are three) in Scotland will become independent from the Scottish union itself.

The clubs will be able to obtain third-party investment and it will place them in a similar position to clubs in Wales and in England. The union will still have an investment, although it will most probably be a minority interest.

The changes will see greater commercial independence and less cross-control between the union and the clubs themselves. Everyone in Scottish rugby hopes that this will lead to positive results where it matters most – on the field.

Continuing on from this, an ongoing problem in Scottish rugby is the link between the amateur clubs, the professional clubs and the union itself. Not surprisingly, many of the traditional clubs had a desire to become professional. When the Scottish union decided to implement the district structure, this led to resentment.

'For a while, the clubs reacted against the professional teams and saw the professional teams as competition,' Jim tells me. 'That's changed now, to a degree.'

The change has come about because professional sides have included the clubs and encouraged them. The professional side is now seen as the pinnacle of rugby in the district and is supported by the vast majority of clubs in the region.

Whether that goodwill remains is one of the major issues facing Scottish rugby. In such a small rugby community, if everyone is not pulling in the same direction then I imagine that the game would not progress to any great degree.

'The clubs need to be kept involved,' Jim says. 'They need to feel as though there is some ownership. That ownership may be tangible, it might involve some shares to be distributed to individual clubs. There need to be programmes in place, whether or not the professional arm develops them.'

Jim is realistic about the need to guarantee outside investment. If a backer of sufficient funds came on board and wanted to shift the outfit to Aberdeen, say, then to Aberdeen it would go. However, this, he feels, is not realistic and any backer would want the entity in Scotland's commercial, political and sporting capital.

Jim says that if Scottish rugby is to progress, then as many people as possible must be introduced to the game. To do that, you need a winning team, something Edinburgh has not had in recent years.

Nor has Scotland for a while, for that matter. Eligible players from overseas have not helped. The argument as to whether Scotland-eligible players from southern hemisphere countries should be selected for the national side was ongoing. Andy Irvine had told me that week that it cheapened the jersey.

From afar, I tended to agree with him. Choosing Kiwi Brendan Laney for the national Scottish side just two weeks after he'd arrived in the country in 2001 was an example of the selectors slapping local talent in the face. In rugby, as with anything, you reap what you sow. I wonder whether the same sort of argument applied to the professional sides?

'It helps us play better and as a result of us playing better we raise the performances of the other guys,' Jim says of overseas players in the Edinburgh team.

'We don't want to bring in those guys unless they are better than the guys in those positions we have already, or if we didn't feel we had enough talent to develop guys who were as good as, or could be as good as, the overseas guy.'

There is no secret as to how Edinburgh Rugby will achieve success, either in the Celtic League, or in Europe. More

The definition of the modern-day hero – Kurow's most famous son,
Richard McCaw, holds aloft the spoils of success after the Crusaders
won their fifth Super 12 title in ten years in 2005. (Geoff Sloan)

All Black coach Graham Henry looks on as his side trains before the first Test against the Lions. Henry, like his side, had come of age.
(Geoff Sloan)

LEFT: Captain under siege – Tana Umaga withstood a barrage of criticism after the first Test against the Lions in Christchurch but responded where it mattered most: on the field in Wellington in the second Test. (Geoff Sloan)

BELOW: Three wise men – All Black coaches Graham Henry (left), Wayne Smith and Steve Hansen ponder tactics before the first Test against the Lions in Christchurch. (Geoff Sloan)

The heart and soul of New Zealand rugby –
George Naoupu from Canterbury (left), Michael
Johnson from Hawke's Bay (top) and Luke
O'Donnell from West Coast dispelling any doubt
that the spirit within New Zealand rugby has
suffered since the start of the professional era.
(Author's collection, *Hawke's Bay Today*,
Luke O'Donnell)

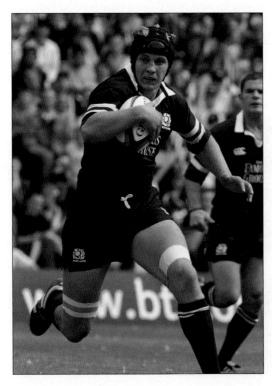

ABOVE: The end of the dream – Lawrence Dallaglio is down against Bay of Plenty in the first match of the Lions tour in Rotorua and out of the rest of the tour with an ankle injury. (Cleva)

LEFT: The unlucky Lion – although selected for two Lions tours, all Scotland's Simon Taylor has to show for it is one appearance as a substitute in 2001. (Gordon Fraser, Haddington)

ABOVE: Lions' captain Brian O'Driscoll's dream of leading the
Lions in a Test match in New Zealand lasted only seconds. The pain
in his eyes and in his reaction in the days subsequent was evident
for all the world to see. (Geoff Sloan)

BELOW: Wales and Lions flanker Martyn Williams had more ups
and downs than a roller-coaster during the 2004–05 season and yet at
the end still had a second Lions tour to show for it. (Cleva)

Sir Clive Woodward was never as good a coach as he was made out to be after England won the World Cup in 2003, nor was he as bad as he was portrayed after the Lions were beaten 3–0 in New Zealand in 2005. Here, the head Lion helps prepare his side for the first Test in Christchurch. (Geoff Sloan)

RIGHT: Southbridge's Daniel Cater gave one of the best ever performances by an All Black inside-back against the Lions in Wellington in 2005. As the cliché goes, a star had been born. (Geoff Sloan)

BELOW: Unassuming, down to earth and a rugby talent as well, Chris Jack helped lead an All Black forward pack that did not take a backward step against the Lions in 2005 and continued the grand traditions established by the likes of Tiny Hill and Colin Meads. (Geoff Sloan)

competitive rugby is one of the more obvious ways that the district can improve its results.

'If you look at the Celtic League, the standard has improved,' Jim says. 'As a result, Celtic sides – whether they be Welsh, Irish or Scottish – have performed better in the European Cup. We've got a bit of a way to catch up in Scotland. We've done reasonably well in the Heineken, while we're currently sitting third from bottom in the Celtic League.'

It seems to me that it just wasn't realistic to expect professional clubs with limited resources to compete with the big clubs in the rest of Europe. Jim says it depends on how the Scottish clubs go about it. The same applies to the Scottish national team.

'One of the advantages that Scotland has is the access that it has to its players. If we get the appropriate development in place, then we could develop good players who are as good as anything in England and France. Both of these countries have tremendous resources but they are disparate.'

Former Scottish coach Matt Williams had been working on the concept of 'Fortress Scotland', in other words, having all of Scotland's best players playing at home. This concept worked well in Ireland and has been one of the major reasons for their recent resurgence.

'I think that might not necessarily be possible,' Jim says. 'We've got three teams playing and that may go down to two next season. With only two teams playing, we don't have the broad base of competition that we need to reach that goal, I believe.'

Three professional clubs may become two because there are not enough quality players in Scotland and because professional clubs need to be based around a commercial centre.

That aside, Jim says it would be wrong to say that professionalism has been detrimental to Scottish rugby. Other factors, most commonly referred to as 'changing demographic trends', have played their part.

I raise a parallel between Scottish rugby and New Zealand rugby. Both countries once relied on men of the land and on the physical aspect of rugby. Professionalism changed that and as a result international rugby became a numbers game.

'The difference is,' Jim tells me, 'that everyone in New Zealand plays rugby. It's the national sport. Scotland will never have that. There will be a section of the community who will retain that passion but soccer will always be the number one sport here.'

The Lions concept gives Scotland's finest the opportunity to shine. Jim hopes that the 2005 Lions will be reflective of British and Irish rugby and that Edinburgh Rugby will be represented. If the Lions can win in New Zealand, it will boost enthusiasm here and encourage the next Simon Taylor or Chris Paterson.

In some ways, I hope the Lions do well because world rugby needs Scottish rugby to be strong. Is there a more moving occasion in rugby than standing at Murrayfield and hearing 'Flower of Scotland'?

THE CHOSEN SON

Friday, 8 October 2004

In 2001, the Lions selectors were brave and selected a young, but immensely promising, Scottish number 8 for their tour of Australia.

He had all the right attributes: athleticism, a physical presence, the appropriate body type, a positive attitude. He was potential personified.

Simon Taylor had stood out in a Scottish environment where world-class players don't come along every day. Playing with the collective talent of the Lions was going to make him a rugby superstar.

The superstar bit eventually happened but Australia 2001 hardly got started. Simon injured a knee in Perth in the first match. He was sent home to recover and his Lions destiny would have to wait.

Australia in 2001 had been unbelievable. He hadn't targeted the tour and his selection had followed his first season as a professional. It was some baptism of fire.

'I just went along not really knowing what to expect,' Simon tells me. 'I would probably be more nervous than most of the guys, certainly the guy who's 30 and done one before. I'm just pitching up. I'd never met many of the guys before and I wasn't sure any of the guys knew who I was anyway.'

I meet Simon in the gym at Murrayfield. It's an appropriate place to talk with the face of Scottish rugby. Others may disagree but when you think of Scottish rugby these days you think of Simon Taylor.

Simon's rugby background is similar to that of many other

Scottish lads. He started playing in Stirling County, had played at school and then for Heriot's club, before being signed by Edinburgh.

Playing club rugby was of benefit. It gave Simon perspective, understanding about not only the traditions of rugby but life in general.

'I loved it. I was playing for one of the best clubs in the country and it was fantastic. We had a pretty decent team as well and we won a couple of national championships.'

It is reflective of the weakness of Scottish rugby that after only a few good games for Edinburgh, Simon was selected for Scotland. Selection for the Lions further raised his profile. He quickly became a big fish in a small pond.

'[Scottish rugby] is in as good a state as it can be. The national team has a good coaching set-up, while some big improvements are being made. It's exciting to watch, as we've had some average years, to be honest.'

Scottish rugby took time to come to grips with professionalism, Simon tells me. It is only now that the necessary building blocks have been put in place that will hopefully ensure future success.

Professional rugby has taken its toll on Simon's body. He's been out with a knee injury for the last six months. He's hoping to be back playing in the next six to eight weeks but he's cautious.

Not surprisingly, he's thinking about getting on the field, not about playing for the Lions. 'Once I start playing, I'm sure I'll be thinking about it but I would just like to get through the first few games first without mishaps.'

Simon doesn't reckon that the Lions have become over-commercialised, certainly from a player's perspective. If he was selected, he would be interested to see how the tour was going to be managed.

'It will be a tour slightly different from any tour before. You can see from a rugby point of view it's a good thing [having 44 players], as you're not struggling to get a team together. I don't think it devalues the tour at all.'

Touring New Zealand would be a fantastic experience, Simon tells me. With the number of supporters coming over, it may even double the population, he jokes.

Professional rugby as a lifestyle suits Simon. Even with an injury, he trains up to twice a day and has plenty of spare time. While he is injured, Simon tells me, the administrators know that he is a captive audience and are sending him along to everything.

The downside of professional rugby is the injuries. 'You are only a game away from having an injury. Apart from that, you can't really complain. You might do when it's the middle of November, or January and you're out there in the freezing cold, but there are plenty of people who are doing that for not as much money.'

Simon is low-key, New Zealand-like, and it's like a mask that hides his natural talent. He's also easy to talk with and relaxed. He has an ease that reminds me of former All Black Rueben Thorne and he is certainly one of the most pleasant rugby players I've met.

Simon would love to be part of a successful Edinburgh side. He'd love to see Scotland do well. He would like something to look back on and be proud of. Some would say that he's got that already.

After rugby, who knows? Rugby will open doors for him, that's for sure. I don't think he'll have a problem adapting. A law degree already earned and a balanced personality will ensure that.

After we've finished the interview, I hobble back down the large, brooding Murrayfield driveway. My foot hasn't got any better and I'm dreading the next 30 minutes as I make my way to the bus stop.

After a few hundred painful steps I look behind me and a large Land-Rover is heading in my direction. Just when I think that it's going to hit me, it stops.

It's Simon. 'Want a lift?' he asks. I'm embarrassed. I decline, as I don't want to put him to any bother. 'You can't go on like that,' Simon says of my condition. He's right, so I jump in and he takes me in to Haymarket.

When I eventually jump out, thank Simon for his trouble and go on my way, I realise that I don't care if Scotland aren't Six Nations champions. There are things more important, like human decency. I wonder whether an All Black, English international or a Wallaby would have stopped. I really don't know.

* * *

A DECADE OF REALITIES

It is unlikely that any sports team has ever endured such an extended period of poor weather as the 1977 Lions did. Regardless of whether they were in Rotorua or Masterton, it rained. New Zealand farmers used to joke that they should hire the Lions as witch doctors to bring rain during summer.

When you combine a growing desire for national independence in New Zealand with poor weather, you begin to understand that the 1977 tour was never going to be the easiest for the John Dawes-coached side.

The Lions didn't help themselves much either. Following in the grand traditions of the 1971 Lions in New Zealand and the triumphant 1974 Lions in South Africa was never going to be an easy ask of any side.

Likewise, the selection of 16 Welshmen in the initial Lions squad raised questions about potential cliques developing, especially as both Dawes and captain Bennett were from the principality.

Still, this Lions side had some terrific players: the world's best full-back in Andy Irvine, the king of centres in Mike Gibson, the flair of Phil Bennett, and up front the power and experience of Graham Price, Fran Cotton, Derek Quinnell and Gordon Brown.

THE PRINCE OF FULL-BACKS
It's early one Thursday morning in October 2004 and the streets of Edinburgh appear almost deserted. It's a beautiful morning and walking down Princes Street and watching the sun hit Edinburgh Castle confirms to me that Scotland is a land of culture and history.

I'm a little early and so I'm tempted to buy doughnuts from a chain store. I resist and instead gaze in the windows at the poor souls who are having their breakfast at a most obvious symbol of globalisation. There wouldn't have been stores like this in New Zealand in 1977.

Andy Irvine greets me at the door of his office with a big smile. He's obviously lost none of his charm nor, it must be said, his boyish good looks that helped make him the pin-up boy of the 1977 Lions.

Andy is busy. His daughter is getting married this weekend and he's got a couple of big deals to finalise at work. And there's this writer from New Zealand wanting to talk to him about a tour some 28 years ago.

Still, he is unfailingly polite and dignified and we go into a rather grand boardroom and talk. Andy says that the 1977 Lions under-performed relative to their potential.

'We had some pretty good running backs. Still, you've got to give New Zealand credit. We had a tremendous scrummage but the New Zealand back row always tended to get to the ball first. I actually think we picked a pack for power rather than pace and agility and I thought we were too slow.'

Goal kicking was also a problem. 'I remember in the third Test, for example, I missed some kicks, Phil Bennett missed some kicks. In the final Test, Dougie Morgan missed some kicks. With a slight bit of luck, we could have come out of that series 2–2, or even 3–1.'

Coach John Dawes had great faith in Andy. 'He never bothered me,' Andy tells me. 'Early on in the tour I asked him what sort of game he wanted and he told me that I was the best full-back in the world and that I should do what was right. I respected him for that, for that was passing on responsibility to the individual and he was very good in that sense.'

Andy tells me that Phil Bennett was a good captain. He wasn't a thunderous individual but he could control a game. He was the best five-eight that Andy played with and, he suggests, was better than Barry John in reading a game and bringing in his full-back.

'Phil was unfairly targeted. When you captain the Lions, particularly in New Zealand, you've got to say the right thing and so forth. Some of the discipline on tour wasn't great. The management was a little bit slack but I would always stand by Phil.

'It's funny that after the 1974 Lions tour Willie John got the plaudits for captaining the side, when in reality the whole thing [on the field] was run by Gareth Edwards and Phil Bennett.

'They didn't say too much but because he did all the team talks and media interviews, Willie John was regarded as being the driving force. But as soon as the whistle went, Gareth controlled things, while Phil decided our kicking game.'

The Lions started the tour positively with eight wins on the trot, including a victory over the All Black-laden Manawatu-Horowhenua. Surprisingly, they were upset 21–9 by New Zealand Universities in Christchurch before the first Test.

As is so often the case, the Lions selectors got the selection wrong for the first Test – Phil Orr was selected ahead of Fran Cotton, Bobby Windsor ahead of Peter Wheeler, and Trevor Evans ahead of Tony Neary. What's more, Gordon Brown was injured, meaning the only two fit locks – Allan Martin and Moss Keane – had to play.

214

The All Blacks awarded first Test caps to Andy Haden and Lawrie Knight in the first Test. The New Zealand selectors also called up debutant Auckland full-back Colin Farrell who was an attacking player but weak on defence.

Playing on a damp, cold, Wellington afternoon, the All Blacks scored three tries to beat the Lions 16–12, all the scoring being done in the first half.

The most dramatic moment came two minutes from half-time, when Grant Batty (who was playing in his last Test) intercepted a pass from Evans to run the 60 metres required to score. The sight of the diminutive winger being chased by Andy and prop Graham Price was the most lasting of the match.

'The thing that disappointed me about the first Test was the wind was so strong that it made the game a bit of a lottery,' Andy says. 'New Zealand against the wind played really well but they didn't score in the second half. The Lions actually did a lot better.

'The wind did spoil it. I can remember chasing Grant. It was frustrating, as if he hadn't scored, we would have scored at the other end. These things happen. Good on him. He was a gutsy wee player and I had a tremendous regard for him. He was fiery all right but off the field I really enjoyed his company.'

Having lost the first Test, the Lions regrouped and came back a stronger unit. Cobner took over the forwards, while Bill Beaumont, Cotton, Quinnell, Wheeler and Brown were introduced into the pack. There was now a hardness about the pack that had been missing in the first Test.

The Lions were one of the first sporting teams touring New Zealand to be hounded by the gutter press. 'Lousy Lovers,' one infamous headline screamed, commenting on the Lions' lack of prowess in certain areas of their private lives.

'For some players, it probably got to them,' Andy says of the media coverage. 'I think it probably got to Phil Bennett by the end of the tour, as he got depressed at times. It didn't bother me at all, because I tend to be strong-minded. It's up to the individual to believe what the media writes.

'I think it affected the midweek players more, the guys who weren't playing at the weekends, when the weather was pretty bad. If you're getting soaked at training and your kit is all wet, it can get you down.'

The second Test, played in Christchurch, saw the Lions at their most desperate. Before they went out onto the field, Cobner got his troops together and said that they would be listening in the valleys back in Wales. The atmosphere in that changing-shed must have been electric, with the success of the tour on the line.

Two Bennett penalties and a John Williams try gave the Lions a deserved lead, before Bryan Williams kicked a penalty. Further penalties by Bennett and Williams made the half-time score 13–6 to the visitors.

A penalty by Williams for the All Blacks was the only scoring in the second half, the Lions running out deserved 13–9 victors. It had been a tough match, with a brawl erupting after ten minutes when Bennett was late-charged.

'Ironically, we probably had more of the ball in the fourth Test, which we lost, than in the second Test, which we won,' Andy says. 'In the second Test, we took our chances. If these two Tests were adjudicated like a boxing match, we would have won both.

'In rugby, the better team only wins around four times out of five. I've seen lots of games where a team has won but it hasn't deserved to win. That's rugby, you take your chances.'

BEING PUSHED AROUND BY THE LIONS

The series was deservedly square. Much would hinge on the third Test in Dunedin. There, as in the first two Tests, diminutive Canterbury hooker Tane Norton captained the All Blacks.

I meet Tane in the heart of St Albans, Christchurch, on a late summer evening. His home is comfortable, relaxed, and after I greet his no doubt understanding wife, we go out onto the patio and talk.

Tane had been an All Black since 1971. He was captaining the national side for the first time, an honour that he took very seriously. 'It had to be the highlight, in a way,' he tells me.

'Being an All Black was unbelievable but being made captain was a responsibility. I wasn't absolutely sure that I wanted it but with people like Kirky [Ian Kirkpatrick] and Sid Going, they helped me through.

'I mean, I remember in 1971 when I was first named for the All Blacks. I'd heard it on the radio and seen it on TV but it wasn't until that last five minutes in the Carisbrook dressing-room before the first Test that I realised I was going to be an All Black.

'I remember the reserves had left and we put our arms around each other. I looked across the circle and saw Colin Meads and Bryan Williams and Ian Kirkpatrick and I couldn't believe I was in that room.'

Tane was 29 when he was first picked for the All Blacks. He'd had a life outside rugby and was undoubtedly better for the experience. By the time the 1977 Lions arrived, Tane was 35.

'After Colin Meads, Kirky had been my captain. He'd been dropped and replaced by Andy Leslie in 1974. Andy came back from South Africa in

1976 and retired. I always believed, and still believe, that the guy who should always have been captain was Ian Kirkpatrick.

'*He should have been captain against the Lions. When I was offered the job, I rang Kirky. I couldn't have had more support from anybody.*'

After the second Test, the All Blacks endured the wrath of a public that expected big things. 'When you don't perform in your own country, it's extremely tough going, and rightly so. I'm a member of the public and we expect so much from our team.

'*When they don't perform like we think they should, we get tough on them. The public was tough on us. When you walk down the street after winning a Test, it's a great feeling. But by hell, it's not so good when you've lost one.*'

The All Blacks dropped mainstay half-back Sid Going and flanker Kevin Eveleigh for the Test and introduced Lyn Davis and Graham Mourie, later to be one of the great All Black captains. The All Blacks started the third Test with a hiss and a roar when Ian Kirkpatrick scored from the first lineout after Bruce Robertson had made a strong break.

Willie Duggan scored for the Lions, before Andy Haden crossed for the All Blacks, to give the home side a 10–4 lead at half-time. Andy Irvine and new All Black full-back Bevin Wilson exchanged penalties early in the second half, before Wilson kicked another penalty and Robertson dropped a goal.

The All Blacks had earned their 19–7 victory, despite the Lions forwards winning the majority of the scrums, lineouts and rucks. The Lions had missed kicks at goal, while the introduction of fresh blood had assisted New Zealand.

THREE-MAN SCRUM

The All Blacks now had a 2–1 series lead going into the final Test in Auckland. The Lions warmed up for the match with wins against Counties–Thames Valley, North Auckland and Bay of Plenty.

The Lions' forward strength was proving too much for a nation that had prided itself on its traditional power up front. In Cotton and Price, the Lions had two props that were amongst the greatest ever, while locks Brown and Beaumont complemented each other. Wheeler was a talented hooker, while injuries forced the long overdue introduction of Tony Neary to the back row. The versatile Jeff Squire was also introduced, alongside Willie Duggan.

A capacity crowd of 58,000 watched the match at Eden Park as a determined Lions side attempted to even up the series. Wilson and Morgan exchanged penalties in the first quarter.

The Lions scored the only try of the first half when Welsh midfielder

Steve Fenwick broke through the line. When he was held up, he sent the ball wide for Morgan to collect and cross for the try. Morgan converted his own score and the Lions had a 9–3 lead at the interval.

In the second half, the All Blacks amazingly put down a three-man scrum when their prop John McEldowney had to leave the field with an injury.

'If that happened today, under the same circumstances I would do it again,' Tane says firmly.

'There was no danger, which was the first thing. In those days, you had to wait for a prop to get clearance from the doctor. John went off and we had to go into a scrum with a man down. I had to put loose forward Lawrie Knight in the front row and against Fran Cotton in a normal scrum that wouldn't have been a fair contest.

'So we put a three-man scrum [down], the Lions didn't pick it up but the point was that they couldn't push until the ball came in. We were lucky enough to win it. I wouldn't say I was proud of it but all I would say is that I would do the same thing again.'

Wilson kicked his second penalty for the home side, ensuring the last quarter was going to be a tense and tight affair. Both kickers missed penalties before the defining act of the game occurred.

With five minutes to go, Phil Bennett missed touch for the Lions. Midfielder Bill Osborne collected the ball and kicked ahead to Fenwick. The Welshman secured the ball but was shunted in a tackle by Osborne. The tackle delayed the pass to Wheeler, who was bowled over by Mourie. The ball popped into the arms of Lawrie Knight, who powered over from ten metres to win the All Blacks the match, 10–9.

The Lions had been unlucky to lose the Test and the series. They had dominated the fourth Test and had deserved better. A 2–2 series would probably have been fair and just, although the All Blacks had taken their chances.

A SUPERSTAR'S LAMENT

Andy Irvine was a superstar in New Zealand, playing in all four Tests and scoring five tries against Wanganui King Country in one of the early matches on tour. He lit up New Zealand's muddy fields with his scintillating pace and incredible anticipation.

Yet he says he played his best rugby on the hard grounds in South Africa in 1974. 'I wasn't a particularly big player and I had to beat players with pace and manoeuvrability. It's an awful lot easier to sidestep when the grounds are hard.'

Andy doesn't dwell on the series loss in New Zealand. He enjoyed the experience because he was very much involved, while by anyone's estimation he starred on the tour, having played some magnificent rugby.

Andy sighs when we discuss the changes that have taken place within the sport. I get the impression that he's no fan of professionalism. He says, for example, that he can't believe that the Lions are taking 44 players to New Zealand in 2005.

'They are only playing 11 games! It's nuts! We went to South Africa with one coach and one manager, no doctors, no physios, no dietician. I think they are going overboard and it's a huge waste of money.'

He doesn't begrudge the modern players their money and the trimmings now associated with rugby, confessing that he would enjoy them. Yet he doubts whether he would have enjoyed it as much as he did his own career.

'I don't envy the playing side of it just now. They train a lot harder, you have to have special diets, while the game is more formula-driven. Rugby in my day was more spontaneous . . . I think the game today is boring and stifles individual decision making.'

Andy says the 2005 Lions won't see New Zealand like the Lions did in 1977. 'It will be more like a business trip, rather than a rugby trip. We played around New Zealand in 1977 and we saw more of the country than most New Zealanders ever would! It was wonderful and it created memories that I will never forget.'

I want to hear from Andy what it means to be a Lion. After all, he is one of the great Lions and I'm certain he must feel amazing pride. His answer is blunt.

'Now, I suppose it doesn't mean so much, because in some ways it has been devalued. When I was first selected, it did mean a huge amount, because it was the pinnacle of anyone's rugby career and it was the very best of the four nations. When you take 44 players [on tour], that to me devalues it.'

Andy toured New Zealand again in 1981, this time as captain of the Scottish team. He retired soon after and played club rugby until he was 40. He then went into coaching for a couple of seasons, business commitments making it difficult to devote himself fully. He's also been involved in radio work.

In the last six years, Andy's been involved in coaching youngsters on both Saturdays and Sundays. He tells me he's somewhat disillusioned about the way rugby's gone and the fact that the bulk of the money in Scotland has been invested in the professional game. He also laments the overkill in international rugby.

'It [international rugby] is a bit like fillet steak. Fillet steak is lovely but if you get it every night you'll soon want to go back to beans on toast. Let's be honest, the reason why there has been overkill is that the [administrators] are trying to generate money . . . there is far too much [money] in rugby going to too few.'

Andy is not a bitter man, and in fact he's doing something about his concerns by recently being appointed president of the SRFU. He just wants to see the money that's flowing about in rugby evenly distributed.

GIVING BACK TO RUGBY

For Tane – who as a kid in 1959 used to stand outside the Lions' hotel to see Lions players – beating the Lions was a great thrill. He retired from international rugby after that series, rounding out his rugby by playing with a World XV in South Africa.

'I remember in South Africa playing on wonderful fields and on beaut days and then coming back to a training session in Christchurch with Tiny Hill. There was like four inches of mud and two inches of water on the field which ran all over my boots and I just couldn't get motivated.

'So I went up to Tiny and said, "Let the young fellow", who was John Black, "take over. I'll go and sit in the grandstand." I'd had my run. It was the right decision. I have no regrets.'

Tane was always one of the most unassuming and modest of All Blacks – one of the most unassuming and modest of men in fact. He never quite believed that he was an All Black. Still, 61 matches (27 Tests) for the All Blacks suggests a proud record.

Tane says that apart from a few freaks of nature, the majority of All Blacks in his time were good players who made their way from club rugby to provincial rugby and then were selected for the All Blacks.

Since he finished playing, Tane has raised four boys with his wife and has worked his way through the administration ranks to become president of the NZRFU. He's well qualified to comment on New Zealand rugby.

'I think what's happened with New Zealand rugby is that we have gone through this professional stage and I thought that we were handling it pretty well. But about two years ago I realised that we weren't. We were seeing young men who were getting into the game and they were looking for the money thing and that was becoming more important than the jersey.

'But I feel this last year, with the foresight of our coaches under Graham Henry, that they are bringing this team up in a way that ensures that they respect the jersey. They have a respect now and a big part of that must go to Brian Lochore and the work that he's done. He's given tremendous value to the team.'

Tane is aware that at the amateur level every rugby club in New

Zealand is struggling one way or another. Clubs are facing financial pressure and he can't understand how all the clubs are surviving, especially those outside Canterbury who don't get a handout after the Super 12 successes. Reducing the number of clubs is not the answer, he says. That would destroy the culture of New Zealand rugby.

Rugby for Tane means far more than just what occurs on the field. It always has done. He tells me definitively that he is pleased he played in his time, when rugby was a good deal more innocent.

'What rugby has given me you just couldn't buy. I wouldn't swap that for anything. I'm glad the young men are being paid today. They deserve everything they get. But I wouldn't make it in today's game and I wouldn't swap the experiences I've had for quids.'

Tane retired as president of the NZRFU in early 2005. He'd spent four years with the union and enjoyed getting around the clubs. He's seen the issues involved, met the people, embraced the spirit of the game. His love for the sport is everlasting.

'Now I've finished with New Zealand rugby, I'll come back to Canterbury rugby and when I've finished there I'll go back to my club, Linwood. Until they kick me out, I'll be there.' A true rugby stalwart.

ANSWERING IRELAND'S CALL

Before I came on this European odyssey, I knew more about Irish rugby than I did about the game in the other three home nations. I'd been living in Ireland when the national side had beaten Scotland in 2000 in Dublin. Peter Stringer, Shane Horgan, Ronan O'Gara and John Hayes had won their first caps that day. The modern Irish rugby renaissance had begun.

The Irish had a rugby tradition to begin with, something the Scots did not have. While rugby wasn't the national sport in Ireland, there was a feel for rugby in Limerick that, outside Wales, was unique to Britain and Ireland.

While I lived in Ireland, I'd seen rugby supporters in Munster do things that I'd never seen in New Zealand. Displays of passion, if you like, that were almost tribal. Rugby was life and I loved it.

Irish rugby was a success story. Centralising the top players has been a master stroke, contracting the players to the union sound

221

thinking. Irish rugby was benefiting from quality, strategic planning, regular European competition and having the good fortune to have two players of world-class standing.

THE NATURAL

Wednesday, 13 October 2004

Ireland has always produced talented individuals: Mike Gibson, arguably in the top half-dozen players ever to lace a boot; Fergus Slattery, one of the best flankers ever; Jack Kyle, magnificent; Willie John McBride, robust and a born leader; Ray McLoughlin, Tony O'Reilly, Ollie Campbell; the list is endless.

I've already prepared for and conducted about ten interviews in Europe by the time I rock up to the Riverview Fitness Club in south Dublin. Yet I'm as nervous as hell, to be honest. The taxi driver doesn't help by ripping me off and as I make my way through Dublin's social climbers, I can't help but wonder whether Brian O'Driscoll is the best rugby player in the world. He's certainly one of the finest Ireland has ever produced.

I'd been living in Ireland when he scored three tries against the French in Paris. I'd been at a breakfast at a rugby club in Northern Ireland when he cut the Wallaby defence to shreds for the Lions in Brisbane in 2001. He was as symbolic of my Ireland experience as Seamus Heaney, Roddy Doyle, the Corrs and U2.

Brian is without question Ireland's rugby superstar. His profile is significant in a culture that likes to bring its heroes down to size. Whether it is his dyed hair, the girl that he is seeing, or whether he is spotted on a night out on the town, Brian is news.

I accept the importance of Brian being a role model but I can't get my head around all the periphery. Somewhere amongst it all, the man's genius appears to be regularly overlooked. It frustrates me and is perhaps a sad reflection of what makes news.

As captain of Ireland, Brian has already been suggested as a possible captain of the Lions in New Zealand. He was a certainty for the Test squad, while being Irish would certainly be an advantage in the public relations stakes. He also seems to be handling the Irish captaincy extraordinarily well. Tana Umaga had proved that a midfield back could successfully captain an international side.

I walk quietly into the members' lounge. Brian is sitting at the far end waiting for me. It feels like an audience with the Pope, which I guess, being in Ireland, is an appropriate analogy.

Brian immediately reminds me of Andrew Mehrtens. Both have a playful cheekiness that is boyish and quirky. They're both individualistic but individuals within the collective fold. They add flair to the game that is almost French-like. It's not surprising that they get on well off the field.

Like a lot of modern players, Brian started to fully understand what the Lions were about in 1997, when they toured South Africa.

'It was enormous,' Brian recalls. 'I was doing my final exams and any distraction away from that to watch games was certainly welcome. Since then, I've looked back and I now know a lot more about the great teams: the 1971 side [in New Zealand], the 1974 team [in South Africa]. Particularly about great Irish Lions like Fergus Slattery but I couldn't teach a class about it.'

Becoming a Lion was never a goal for Brian as a kid. Rugby was fun, not an all-encompassing burning passion. His rugby career happened so quickly that his goals were only formulated once he became an international.

'I've never been one to sit down and really think about what I really want to achieve. I don't put myself under that sort of pressure. I just try and let it happen and if it happens, it happens.'

In saying that, making the Lions had become a goal the year of the 2001 tour. Brian by that stage had played international rugby for a year and a half and felt he was playing well. The Lions seemed a natural progression.

It was a nervous time. Some of Brian's pals were also in the running for the squad. Some made it, others didn't. As a result, when the squad was selected it was a mixture of elation and disappointment. Then there was that awful period between being selected and going on tour, hoping you wouldn't pick up an injury.

Being selected for the Lions meant a lot. Yet, Brian tells me, it would have meant a good deal more had the Lions won the second and third Tests. 'As much as the series was remembered for the first Test, when the Lions took Australia apart, we didn't win the series. No one remembers teams that don't win the series.'

Being selected for the tour of New Zealand later in the season will be a different experience, I suggest, than 2001. Brian's a certainty and it would be a huge surprise if he wasn't in Clive's squad.

Brian doesn't agree. There is no such thing as a certainty, he says, regardless of who you are. A poor Six Nations and an individual will give Clive Woodward a sound reason not to select him. The pressure remains.

Just like he's always done, Brian's not putting any pressure on himself. If he can continue to do the basics right, to play well and make few mistakes, then he'll maximise his chances of making the tour. Still, I couldn't imagine a Lions squad without Brian in it and I guess, if he was honest with me, neither could he.

A great thing about modern Lions tours is the support touring sides get, both in the host country and back home. I wondered whether the players were aware of it in the heat of the battle.

'You are but you're still cocooned out there from what's going on. There was tremendous support in Australia but we didn't really appreciate how big it got back home. You're just getting on with the job.

'In saying that, they love sporting success in Ireland. Recently with the Olympics, everyone in Ireland was glued to the telly watching Cian O'Connor win gold. I've never got so excited about equestrianism in all my life, I was shouting at the telly.'

Brian is a better player now than he was in Australia in 2001. Aspects of his game have significantly improved. He's a more rounded player. He does more of the grunt work, hits more rucks. He's defensively more solid. Still, age has probably ensured that he's lost some of that reckless free spirit that made him difficult to defend against.

'You play with a free spirit when you're young because you know no different,' Brian says thoughtfully. 'You don't know about the hard parts of the game, you just go out and play. That was pretty much what I was about then.

'I think there's an element of ignorance to youth but it's a breath of fresh air, too, because, no matter who you are, the older you get the more you're going to lose that. That won't continue for ever.'

I get the impression that while Brian has matured as a player, he's also matured as a man. Captaincy would have helped that process, as would being his country's finest rugby talent. He's put the disappointment of the 2001 Lions tour to bed but it's undoubtedly back there somewhere providing motivation for 2005.

'I would gladly give up personal adulation if I were to be part of a Lions side that won the series. That's what it's all about. People judge you on your success. I really don't like talking about it because I'm not selected for the Lions yet.

'Still, New Zealand is probably the toughest place to tour because of their tradition. Not a lot of sides win down in New Zealand. It's a very special place and if you won a series there you'd be in a unique enough club as there aren't too many people who can say they've won a series in New Zealand.'

Brian's goals aren't to play 199 Tests for Ireland and the Lions or to score more tries than anyone else in world rugby. Brian wants silverware. He wants to remember the sweet feeling of winning matches and titles.

As we are talking, I can see people glance across at Brian. People at this fitness health club have too much money to stare openly. Brian appears oblivious to it. He's probably used to it.

It would be easier being an All Black, I think. There is a bigger pool of world-class players. Brian, alongside Paul O'Connell perhaps, is it in Ireland. It must be difficult for him trying to lead a healthy, balanced lifestyle.

'Of course there are fantastic things that people have to say to you and there's not so nice things. There's always going to be a few who will cut you down, whether they are a little bit jealous of your success or whether they are envious of what you have.

'I've probably become a little more hard-necked, to be honest with you. I don't take everything I hear to heart any more . . . otherwise it would start playing with your mind.'

The public attention has been made worse by the fact that this Ireland side has been successful, that Brian's now captain, and that he's the David Beckham of Irish rugby.

'Being captain is more a title than a job. People make more of the role of the captain than I think there needs to be made of it. These days, a captain makes the toss and has a few words of encouragement. It's not as though you do anything hugely different. You look to the experienced players to captain along with you.'

Brian is right. These days leadership is shared, with pivotal playmakers like the half-back and the first five-eight often having more say than the captain. However, from what Andy Irvine told me last week, that was also the case on the Lions' 1974 tour of South Africa.

Brian has enormous respect for Martin Johnson as a captain and as a player. Johnson spoke when he had to, not for the sake of it. Captains can encourage either with a few quiet words or through their actions. Verbosity never equated with real leadership.

I've got to ask Brian whether he would accept the captaincy of the Lions to New Zealand if he was offered it. It's a difficult question to ask: the Six Nations are still to come, while a sizeable proportion of Leinster's season remains. I can't blame him if his mind is elsewhere.

'I would have to think about it,' he says honestly. 'It's hard for me to say that I am a contender but because I'm captain of my country it puts me in the picture, I guess,' he says modestly.

I surmise out loud that he would be a good choice and that the New Zealand public would love him, much the same way they have some other Irish captains of the Lions. He would also be a nice contrast to Clive Woodward's more upright approach.

Brian looks at me and then smiles gently, like he must have done as a kid when he didn't tell his mother the whole truth. It's partly because I've answered my own question and partly because, I think, his ambitions are understated but obvious.

THE GRASS ROOTS OF IRISH RUGBY

Thursday, 14 October 2004

As in Scotland, Irish rugby has a tiered system: clubs (either amateur or semi-professional), provinces (in Scotland they are districts) and national sides. I'd enjoyed hearing from Brian about what life was like at the professional end of the game but to get a fuller picture of Irish rugby, I needed to look at the club and provincial game in Ireland.

So I'm going back to my old hunting grounds. I'd spent one and a half years in Dublin and two years in Belfast. In Dublin, I'd ended up living in Monkstown, on Dublin's south side. They'd had their own club but I'd tentatively supported Blackrock, just down the road.

Rock (as it was commonly known) was also Brian's club and had produced a host of other Lions, including Ray McLoughlin, Willie Duggan and Fergus Slattery.

In Belfast, I'd lived on the Ravenhill Road, about three-quarters of a mile from Ravenhill, the home of Ulster Rugby. On Friday nights in winter, my flatmate, his son and I would often go to European Cup matches at the ground. We'd watch Ulster play, enjoy the intimacy of the ground and the sense of collective spirit of the Ulstermen. Those were enjoyable times.

Back in Ireland some two and a half years after I was last here, my first stop is Ravenhill. The first thing that I'd always noticed on arriving at Ravenhill was the Union Jack swinging proudly at the front gates. It emphasised that Ulster rugby is a Protestant sport and traditionally strongest in the Protestant schools. Yet it was not flying today.

Still, despite regular informal accusations of bias, Ulster had a positive working relationship with the other three provinces in Ireland. Of course, technically three of Ulster's counties were in the Republic anyway, although the heart of Ulster rugby was certainly in Belfast.

Ulster had produced numerous champion teams, and, in the likes of Gibson, McBride, Kyle and Dave Hewett, individuals of world-class ability. In 1999, they'd won the European Cup and Dublin had been a sea of red and white banners and streamers on the afternoon of the final.

Michael Reid, chief executive of Ulster Rugby, greets me with a hearty handshake. He'd been initially reluctant to see me. The reason was that a host of school kids had been using Ulster Rugby as a case study. They'd all wanted interviews too. It had been easier to give a blanket no.

Michael tells me that winning the European Cup was the best and worst thing that happened to Ulster. On the positive side, it was fantastic for marketing and recruitment. The game is now played in 200 schools throughout Ulster, including a number of Catholic schools that previously had not been involved with the sport.

'As an example, the Ulster Under-18 side now has boys from all nine counties in Ulster, which is a big, big step forward from where we were,' Michael says. 'So development-wise it was a massive boost.'

Rugby-wise, the European Cup victory might have put Ulster on a pedestal before it was ready, Michael tells me. The result was that a couple of lean years followed. In that sense, the European Cup did nothing for Ulster.

The cultural diversity in Ulster rugby interests me. It is telling that there are three players in the current senior Ulster squad who have gone through the Catholic education system. There could be other Catholics in the squad, although the three are enough confirmation that rugby in Ulster may be changing.

Ulster Rugby has purposely not made a big song and dance about their push into Catholic schools. The aim is to change the base, without drawing public attention.

This is sound thinking and will not offend, in the short term at least, the Protestant majority that forms the foundation of Ulster Rugby. Yet the symbolism is still British and my mind goes back to the Union Jack that used to fly outside Ravenhill so proudly.

Michael says the four provinces' flag is now flown outside the ground. Inside the ground, the flag sold is the Ulster Rugby emblem which is two rugby balls within the Red Hand, which is a Gaelic symbol also used by the Tyrone Gaelic Athletic Association.

'Flags and emblems will always cause a problem in Northern Ireland,' Michael admits, 'but we are lucky that it is more of a talking point than an issue here.'

That aside, the spirit in Ulster Rugby has always been strong. You could suggest that it was a sport played by the Protestant majority but you couldn't deny that a packed Ravenhill was quite a sight. I wondered why this was the case.

'I think because there wasn't anything else to do here, to be honest,' Michael says with a laugh.

'Due to the history of the Troubles, there hasn't been a lot of sport of any sort [played here]. We were the best supported team in the Celtic League last year. This season, despite some bad results, we are the second-best supported team.

'There is nothing else like it,' Michael says of the Ravenhill experience. 'Standing on an open terrace when it's freezing cold and there is snow and ice and you have to queue for an hour and a half for a burger and a pint, but people still do it. Although the ground is old, on a Friday night it lends itself to an atmosphere because it's close to the pitch.'

Being originally a Protestant grammar school sport, it was natural that rugby would appeal to local businessmen. This connection grew when rugby went professional. As a result, 650 people would pack into two large marquees, paying £130 a head, when Ulster played Cardiff at the weekend.

As in the rest of Irish rugby, Ulster knows that it cannot offer the big money of the French and English clubs. The secret to competing with these clubs on the field is creating efficient player development methods.

'We're probably about a year to 18 months away from having a successful season,' Michael tells me, 'but we have a number of talented young players who will one day be Irish internationals.'

As part of their development, Ulster has to have a reasonable number of competitive games. In that sense, the Celtic League is working. 'We need a 30-game season for our team and thankfully that's what we have at the moment,' Michael says.

If Ulster is going to be successful at a professional level, it is essential that the local clubs are involved. As in Scotland, there has been an 'us' and 'them' mentality between the professional and amateur game.

Michael admits that Ulster Rugby hasn't fully sorted this out yet. For example, Ulster Rugby pays the players and as a result the clubs feel like they are missing out.

While Ulster was taking players from their clubs, the IRFU was taking players out of the provincial environment. This season, the IRFU had taken the elite players out of the Ulster set-up for ten weeks for conditioning and pre-season work. The parties all understood each other thanks to greater levels of communication. Michael tells me that this is what needs to happen between Ulster Rugby and the clubs.

The issues faced in club rugby in Ulster Rugby appear similar to those in other places: that is the club fraternity understanding that the game should not be professional at every level.

'A lot of the clubs have realised that, yes, the game is professional and you can't stop money being paid but realistically it isn't a professional sport at club level.'

Ulster Rugby has enforced this by placing a maximum earning level of £3,000 outside the one professional player that the club is allowed. The system promotes equality and reduces the chances of victories being purchased.

It is reassuring to see Ulster Rugby give the club game the emphasis that it deserves. As elsewhere in the world of rugby, it's essential that the club game prospers. If it doesn't, then the professional game will have no future and certainly no heart or soul.

They know that in Dublin, for sure. I'm standing in the autumn rain at the Blackrock club three days after talking with Michael Reid. The club chairman, Ken MacDonald, is running slightly late so I go inside and make myself acquainted with the surroundings.

The club is a treasure trove of Irish rugby history. Photos of ex-internationals line the walls like relics of the past. Club plaques from around the world signify the club's outreach. A large framed drawing celebrates the club's contributions to Lions teams down the years.

When Ken arrives, he tells me that the club hosted a dinner to mark Blackrock's contributions to Lions teams a couple of years ago. The dinner, which had Jack Kyle as its special guest, saw all Blackrock's living Lions attend. It was some night, Ken tells me, and I don't doubt him.

I want to know about the Blackrock ethos. I can sense it in the clubrooms but I wonder whether it can be put into words. Ken tells me that it involves an emphasis on sportsmanship and quality running back-play. This is reflected in two of their most recent Lions – Brendon Mullen and Brian O'Driscoll.

Having a feeder school in Blackrock College has been of huge benefit to the club. The school was set up by a French priest in the nineteenth century and rugby was one of the first sports introduced. The school has been the most successful in Leinster, a virtual production line of future Leinster and Ireland representatives.

As a result, the club has a successful Under-20 side and boasts a competitive senior squad that competes in the All Ireland League. Two Blackrock players were in the Ireland Under-21 side that made the final of the world tournament this year.

As a club league, I wonder whether the All Ireland had been a success. On the face of it, it should have been. The distances clubs have to travel aren't huge, the standard seems reasonable and there is a healthy rivalry between club sides within the different provinces.

'Blackrock has just had its best season in the All Ireland and narrowly missed a top four place,' Ken says. 'Last year we finished as the best team in Leinster. It has been good for creating a competitive atmosphere and allowing Blackrock to compete against the best teams in the country.

'Still, there are a number of reservations that Blackrock, like all other clubs, have about the funding of the league and the funding of clubs generally. It's becoming harder and harder to make ends meet and there is a lot of debate going on about that.'

Ken tells me that on the whole clubs in Ireland are struggling to keep going. Blackrock, for example, has had to make huge efforts in the last 12 months, just to keep things on an even keel. A couple of years ago they were €100,000 in debt. They got out of it by organising a number of functions. Still, the club only has six senior sides this season.

Professionalism has had an impact on Blackrock. Their best players have been snapped up by Leinster or the other provinces. Without their best players, the club struggles to get the crowds to attend. The result is, of course, that it is harder to fill the bar.

The club's financial allocation from the IRFU has been decreasing all the time, making running a club more difficult each year. 'I think the IRFU has to appreciate that if they don't support the clubs financially a number of the clubs will disappear and that will affect the flow of players onto the Irish team. Funding remains the most crucial issue. It's a constant chore for clubs.'

Ken says that it's become a critical 'us and them' situation. Many clubs are running up big debts and the end may be in sight for some unless outside help is forthcoming.

Amalgamation remains a possibility in the years ahead, although Blackrock itself is being proactive in other areas, such as appealing to other schools beyond Blackrock.

Ken sees amalgamation as an inevitable consequence for many other clubs. Some of these clubs have produced Irish internationals and been part of the folklore of Irish rugby. Still, there are economic realities that need to be adhered to.

Clubs in Ireland have generally pulled back from paying players, as they can no longer afford the salaries. As a result, club rugby has returned to being an amateur sport and the gap between professional and amateur rugby is consequently growing.

Especially when the top players are seldom seen in club colours. There is no denying that when an international is playing in club rugby in Ireland, the crowd attendance rises significantly.

'When some of the Six Nations matches were called off a few years ago [due to an outbreak of foot and mouth disease] Brian [O'Driscoll] immediately made himself available for the club and it certainly boosted the crowds. He's hugely popular.'

Ken says the club would naturally love to see Brian as captain of the Lions in New Zealand and Shane Byrne as one of the hookers.

Yet I wonder in the future, with international players playing less and less for their clubs, whether the clubs themselves will feel the same affinity with any internationals that they are lucky enough to have.

My point here is that the next generation of stars is likely to be produced by academies and not clubs. Who will the upcoming players at Blackrock aspire to be like if the internationals have never played for club teams?

Financial problems aside, Ken is adamant that the spirit of rugby is still alive and well at Blackrock. When the Lions tour New Zealand, there will be breakfasts held at the club for each of the Test matches. The club faithful will come along and cheer on one or two of their finest. Those players on tour will have taken a little bit of Blackrock with them. The heart and soul of amateur rugby in Ireland. Priceless.

THE SOUL OF IRISH RUGBY

Saturday, 16 October 2004

It amazes me that in the time I lived in Ireland I never visited Limerick. I'd seen Limerick club sides in action in Dublin but I'd never travelled across to visit the spiritual home of rugby in Ireland. So here I am, one Saturday morning, on a rickety old train and wondering what I'll find at the end of the line.

As we cruise across the Irish countryside and I scan the weekend newspaper, I think about that morning in 1978 when I mistakenly heard that the All Blacks had beaten Munster 12–0. It seems such a long time ago. I wonder whether I'm the person I thought I would turn out to be. Still, rugby remains at the centre of my life.

As a result of my expectations, Limerick is initially a disappointment: it is grey and there are no faces of joyful optimism. Just a main street with terraced housing and little sign of life. I recall that this was once a garrison town. It appears decidedly working class.

I struggle to find somewhere to stay. When I go into the first bed and breakfast, I'm told the proprietor is away and won't be back for another 25 minutes. A few minutes later, that changes to one hour and 25 minutes. I've learnt, however, not to get frustrated by such indecision but to accept it as part of Ireland's charm.

After finding the most expensive bed in town, I make my way to Thomond Park. I'm truly excited to be visiting the ground. It may not be one of the biggest rugby grounds in the world but it is one of the most symbolic with regards to reflecting the spirit of rugby.

As I make my way through the streets of Limerick, all the signs are there that this is a rugby town: the specials at the pubs, the red balloons that hang in some shop windows, the look of expectation on the faces of the locals.

This is not a beautiful city but there is a working-class roughness that I like. It feels a lot like west Belfast. I pass a small church where a wedding is taking place. The bride is a picture of loveliness and proof that not everyone in Limerick is going to the rugby tonight.

Thomond Park isn't Twickenham or the Stade de France. Yet with the sun setting it reminds me of Carisbrook in New Zealand – purpose built, not flashy but immensely practical. Reflective perhaps of the fundamentals that make rugby great.

When I buy my programme, I notice that a plaque has been erected above the booth and dedicated to the Munster team that beat the All Blacks in '78. The plaque contains the names of the players and the score. I smile to myself and realise that that game will never be forgotten in these parts.

Tonight, Munster are playing Cardiff. It's bitterly cold and it looks like it's going to rain. So I go up into the stand and do what I can to stay warm. Nobody else seems to have that problem – they are either well rugged up or right into the atmosphere.

As the lights take over, the conversation amongst the crowd is earthy: everyone seems to know everyone here. It's also clear that these Munster players are gods in the eyes of their public and that regardless of what they do on the rugby field, they can't do any wrong.

Apart from two hearty souls shouting for their 'Cardiff boys', the support is entirely for the home side. As a result, it feels a lot like Lancaster Park in Christchurch used to feel like – parochial, collective and, almost, primitive.

Christian Cullen is playing at full-back for Munster tonight. He's one of the great All Black talents of my generation but they tell me he struggled with injury in his first season with Munster last year.

Tonight though, it's his night as he scores two tries and drops a goal to lead Munster to victory. Through the cold and the rain I'm beaming with pride at his performance. He's earned his pay cheque this evening and nobody could be happier than this Kiwi far from home.

Even though the night is miserably cold and wet and I've sat by myself in relative silence, it's been memorable. Watching Munster win and Cullen play superbly is a joy. Getting a feeling for rugby in Munster is unforgettable.

Still, tonight for me is about much more. Somewhere amongst the occasion of a European Cup rugby match I feel I have discovered what I set out to find when I started this book. I'm not exactly sure how to describe it – perhaps it is that old chestnut of professionalism combined with amateur values that I keep harking on about.

When I look at the faces of the kids supporting Munster, I see fellowship with the players. When I hear the yells of support throughout the game, I feel identity. The connection between the players and their fans is strong and intimate. Ronan O'Gara, Pete Stringer and John Hayes aren't entertainers tonight; they are rugby players representing their province with pride.

I leave Thomond Park shaking – and I don't think it is because of the cold. Rugby and identity is the thing tonight. There are no corporate tents. No cheerleaders or expensive wine being sold. No one seemed to mind.

Yet what there is in bucketloads is honesty. Yes, honesty from the players and from their supporters; honesty in the traditions and in what the people talk about. Rugby is about the people tonight and I for one cannot get enough of it.

* * *

Despite the expensive hotel bed, I don't sleep well. I'm feeling a bit lonely and now missing loved ones back home. Limerick's greyness is affecting me.

Still, there is more rugby to look forward to. After packing up and having brunch at a friendly café in the city centre, I head back to Thomond Park.

Today, the home club, Shannon, are taking on Blackrock in the first round of the All Ireland League. In broad daylight, there is not the same atmosphere as last night but there are still plenty of spectators and more than you would get to a club game in New Zealand.

As the weather has cleared, sitting in the stands this afternoon is more pleasurable. As this is the first round and club rugby, the standard of play reaches no great heights but is entertaining nonetheless.

Sadly, Blackrock go down, although they compete well and with an ounce of luck could have won. As I sit in the stand and watch, I enjoy the festivity of the occasion. Shannon is obviously a family-orientated club. Today, it seems not just about the rugby but about the community. I like that.

As I watch, I notice that Munster and Ireland half-back Pete Stringer is sitting behind me. Having played last night, he's not playing today but is helping with the coaching of his club. I like the fact that he's come along to support.

I'm disappointed that Blackrock have lost but I'm pleased I've come along. It's clear that in Limerick at least, the club game is strong and in good heart.

Shannon is this season being coached by former Irish international Mick Galway. He has recently hung up his boots for the last time (perhaps) and has now set out on a coaching career. It appears only a matter of time before he's at the helm of Munster.

My lasting memory of Mick is during the national anthems before Ireland's international against Scotland in 2000. Here was this grizzled veteran standing between two of his Munster charges – Ronan O'Gara and Pete Stringer – playing in their first Test. He was like an unofficial chaperone. A man of character and, as they might say in New Zealand, salt of the earth.

When I find Mick, journalists, club officials and adoring school children have besieged him. He reminds me of former All Black Todd Blackadder in that he is amazingly charismatic. It's great to see but annoying as I want a word and I don't have long before I've got to catch the train back to Dublin.

Along with being an Irish international, Mick was a member of the 1993 Lions squad in New Zealand. He didn't make the Test team, yet has some interesting insights into how the game has changed in Ireland.

'It's a good win for us,' Mick tells me in his BMW later on, 'even though we didn't seal it until the last five minutes. When you're defending champions, everyone wants to beat you, and I'm sure it's the same in New Zealand rugby.'

Shannon have no senior locks and instead played five back-rowers today. I tentatively ask whether Mick may make a comeback at some stage in the season.

'God no,' Mick laughs, 'rugby's a young man's game. I'm 38 now and so I'm not going to be turning the clock back. I'll leave it to the young lads.'

Still, I could imagine Mick lacing up his boots again, even at 38. Rugby has been his life since he was 17. It had given him confidence as a person and allowed him to mix with all sorts of different people.

As a player, Mick was a no-nonsense sort of a forward. He played most of his rugby as a lock but was selected for the Lions in 1993 as a flanker. He also toured New Zealand with the Irish national squad in 1992 and has a high regard for the rugby there.

'The thing I liked about New Zealand rugby was its competitiveness,' he tells me. 'Whether you played Auckland, or Hawke's Bay, the commitment was always there. There are no soft games. They're a proud race and as New Zealand is so isolated, when teams visit they want to put on a good show.'

Mick speaks with great fondness about touring New Zealand in 1993. His memories are romantic reflections of a time when things seemed much simpler. He says it was a trip of a lifetime. He made friends for life, saw the country from north to south and enjoyed himself immensely. It's a long way from professional rugby these days.

'From a personal point of view, I got six or seven years out of professional rugby and I really enjoyed it. The Irish set-up is going well. The provinces are the way to go [in Ireland]. We have close on 30 contracted players to each province, so in total we've got about 100 professional rugby players in Ireland and the rest are clubs players, like you saw today.'

Mick believes club rugby is a great stepping stone for players who have ambitions of a professional career. Playing with Shannon is a perfect shop window for the ambitious in Munster. In that sense, the link between the professional and amateur game appears to be beneficial to both parties.

Mick is aware of the issues facing club rugby in Ireland, issues primarily to do with funding. Yet Shannon, with its proud heritage and huge support, is keeping its head well above water. As the All Ireland club play-through champions, it's clear they are doing things right on the field as well.

I ask Mick about whether in future professional rugby will produce charismatic individuals like him, players who could inspire their community with not only their playing ability but also their strength of character. Mick laughs at my question.

'I've been around and been involved with this club for 20 years. It [respect] is something that you get along the way. My philosophy is that it costs nothing to be nice and I would like to think that I don't have too many enemies out there. When you play, you put in an honest performance and people respect that.'

Having played both the amateur and professional game, I wonder which Mick has enjoyed the most.

'Looking back on it, for fun the amateur game was better,' he says. 'At the same time it was great to play professional rugby and have the opportunity to train and be a professional sportsperson and do something you enjoyed doing. I mean, as a job it doesn't get much better than playing rugby does it?

'I enjoyed the professional game because you took more out of it in the sense that you had to put in more of an effort. I enjoyed both but from a rugby point of view the professional game was better.'

I'm pleased that my last interview in Ireland was with Mick. He's larger than life and has a word for everybody. Sometimes rugby turns up men like Mick, men who can reflect the human condition by their charisma and sense of belonging.

* * *

OLLIE IN WONDERLAND

Although the New Zealand that the Lions found in 1983 was a country on the brink of puberty, it was still a giant in rugby. The All Blacks had destroyed Wales in 1980, beaten the Springboks in '81 and Australia in '82. They were the world's best.

This was partly because of the side's stability. Captained by Andy Dalton, the vast majority of the pack had been around for a number of seasons. The back line was perhaps less experienced but in Stu Wilson, Bernie Fraser, Allan Hewson and Dave Loveridge there was plenty of experience.

British and Irish rugby, on the other hand, was going through troubled times. Gone were the glory days of the 1970s when the isles produced some of the greatest players ever. British rugby in the 1980s reflected the political climate of Thatcherism: solid and reliable, yet with no flair.

Having won the Triple Crown in 1982 and the Championship in 1983, Ireland were odds-on to provide the captain and that they did in army officer Ciaran Fitzgerald. Whether Fitzgerald was the best hooker in Britain and Ireland is a moot point but nobody could question his captaincy credentials.

Likewise, nobody could question the lack of depth in the Lions squad. Quite simply it was a team marked by its mediocrity. History has confirmed this in the backs especially, with only Ollie Campbell, Terry Holmes and John Rutherford of any real quality.

As I mentioned earlier, I'd idolised Ollie Campbell as a kid and had had the privilege of meeting him when I lived in Ireland. Consequently, when we arranged to meet in Dublin late in 2004, I was expecting to see an old friend, not a rugby hero.

We meet at his office in downtown Dublin. It's appropriate that one of the most stylish rugby players is now involved in the fashion business. Ollie Campbell Limited markets and distributes, amongst other things, Pierre Cardin shirts and ties.

'When we last met up did I give you a Six Nations tie?' Ollie asks at one stage during our interview.

'You did but I think it was the Five Nations back then,' I smile.

So Ollie gives me a Six Nations tie and I am as proud to accept it from my hero as I had been back in 1999.

In 1983, Ollie was at the peak of his powers. He'd toured South Africa with the Lions in 1980 and like almost half the squad, had been injured. After shrugging off the challenge from Tony Ward, he'd established himself as the best number 10 in Europe and had been a pivotal cog in Ireland's success in 1982 and 1983.

'There is just some unique aura, some inexplicable X-factor about the prestige and the whole concept of the Lions,' Ollie says. 'As a kid in every playing nation in the world, you really do dream about playing for your country, and that's no different in Ireland. Yet there is something remarkable about the Lions. It's the ultimate experience for someone from this part of the world.'

Ollie grew up with romantic tales of the '71 and '74 Lions, the great players and the stories. As he tells me this, he's clearly emotional, as if we are going back to a more innocent age.

'The 1971 Lions especially were one of the major influences in my whole rugby career. Just the personalities involved in that tour, the fact that it was the first successful Lions tour to New Zealand. For me, what added a whole new dimension to it was the Carwyn James mystique as well and the way the side played. It wasn't just because they won.'

During the 1974 tour, Ollie would do his best to tune in to the radio commentaries from South Africa. The BBC from England was difficult to get, the rugby from South Africa that much harder, but listen he did and that tour again caught his imagination.

For Ollie, being chosen for the 1983 tour was not the surprise that being chosen in 1980 had been. By 1983 he was reasonably well established, the Irish had won a Triple Crown, he was playing well and he knew he was in with a good chance of making the trip.

New Zealand was Mecca for Ollie. 'Again, I don't have the words,' he tells me when I ask him whether he was looking forward to touring New Zealand.

'The first international that I was brought to by my dad was Ireland versus the All Blacks, 1963, Lansdowne Road, 6–5 . . . even thinking about it now, it was like it only happened last week.

'I was hooked by the All Blacks, by the silver fern, just by the whole aura of the All Blacks and it is with me to this day. In my final year of school, we watched the highlights of the 1967 All Black tour to this part of the world time and time again. Not on a video but with a white sheet and an old black and white thing that shook.

'I would have about 200 rugby books at home and about 90 per cent would be about New Zealand rugby, T.P. McLeans, and the old tours. New Zealand has had a massive impact on me.'

The Lions narrowly lost to Auckland in the second match of the tour before four wins prior to the first Test in Christchurch. As it turned out, it would be the Lions' best chance of success in the series.

Crucial players Terry Holmes, Ian Stephens and Jeff Squire remained fit, while the All Blacks hadn't had any warm-up matches. Playing in fine conditions, the Lions threw everything they could at the All Blacks.

After leading 9–6 at half-time, the Lions looked on course for victory. Yet in the second half Allan Hewson kicked a penalty and dropped a goal, while Mark Shaw scored a try for the All Blacks. Ollie kicked a penalty but when the final whistle sounded the home side had won 16–12.

'The biggest single disappointment of the tour was probably to have lost the first Test,' Ollie tells me. 'It's a match we probably should have won. You know that if you win the first Test the series is open to the last Test. You lose the first one, especially in New Zealand, and you know that you have lost your best chance. If we had won that Test, the series would have taken a whole different complexion.'

Ollie recalls thinking the day after the first Test that the whole tour was now going to be an uphill challenge. Had the Lions won the first Test it would have created strong interest in New Zealand and would have made for an outstanding series.

After losing in Christchurch, the Lions had three comfortable wins before building for the second Test in Wellington. The Test, played in a howling southerly, was as a result a game of two halves. Winning the toss, All Black captain Andy Dalton chose to play with the wind in the first 40 minutes. Thanks to a Dave Loveridge try, a Hewson conversion and penalty the home side led 9–0 at the break.

'We were only losing 3–0 going into injury time in the half,' Ollie recalls. 'Dave Loveridge then slipped down the blind side to score and with the conversion we were 9–0 down. We were certainly in the match but as it turned out I literally did not see the ball in the second 40 minutes. Again, it was Loveridge running down the blind side, feeding back inside and it was ruck to ruck. It finished 9–0.'

The All Blacks had been clinical in the second half. With Wellingtonians Murray Mexted, Stu Wilson and Bernie Fraser in the starting line-up, the home side knew how to play into the wind and had in the end deserved their victory and 2–0 series lead.

A LEADER WITH CHARACTER

When I was growing up, there were three outstanding All Black captains at different stages. Graham Mourie is, along with Wilson Whinerary, rightly regarded as being the best of the best. Analytical, removed and a born leader, Mourie was special. Wayne 'Buck' Shelford was more from the 'lead from the front' mould but no less effective. He was also inspirational.

Then there was Andy Dalton. The Counties hooker was a player's sort of leader. Widely respected by his troops, he led the All Blacks against the Springboks in 1981 when Mourie made himself unavailable. He'd taken over the reins full time when Mourie retired in 1982. When Dalton spoke, people listened. He had a calm, reasoned approach to rugby and life, and was another one of rugby's outstanding individuals.

I meet him in Auckland one Friday morning in April 2004. He is not a big man and I wonder how he would have got on in the heat of the front row. Still, he obviously managed. He is unfailingly polite and generous with his time and comments. The word 'great' is overused. Yet Andy, like Ollie, is a great man.

Andy was captain of the All Blacks in the 1983 home series against the Lions. He'd played for Counties against the 1977 Lions and credits his performance against the Pontypool front row as thrusting him into All Blacks contention.

'We were blessed with a lot of experienced players in 1983,' Andy tells me. 'It made my job a lot easier because of that. We'd copped criticism that *we were actually too old and that the front row especially was past its best. Yet those guys were playing at the top of their abilities. We were never overconfident going into those games but we thought we could match them in the forwards.'*

Dunedin, in the south of New Zealand, is not the type of place that you want to play rugby when it rains. Especially when it's so cold that hypothermia is a distinct possibility. With the Lions needing to win to have any chance of squaring the series, the last thing they needed was atrocious weather.

The Lions lost the third Test 15–8, despite tries by Roger Baird and John Rutherford. The All Black pack was again outstanding and in such conditions was always going to dominate. The Lions had led until halfway through the second half but a Stu Wilson try had turned the tide and yet again the Lions had blown it.

'It was so cold,' Andy recalls. 'When we got onto the pitch a huge hailstorm hit us and we were freezing cold even before we kicked off. It must have been terrible for the backs, because there was no way that we were letting the ball out there! Most of the backs were wearing these [new] vests, which we thought made them pussycats, but two minutes into that game we were all looking for one to wear!'

FAIR-WEATHER LIONS

As it had rained the whole week, the Lions were offered similar wet weather gear. 'I will never forget as long as I live, running out onto this red carpet and as soon as my foot came up to the grass, over the boot came this absolutely freezing water,' recalls Ollie. 'Then the other foot went in and before the match the feet were frozen. How are you supposed to catch a ball and make tactical decisions in those conditions?'

The Lions had lost the series and with a rising injury toll, had only a dry ground in Auckland to look forward to. While the 1959 Lions had come back to win the fourth Test in Auckland, there would be no such fairy tale for the 1983 Lions.

The All Blacks won 38–6, Stu Wilson scoring 3 tries and Allan Hewson 18 points. They had been significantly better in the finale. It had been a sad way to end a tour that had promised much. The Lions had been competitive in the first three Tests and, rightly or wrongly, their tour has been remembered for the pasting they got in Auckland.

'I think that was one of the better All Black performances in the era that I was involved in,' Andy tells me. 'Certainly it was a complete performance team-wise and I think the scoreline said it all. It was just a really good feeling. That team in that era peaked in that Test.'

Ollie, not surprisingly, does not recall the Test so fondly. He tweaked a hamstring the week before the match, which was the beginning of the end of his career.

'*I really shouldn't have played but it was last man standing, really. There were so many injuries, people going down like ninepins. The less said the better. To finish a tour on such a disappointment was tough. I don't think we were that bad.*'

The Lions had never got out of first gear. They had deserved better than what occurred in Auckland, yet aside from Ollie's kicking, they didn't bring anything unique to New Zealand.

Ollie rejects criticisms of the coaching and management. Manager Willie John McBride taught him how to switch on and switch off from rugby. Coach Jim Telfer's outstanding coaching career was, meanwhile, in its infancy.

Injuries had not helped – the Lions had brought out eight replacements – yet they had not taken their chances. Had they won the first Test in Christchurch, the series result might have been different. Still, it is difficult to imagine this All Black side being beaten.

Although critics were quick to identify the Lions' shortcomings, they were up against one of the great All Black teams. It is questionable whether any Lions side – even the 1971 side – would have beaten this All Black team. They were supreme.

GREAT PLAYERS ARE OFTEN GREAT MEN

Ollie subconsciously knew the writing was on the wall for his career after the tour finished. The hamstring, the dreaded hamstring, was causing him problems. With hindsight, perhaps he shouldn't have played that final Test.

Despite the series result, he came back from New Zealand inspired. It had been what he'd imagined it would be like. He'd also seen how rugby could be played and how a team could dominate. He wanted more of international rugby.

It was not to be. The next northern season he played in only two Tests and those were his last internationals. He played three seasons for his beloved Old Belvedere club and finally retired in 1987. He'd reached great heights as a player. If injury had not shortened it, his reign could have lasted until the 1987 World Cup.

Being cut down in his prime remains a lasting regret. 'I've never really expressed this before but when I came back from New Zealand in 1983 people thought I was a bit tired. They couldn't have been more wrong. I was rejuvenated by the experience.

'*I learned the game did not have to go from set play to set play. On that tour, I was reminded of the possibilities. I was rejuvenated but rejuvenated with a chronic hamstring problem. There's a combination for you.*'

After his career finished, Ollie admits that he got caught up in his business, having the same sort of obsession that he had with his rugby.

'*I guess you could say that it's part and parcel of being an amateur player in the sense that I had to catch up for lost time. In saying that, you don't get the same sort of adrenalin rush from business as you could do from rugby.*'

He works too hard, he tells me. He wants more balance in his life and wants to watch more rugby. He's been back to New Zealand since 1983, touring as a spectator with Ireland in 1992. When he visited Dunedin on that occasion, the sun was shining.

Ollie is a fan of the modern game and thinks it's a better spectacle. He wouldn't have swapped his era for the professional age and yet he would have loved to have played in this age where the five-eight gets the ball perhaps up to four times more often.

To Ollie the current concept of the Lions is miles away from 1983. '*A Lions tour now bears no resemblance to the tours that we went on, good, bad or indifferent,*' he tells me. '*Martin Johnson was saying that even between 1997 and 2001 they were like two different eras. The whole commercial side had clicked in and that was only four years.*

'*I remember in 1983 we went on an 18-match, 10-week tour and the old Lions were saying that it wasn't a real Lions tour! I mean, what would they make of the current tours?*

'*Our tour in the bigger scheme of things was a real tour. It's reality, things change. I don't think it would be possible in this professional age for guys to go away for that length of time.*'

After we've finished talking, Ollie drops me at my friend's place where I'm staying. The music he plays in the car is moody and melancholy. There are moments when you realise that life is wonderful. That the occasion is to be enjoyed. Talking about rugby with my boyhood hero on a Friday evening in Dublin was a series of splendid moments.

GOLDEN ERA OF ALL BLACK RUGBY

Andy Dalton went on to captain the All Blacks to a series victory in Australia in 1984. He was then chosen to captain the All Blacks on their eventually aborted tour of South Africa in 1985, before being appointed leader of the Cavaliers to the republic in 1986. When his jaw was broken in the second match, his career looked over.

Yet Andy was the man chosen to lead New Zealand's bid for World Cup glory in the inaugural event in 1987. In another cruel twist of fate, a *hamstring injury also let him down and he was unavailable for the pool matches. By the time he had recovered, a young buck named Sean Fitzpatrick was irreplaceable.*

By that time Andy had established his credentials as one of the great All Black captains. He had great teams to captain, sure enough, but he also stamped his own mark on the role, thanks to his special individual traits.

After rugby, Andy's focus moved to farming in Bombay, South Auckland. His was a tough property to farm, he tells me, and so he became a coaching coordinator with the Counties union.

He then began working in a waste business, eventually becoming a shareholder. Today he works for Sportsbrand, a company that organises signage and the big screens around the rugby grounds.

Andy's also had a spell coaching Counties, while he has made his mark in administration, eventually becoming a well-respected president of the NZRFU. Rugby has remained a big part of his life.

'I love the game. We all have to change direction as we have to make a crust somehow but it's still a big part of my life and the people I'm involved with.'

Andy still keeps in touch with many of the players he captained down the years, fellow front-rowers Gary Knight and John Ashworth amongst them. He's also caught up with John Rutherford and Colin Deans, both of whom were on the '83 Lions tour. He's never become reacquainted with Ciaran Fitzgerald and isn't sure what he's doing now.

Andy fears for the game in some respects. He's concerned about the attitudes that some of the players and their agents have towards the game.

'It's very much a "what's in it for me" sort of picture and for the long-term good of the game I think that's quite threatening. I would like to see that change.'

New Zealand runs the risk, Andy believes, of continuing to lose players overseas. New Zealand can't compete with the money being offered to its finest, so it has to find creative ways to keep its players at home. This is going to be crucial for New Zealand to remain a rugby superpower.

Andy laments the changes that have weakened rugby's place in New Zealand society and believes central government has an important role in ensuring people remain actively involved in sport. Rugby, amongst other things, teaches humility, something that Andy has in bucketloads. I ask him what's been the secret of his personal success.

'I think you've got to be careful about how you define success. People say I've been very successful. When you look at things like family, I've had a broken marriage and so I keep my feet on the ground.

244

'As a rugby player, I had a lot of experienced players around me who helped share the load. I don't get too carried away: whatever success I had as a captain was a shared success and a lot of people contributed.'

As I'm in Auckland for the weekend, Andy offers me a ticket for a corporate box at that night's Blues versus Stormers match at Eden Park. He didn't need to do that but his generosity was greatly appreciated. I couldn't help but wonder again whether the modern game will produce individuals like Andy, men who by their personal actions symbolise how great the game can be.

THE PASSIONATE RED DRAGON

Tuesday, 19 October 2004

I shiver when I arrive at Cardiff Airport on a cold autumn morning. After I've grabbed my bags and found a bus to take me into the city centre, my mind turns to the enduring Welsh love for the game of rugby. I can almost feel the passion in the busy streets.

Memories come flooding back. I remember when Andy Haden fell out of a lineout to help deprive Wales of victory in 1978. I can recall Graham Mourie's magnificent try against the Welsh in 1980. I was at Lancaster Park when the All Blacks thrashed the Welsh in 1988. I appreciated Graham Price, Bob Norster, Phil Bennett and Terry Holmes, amongst others.

Then there were the stories I was told about how the Welsh loved their rugby. They embraced the sport like New Zealanders, appreciating what it meant. When you thought of Wales, you thought of coal mining, singing and rugby. These were a passionate people and, in my view, they had their priorities right.

Still, the proprietor of the bed and breakfast where I'm staying doesn't like rugby. In fact, he doesn't like New Zealanders much either. Apparently a group of Kiwis came down from London recently and caused him trouble. We are not off to a good start.

I don't know what it is but you can always tell whenever you're in a rugby country. Maybe it's a subjective thing but I feel it walking into central Cardiff. It could be that there is a rugby shop near Cardiff Castle, yet I think it goes much deeper. It's as if rugby is a reflection of the outlook of the people and what they regard as important.

It could also be how people in a rugby country appreciate the New Zealand accent. Everywhere I go I expect the locals to ask me about Bob Deans's controversial no try in 1905, the Haden dive in '78. In some ways, I want some association, as I am a New Zealander and want to be part of that rich history by association.

The setting is certainly a factor: the Millennium Stadium dominates the Cardiff ground like a beacon to visitors to the city. It's a magnificent stadium sure enough, with the more traditional Cardiff Rugby Club tucked neatly in front.

THE BEST OF THE NORTHERN BEST

Wednesday, 20 October 2004

'Every young kid in Wales aspires to be an international, even though it's beyond your wildest dreams,' Gareth Edwards tells me from the comforts of the Cardiff Blues' offices.

In these parts and throughout Europe, they reckon that Gareth is the best player the world has ever seen. New Zealanders tended to say Colin Meads. Of course, it's a subjective argument. Regardless, Gareth is certainly one of the best.

'Likewise, when you're young you aspire to be a Lion without actually knowing what it means,' Gareth says. 'You read about great matches. I think the first tour I became aware of the Lions was the 1950 tour and about Jack Matthews and Bleddyn Williams. I was a lot more aware of the 1966 tour. I was still at school but just starting to cut my teeth in rugby.'

Gareth was at college when he heard he had been selected for the Lions in 1968. The preparation was made easier by the fact that some of his Cardiff teammates (including Barry John and Gerald Davies) were on the tour.

'More than anything it was an adventure for young kids, before we really appreciated what the series was all about. It was only with hindsight that we were able to look back and realise what the series really meant.

'It was a fantastic tour and I had the most wonderful time. It wasn't just playing on the field, it was the whole education bit, the meeting of the people and the culture, everything that's probably lost in the modern game [in reality].'

Gareth went on to star on the 1971 and 1974 series-winning Lions' tours of course, becoming a rugby icon in the process. I wonder whether he now feels that the Lions these days have become over-commercialised.

'Yes,' he says, before adding, 'I think you make the most of the opportunity when it presents itself. It shows you there is something special about it and that as a result it has become commercialised. I think it was inevitable because it's such a fantastic brand.'

'Forty-four players?' I ask.

'The point is that it's not for me to criticise that because I might always have the view of what we were. Still, 30 players weren't enough when we had a few injuries. However, if that's what the modern game demands, so be it.'

I could talk to Gareth all day about his Lions experiences. Yet he's got a Cardiff board meeting to attend shortly. So we move to Welsh rugby.

'It's been through a pretty dramatic period for the last 25 years,' he tells me. 'There is some light at the end of the tunnel, however. The game means so much to the people of Wales. Having been to New Zealand, I know what it means to the people there. In that sense, we're similar, which is why we've a shared affinity.

'It's sad how the demise came. It probably came when there was a change in our schools system in the 1980s. The game was based in a small locality, which encouraged patronage, identity and competition. We are a small country and each village had a good team that competed against each other.

'The school system produced those players with great care and skill. The teachers all played a part. The school system changed to the more comprehensive system of larger and larger schools. I think at that time we lost a grip of the game. Teachers wanted to get paid for their work after hours. Before you know it, we had a three-year strike where kids didn't play.'

There are other factors, Gareth tells me. 'The era emerged where there was more competition from other sports and where television was making people aware of other things. Whereas rugby used to have a hold on the young people of Wales with its history, background and tradition, that had changed.

'I don't think the [Welsh Rugby] union was really grasping the problems that were arising. My brother worked as a PE master. He used to say to me, "If you think you've got problems now, just wait five or ten years down the road, I can see it happening." He could see the pressure being put on him to widen the school curriculum for other sports.

'As a result, rugby suffered. The union thought the game would stand the test. I think we've been mismanaged for the last 25 years but I think what we are doing now is a definite move forward.'

Thanks to the likes of Graham Henry and Steve Hansen, Welsh players had come to terms with professionalism, which, Gareth says, the Welsh in general were slow to respond to.

'I'm a lot more confident about the future. We've got a structure in place that has to work and I would like to think that we can start off by really challenging the All Blacks next month.'

Gareth struck me as having a poise that is only held by the greatest sportsmen. Australian cricketer Don Bradman had it, Colin Meads too. It's a confidence perhaps, but to me it is symbolic of what makes Welsh rugby great.

RUGBY'S ARISTOTLE

Wednesday, 20 October 2004
Earlier that morning I had spoken with another legendary Welsh international – Mervyn Davies – in the clubrooms of the Cardiff club. It's enemy territory for Mervyn (he's a Swansea man) but when he walks through the door he's looking as athletic as he's described in the rugby books.

He's an articulate man, is Mervyn. There is also a touch of Aristotle about him and I like him a lot. He tells me he grew up during Wales's five-match tour of New Zealand in 1969.

'I was 21 years of age, thought this was easy. I'd just been part of a Triple Crown-winning side. Wonderful. All Blacks? Who the hell were they, sort of thing. After two Test matches and a real drubbing you realised that you weren't good enough.

'I vowed along with a few people who were on that tour – like Barry John and J.P.R. Williams – that that was never going to happen to us again. We're really going to change our attitude as rugby players. We're going to have to be bigger, fitter, faster, whatever, to compete with the likes of New Zealand.'

The lessons were learnt. Mervyn starred with the Lions in 1971 and became one of the greatest exponents of number 8 play before his career was ended by a brain haemorrhage in 1976. Still, I get the impression there's far more to life for Mervyn than rugby.

'When we toured New Zealand, we met the people,' he tells me. 'Auckland is like any big city in the world but Greymouth on a wet Thursday afternoon isn't too clever sort of thing.

'I often talk with Colin Meads about touring and he would say the same: "It's bloody great." He'd go to the local pubs, the local clubs, sing songs, meet the people, make love to the local women, whatever. You got to know the culture and it's the same in New Zealand. It was a fantastic three and a half months.'

Touring for that amount of time and concentrating on rugby full time was the closest Mervyn ever got to being a professional. 'You spent your life playing rugby, which is what the modern rugby player does today, except that in 1971 we got ten shillings a day!'

Mervyn tells me that in his time rugby players were ambassadors for their country and that the old colonial attitude persisted. As a result, the players visited schools and the local Welsh societies and sang wherever they went. Of course spending three and a half months in a country gave the players time to do this.

Mervyn speaks passionately about the days when he played and toured New Zealand and South Africa. I get the impression though that while a rugby romantic, he's also a realist. I ask him whether he lamented what had occurred in Welsh rugby.

'To a certain extent, yes. It [Wales] hasn't totally embraced professionalism. We are a small nation in reality and when the game became organised in the northern hemisphere it was a bit of a blow to Welsh rugby because we haven't got the numbers to choose from, which I guess you could say the same about New Zealand.

'I played in a period of success for Welsh rugby. I resent in many ways the fact that the Welsh era that I played in is eulogised in so many ways. I find it frustrating and I would like the mantle to disappear and for a new era of success for Wales. They'll still be dragging us out in ten, twenty years' time if Wales doesn't have some success in the meantime.'

I surmise and suggest that the reason Wales have struggled in general in recent years is the fact that their players are simply not good enough. There has been no Barry John, J.P.R. Williams,

249

Mervyn Davies. Mervyn laughs and I admit that it's a difficult question to answer without sounding immodest.

'You could actually say that in the 1970s it was a fluke that all those people came together at the same time, perhaps never to be repeated again. If you're looking for reasons why these people were around, you could possibly say that a lot of them were grammar school kids. Grammar schools in Wales played rugby and cricket, not soccer.

'I was never coached. A lot of us were brought up in that sort of atmosphere and so a lot of us developed our abilities without intensive coaching. I think a lot of youngsters today are over-coached.

'You might say the demise of the coal mines is a reason. But then it's a fallacy to suggest that the Welsh team of the 1970s were based on the steelworks and the coal mines and the farmers, because they weren't.

'Ninety per cent of them were white-collar workers like myself, teachers, doctors, lecturers and solicitors. Most of them were sitting on their arses and weren't at the sharp end sort of thing.'

All these clichés of yesteryear do get built up over time and become inaccurate. In New Zealand, the image of Colin Meads traipsing over the hills carrying a sheep under each arm to train has become folklore. Yet it's simply not true (they were fence posts).

Overseas coaches have not helped the Welsh game, Mervyn believes. Henry and Hansen have brought in a greater level of professionalism but not a lot else. 'I think you have to be Welsh to coach Wales. Can you imagine that happening in New Zealand?'

'Yes,' I answer honestly. Australian Steve Rixon had coached the New Zealand cricket team. The English have a Swede coaching their national soccer team.

Mervyn concedes the point. 'They have put certain parameters in place where hopefully it [Welsh rugby] might develop. The regional rugby in Wales is one result. I think it's the way forward but it's only part of it. There's no A team rugby, no Under-21s rugby.

'I also don't know what level of coaching there is in schools at the moment. The issue is not just the top of the pyramid but how broad a base the pyramid has. I don't think we're spending enough time with kids.'

The Welsh national side will continue to improve but so too will the likes of England and New Zealand. As a result, Mervyn does not believe it is realistic to expect Wales to be as dominant as it once was.

'We would hope that we would regularly beat Argentina, Samoa, Scotland and perhaps Ireland. But we need to be beating England, South Africa and New Zealand regularly if we want to be in the top echelons. At the moment, we're below that.'

Regardless of the results, Wales remains a rugby country. Test matches are sold out and it's still embraced by the majority. However, the reality is that more people in Wales play soccer than rugby.

Like two lost souls standing at a bar on a cold Friday night, Mervyn and I lament the demise of the long tour: when an amateur player could leave the worries of the mortgage, job and wife for a time and concentrate on what he did best. Learning about the culture of the country they were visiting and contributing something was almost as important as the results on the field.

Innocent times. 'That tremendous togetherness,' Mervyn says of touring. 'It's you against the rest of New Zealand. You're living in this little bubble and you feel like it's you against the world. You make friends on tour that you'll have for life because you've shared something special. It was special, all right.'

FROM LINEOUT TO BOARDROOM

Wednesday, 20 October 2004

When I was 12 years old and went along to watch the All Blacks play the 1983 Lions in Christchurch, lock forward Robert Norster was a standout.

Not only was he a magnificent lineout forward but he was a charismatic Errol Flynn-like player who was highly regarded by the All Blacks. He was a star.

Twenty-one years on and I'm sitting with Bob in the Cardiff Blues' boardroom overlooking the club ground. It feels a long way from Christchurch and an even longer way from 1983.

Bob's now chief executive of Cardiff Rugby. After finishing playing he'd gone into management with Cardiff and the Welsh national squad. He'd worked for blue-chip companies in Wales, before making the switch to rugby administration.

Welsh rugby has seen so many false dawns. 'We've all made so many errors since the game went open,' Bob tells me. 'I think we could have had the start we are having now with the new regional set-up and we could have been much better off. We've bumbled along and cost ourselves a lot of time. What we have to do now is make the best fist of this new arrangement that we have here in Wales.'

The regional set-ups are based on the main commercial centres in Wales. That made rugby and financial sense. If professional rugby had proven nothing else it was that you can't base a team where there is no corporate backing.

Bob says that Welsh rugby has got to look forward, not back. That it is pointless looking at the demise of the clubs as the central focus of Welsh rugby.

'But, yeah, I've come through that system and this [Cardiff] has been my club man and boy and I've got prejudices I guess, but we've got to look at the youngsters and make sure that they buy into this new system.'

This meant that players within the extensive Cardiff Blues region had to aspire to play for the franchise, much the same way lads of Bob's generation aspired to play for Cardiff. The change wasn't hugely significant: after all, the franchise still had the name Cardiff and was based at Arms Park. Still, the change of emphasis was symbolic and it was real.

The great traditions within Welsh rugby had made the changes that had to be made more difficult. Wales appeared hamstrung by its illustrious past.

'We've had a lot of heartache and lot of embedded battles between the various factions in trying to move the game forward,' Bob says. 'We've got ongoing constitutional issues that we've still got to sort out.'

These involve sorting out the needs and demands of the professional and amateur games, which are often not the same. Trying to work out a common path forward is one of the greatest goals of Welsh rugby.

It also involves embracing the different competitions that come about through the need to ensure the right number of matches for the professional players.

Bob says the Celtic League has taken time to catch on. The Welsh are used to the tribal rivalries within the principality, something the Celtic has expanded on.

'The Celtic has put a different spin on it. Obviously we take good revenues from the broadcasters but we can't have it both ways. We have to get the balance right between getting the revenues and playing too many matches.

'I think the Celtic is starting to grow. What we have to realise here in Wales is that we haven't had the consistency that they've managed to establish in the Zurich in England. They've had a well-funded competition and they've stolen a march on us.

'We've chopped and changed a lot here in Wales. We've gone from nine clubs to five teams, now four regional teams. We do need a period where we have a good number of sides who remain stable for people to understand the competition, recognise the faces and get behind it. We stand a good chance of making it a really strong competition if we pull together.'

The European Cup has perhaps been more successful as a competition for the Welsh teams, even though they hadn't achieved overwhelming success on the field.

'It's been a real challenge,' Bob says. 'It's a great competition and it has done us no end of good and I think it's helped in the English success story. It's the competition teams build and prepare for and I think it's a real rival for anything else that's out there.'

Although Bob says there may have been a lack of truly outstanding Welsh players in the last 20 years, that may be changing. The success of Welsh youth sides suggests structures are in place to develop individuals into quality professional players.

Having a vibrant, dynamic city also helps. Cardiff has become a tremendous place to live thanks to investment in the city's infrastructure. That undoubtedly flows through into what sociologists describe as the 'feel-good factor'.

Even though the Cardiff Blues is an independent business, if the franchise achieves success there will undoubtedly be a flow-on effect to the national side.

'Obviously what we want to do is work in partnership in a helpful way with our governing body because we both have to be successful together,' says Bob.

By introducing a regional system, Welsh rugby appears to be on the right track. It's too early to say what the long-term prognosis will be but it's certainly a step in the right direction. It's nothing short of a tragedy that it took the Welsh nearly ten years to get their infrastructure right.

It seems a long time ago since Bob laced up his boots. Then, with the game still amateur, players had their own ways of making some coin. On the 1989 Lions tour of Australia, for example, the players signed T-shirts and sold them at the local shops.

'It was inevitable that the game was going to change,' Bob says. 'I think we'd had enough of the shamateurism at the time. I remember in 1988 when we came back from New Zealand, Jonathan Davies and I put a paper together for the WRU as we'd seen the All Blacks doing their thing [earning income]. There was a gulf opening [between the amateurs and the semi-professionals] and the sooner that became legitimised the better.'

This proud Lion still values the jersey and takes pride in being a Lion. He feels the 44 who tour New Zealand will be worthy of the jersey but wonders whether the concept is being devalued as a result of the number. Rugby has evolved, he tells me, but the passion for the sport in Wales remains as strong as ever.

After we've finished talking, Bob brings out a scrapbook in which many of his achievements are reported in words and photos. It's a hark back to the amateur era, reflective of a great career and a wonderful reminder that, issues aside, there's still a delightful innocence within rugby.

THE OPENSIDER

Friday, 15 October 2004

The opensider's role is rarely adequately defined in the rugby books. Still, he's arguably, along with the five-eight and the tight-head prop, the most influential player on the paddock in most games. I'd seen earlier in the year the impact that Richard McCaw had had on matches and wondered whether there was a northern hemisphere equivalent.

In many ways, the redheaded, balding Martyn Williams reflects modern Welsh rugby. The opensider may not be the most skilful player in the game but he's one of the most wholehearted and he never gives up.

He is also symbolic of the changes that have taken place in the sport and the fact that although the national Welsh side has had its ups and downs, there is always plenty of spirit and old-fashioned guts displayed.

Martyn was a star player during Graham Henry's tenure. Graham wrote of Martyn in 1999: 'There's a young fellow of promise in Wales, Martyn Williams from Pontypridd. At 22, he's swift and intelligent and helps provide that essential continuity good teams need.'

Graham and the Lions selectors chose Martyn for the 2001 tour of Australia. Martin Johnson has written that he was affected when Martyn recounted the death of his brother in team-bonding sessions before the tour began. 'It was quite moving and it helped us grow closer,' Johnson said.

Yet Johnson, writing in 2003, also felt that despite Martyn being a 'good guy' he should not have been selected ahead of Scotland's Budge Pountney or Ireland's David Wallace on that tour. He did point out, however, that Martyn had become one of the best Welsh forwards following the tour.

I love the way Martyn throws himself at opposition players, as if his life depends on it. He is an old-fashioned player, playing to the letter of the law perhaps, but invaluable to his team.

I meet up with Martyn in Limerick of all places – after Cardiff have lost to Munster. He's captained Cardiff tonight. It's a cold evening sure enough, the Welsh side have lost and not surprisingly spirits are not high. You can see it on the faces of the Cardiff management that stand outside the changing-shed. They collectively look like someone in the family has died.

Martyn has just fulfilled his television commitments under the stand in a poky back room. As a result, we talk in the corridor of Thomond Park. He's bare-footed, looks too small for professional rugby and, quite frankly, looks like a beaten man, literally and metaphorically.

'We were in the game in the first half but for whatever reason we struggled in the last 40 minutes,' Martyn says.

Martyn tells me that being picked for the Lions in 2001 was one of the highlights of his rugby career, right up there with being first picked for Wales.

'It was an awesome experience. It was a pity that we didn't go on to win the series in Australia but it was a great feeling and I was proud to be involved.'

I ask Martyn what memories he has of that tour. He says that it was exactly what he expected it would be – unrelenting and challenging.

'It was very tough. Training schedules especially were very tough and we were training three or four times a day but it was good craic. The boys were a good bunch of lads off the field as well.

'The thing was that we were going out there [Australia] at the end of a long season for us and a lot of the boys were going out there injured, which made it tough really.'

Martyn tells me that touring as a Lion was an invaluable experience. He says that not only did he develop his game but he also had the opportunity to learn from his fellow tourists.

Although he had not made the Test team in 2001, playing for the Lions had made Martyn a better all-round player. I wondered whether that experience had made him keen for more Lions rugby in 2005.

'I think it's every rugby player's dream in this part of the world to make the Lions. I've got to look at the immediate things, to be honest. I've got to make the national side and if that happens then I've got to play well and hope I get selected [for the Lions].'

'Is it a goal to be part of a squad that wins a series in New Zealand after losing the series in 2001?' I ask.

'Obviously, yeah. If I get selected, it would be massive. Touring New Zealand would be a fantastic experience, there is no doubt about that. Right now, though, my focus is on getting selected for Wales. I'm really concentrating on that and hopefully the rest will take care of itself.'

The irony in playing against All Black teams coached by Graham Henry and Steve Hansen, for Wales or for the Lions, is not lost on Martyn. It is merely reflective of modern professional rugby.

Making the Welsh squad is never easy. Although he's an established player, this season newcomers are staking strong claims for the famous red number 7.

'All you can do really is keep your club form up and hope that you don't get a knock,' Martyn says quickly, getting colder by the second. 'So fingers crossed I'll make it but it's a long way off.'

Although I noticed that there seem to be a lot of knockers in Welsh rugby, Martyn isn't one of them. He tells me that rugby in Wales is in good heart and there is a real positive vibe with so many talented youngsters coming through the ranks.

Martyn is a fan of regionalism in Welsh rugby and believes that there was not enough money in Welsh rugby to continue to fund 10 or 12 clubs. He believes Welsh sides will rapidly improve as a result.

A hot shower is waiting for Martyn. He's earned it tonight, as he does after each match he plays, for like all good opensiders, Martyn leaves something on the track. There is a lot to like about Martyn.

ANNOUNCING THE GENERALS

Thursday, 21 October 2004

My European odyssey ends appropriately in Cardiff, one of the spiritual homes of rugby. The city has been what I'd expected and more. There may be a rugby renaissance happening here because the mood is upbeat and positive.

I've purchased a second-hand copy of one of Gareth Edwards's books in Cardiff. I've explored Cardiff Rugby Club and drooled at the old teams and the famous names highlighted. I've stood outside the Angel Hotel, where All Black Keith Murdoch brawled in 1972.

My relationship with the proprietor of my bed and breakfast hasn't improved any but that doesn't matter, as I'm in a rugby Mecca.

To be honest, I'm also tired. I reckon I've organised and conducted around 30 interviews in 17 days throughout Britain and Ireland. It's been invigorating, it's been a labour of love but it's also been tiring.

My last day of interviewing has been planned to coincide with the naming of the Lions coaching panel for the tour of New Zealand. Clive and his new management team like their press conferences. I get the feeling that if the Lions were wearing new undies on tour they would have a press conference to announce it.

I traipse my way through the corridors and conference rooms at the Millennium Stadium to find the suite where they are making the announcement.

When I arrive at the venue, the well-oiled Lions PR machine stresses that there will be no one-on-one interviews today. I'm frustrated. I've come from New Zealand and Clive Woodward and Bill Beaumont are apparently off limits.

I grab a seat and wait for proceedings to begin. There is a subtle difference between a rugby press conference in New Zealand and one in Britain. In New Zealand, the journalists are emotionally involved in the game. It means something to them. Here, they

257

appear, in general, removed from what they are reporting on. I guess it's something to do with the size of the countries and what rugby means to each.

Eventually, Bill Beaumont welcomes the journalists to Cardiff and then makes his first mistake, referring to the Lions as the British Lions. This frustrates me and I'm not even Irish. For the tour manager, it's not a good start to the day.

'We know how difficult it's going to be down in New Zealand next summer,' Bill continues. 'We know and appreciate the history of the Lions. There is only one side, in 1971, who has ever won a series down there. Obviously we are here to repeat that.'

Bill announces that the Lions will play Argentina in Cardiff on 23 May. Again he refers to the Lions as the British Lions. The Lions don't play much at home and so the game will be a treat for the home fans.

Irishman and chief executive of the Lions, John Feehan, then sets out to thank all the sponsors of the tour. It all sounds like the build-up to a heavyweight boxing match or a Gwyneth Paltrow speech at the Academy Awards. It is, though, merely professional rugby.

It's now Clive's show.

'I know there's been a lot said about the numbers of staff and the coaching. If you look at match schedules one, three and five, they will be headed by Ian McGeechan, Gareth Jenkins and Michael Ford. The even games, which include the three Tests, will be headed by Eddie O'Sullivan, Andy Robinson and Phil Larder. I want to stress that those coaches will be working closely together.'

Clive makes it clear that there will be one pool of players and spells out the reasoning behind his decision before stressing again: 'two coaching teams, one pool of players'. Clive would have made a tremendous primary school teacher – I'll recite those seven words in my sleep tonight.

Clive says he's got four clear objectives in heading up the coaching team. 'One, to get a series win. It's not going to be easy. The last Lions side left these shores the most talented group of players we've ever had but they still lost. We are fully aware of the difficulty that is ahead of us but that's the key objective.

'Secondly, and very closely behind, I do think it's critical that everyone comes back from this trip, whether player, coach, doctor or manager, having enjoyed the experience of Lions touring. We are all given the huge responsibility for Lions touring. That's why I put it to the Lions management committee that we had to do this in another way in the professional age, and that's what we achieved.

'The third objective is that the four countries contributing to the Lions all benefit from this. When we come back and we debrief to the home unions, it's important that all four countries benefit from the Lions year.

'Lastly, I just hope that we put in place the blueprint for future Lions tours. When this is finished in July and we look back at how this [tour] was run, managed and organised [we will hopefully find] that it has been a huge step forward in terms of the way Lions tours are run.'

We're told that the four coaches from the four unions will be the selectors, with Clive heading the selection panel.

Getting Ian McGeechan on the coaching panel is a huge coup for Clive as McGeechan has been there and done that with regards Lions tours. He'll not only head the coaching of the midweek side but he'll also provide Clive with an important sounding board.

Although taking 7 coaches and a 27-strong management team would appear excessive and takes away from some of the romance of Lions touring, that doesn't concern me.

What concerns me is the fact that if this press conference is anything to go by, Clive and manager Louise Ramsay aren't preparing for a rugby tour but for World War Three. It's nothing that is said directly, it's more the general feeling that seeps around the room.

I'm therefore wondering what Clive and the Lions are going to do to promote the game in New Zealand. After spending recent days interviewing some of the past greats of the game, I'm naturally nostalgic.

'Clive, what steps will the 2005 Lions take to promote the game within New Zealand on tour?' I ask. 'Will they be attending schools, doing the things other Lions squads have done?'

I feel like a slyly disguised fox in a chicken house. As the only New Zealander at the press conference, my accent makes me the closest thing within 12,000 miles to a young-looking Graham Henry.

'We'll be doing a tremendous amount. That's why Louise Ramsay is already going over there next week and three weeks in January to make sure we get the balance right. As I said earlier, an objective is to enjoy the tour and enjoy everything we can about the game in New Zealand within reason.

'Not to affect the preparation either side of games but there will be more downtime for players to pass back some responsibility and to attend schools and do other community activities.'

'There's the perception in New Zealand that this could turn into a military operation rather than a rugby tour. Would you disagree with that perception?' I ask.

'I'm disappointed people are saying that, as we are working with the various unions.

'If we had gone there with a small group of players we could not have done what they have asked us to do. Because we have a larger squad, we can do that. I think there will be far more interaction with the local communities than on any other Lions tour.'

Throughout the rest of the press conference, Clive stresses not only the great history of the Lions in New Zealand and the emphasis on winning but also the enjoyment factor. He's right to stress that happy Lions squads are normally winning Lions squads. He wants his squad to have fun.

This has been more of a fact-finding mission than a searching press conference. I can't help but think about the previous teams – in 1950, 1959 and 1971 for example – and how their preparations were much more basic.

After the main proceedings are over, the coaches go into pairs for interviews. Ian McGeechan and Eddie O'Sullivan are, together, other than Clive, perhaps the two most astute of the coaches announced. Ian steals the show, his experience and passion for the Lions obvious.

'The great thing is that we are now looking at the environment that we are now in professionally,' he says, 'and saying that, this is the best opportunity to make sure that the players who get picked for the Lions have their best chance of success. That's what we're all about.'

THE HEAD LION

Thursday, 21 October 2004

'Winning the World Cup was obviously something very special but in a different way the Lions is something just as special,' Clive Woodward remarks like only someone who has played for the Lions can. 'There's a huge history to it; without doubt all the legends in this part of the world have made their names through playing for the Lions.

'The enthusiasm of the players and coaches to go on a Lions tour, especially to New Zealand where it is so difficult, is huge. It's the ultimate for a Lion. Because the history and traditions are so strong in New Zealand, it is a huge privilege and honour [to coach this team]. It's totally different to coaching England.'

Despite the instruction of no one-on-ones, I see Clive standing by himself and so I go on over for a chat. Clive is all smiles. I like successful people. Not only are they pleasant to be around but they also radiate a positive attitude. You can read all you want about somebody, watch them on television, do your best to read their body language, but until you look them in the eye you can't judge them.

Clive has an aura about him and a presence that promotes instant respect. He's not a large man and he doesn't have the physical presence of a Meads or a McBride. Nor does he have the mana of an Edwards or a Michael Jones. Yet what he does have is self-belief and that's also an instantly likeable quality.

Still, if you were nominating the most likely contender of the 1983 Lions to be head coach of the 2005 Lions it would not have been Clive.

He didn't star on that tour, nor did he live up to the fine reputation that he'd established in South Africa in 1980. While the other centres on tour had all been selected for at least one Test match, he missed out.

'Came as probably the best-qualified centre, having produced the goods against All Black touring teams in England and for the Lions in South Africa in 1980,' New Zealand's *Rugby Annual* reported. 'But that was before he broke his shoulder and plainly that injury affected him psychologically, for he shied clear of physical confrontations, passed erratically and generally performed with such little control he was quickly labelled "midweeker only" . . . '

Clive says the 1983 tour taught him a lot about New Zealand rugby. 'We lost the Test series 4–0. I still enjoyed it, and it was a great place to go but it was tough. Every game was tough, while the Test matches were very hard. That's why I'm so pleased to have taken England right up there [to the same level] as the All Blacks.'

Clive was awarded 21 caps for England between 1980 and 1984. He was part of England's Grand Slam-winning squad in 1980, although you get the feeling that he didn't reach his potential on the field.

Clive's limited time as an international undoubtedly taught him that time is precious. A motivation as a coach, perhaps, is to get the best out of his players and ensure that they make the most of their time.

He'd made his fortune in business and learned there the management structures that he would apply so successfully in rugby.

His coaching career had begun with Henley, then London Irish, then Bath. Players who played under him say that it was clear that these were mere stepping stones. His ambitions were always higher.

Clive's reign with England was a success for he won the World Cup in 2003. He deserved the plaudits, the ticker-tape parades and perhaps even the knighthood for restoring some degree of pride to English sport.

Yet before the success came plenty of failure. Being bundled out of the '99 World Cup at the quarter-final stage was a disappointment. Losing three, what would have been Grand Slam-winning, matches to Wales, Scotland and Ireland respectively suggested that England were chokers.

In his last two seasons at the helm of England, Clive's team had matured to be the best team in the world. In Martin Johnson and Jonny Wilkinson he'd had two world-class players who led what was essentially an experienced band of internationals.

Johnson's and Wilkinson's absence from the 2003–04 Six Nations squad had been reflected in losses to Ireland and France. It was time for England to rebuild and it was becoming increasingly obvious that it was virtually impossible for a national coach to properly prepare for a Lions tour at the same time.

It was therefore not surprising that Clive stepped down from the England position. He'd achieved his Everest. Like James Cook in the eighteenth century, he would now focus on New Zealand.

'If I stayed on as English coach I would have stepped down for this Six Nations and concentrated on the Lions, as you can't do both,' he tells me. 'I didn't do it because of the Lions but it's a huge advantage now.

'I'm so busy now with the Lions, I wonder how I would have done England. To have a complete free go at it is something I couldn't imagine I would be able to do. It's great. So I'll try and throw the kitchen sink at it and give the players every chance of being successful down there.

'I'm [also] determined that we'll go down there and enjoy the country and at the same time promote New Zealand and world rugby.'

The Lions tour would be different to an English tour. Clive concedes that his planning ahead of the 2003 World Cup was akin to a military operation, as I'd suggested at the press conference that this tour may be like. The Lions in New Zealand was different.

'It's a different culture than a World Cup. It's about getting all four countries together. While the World Cup was like a military operation, on a Lions tour you've got to enjoy it and relax and I believe you've got more chance of winning Test matches that way.

'I'm certainly changing my approach to this tour. It will be totally different from the way you saw me during the World Cup. There are different sets of rules, a different set of criteria.' Clive knows that the last time he came across the All Blacks they smacked his English side by 30 points. 'I just look at the quality of the coaching team, from Graham, to Wayne Smith, Steve Hansen, you've got real quality coaching and real quality players.'

Clive says there is no animosity between him and Graham Henry. This despite the fact that Clive has obviously been critical of Graham's coaching of the 2001 Lions.

'I don't know where this sort of thing comes from,' Clive says amazingly. 'I was told I've had animosity with [Australian coach] Eddie Jones and yet we're having dinner together soon. It's all media stuff. I've got no issues with Graham at all. In fact, the complete opposite, I've got huge respect.

'I remember ringing him [Graham] up on the last Lions tour when Daws [Matt Dawson] had stepped out of line and wrote something stupid, and telling him that he had my complete support.

'At the end of the day you end up competing with these guys and sometimes you've got to compete with the media. I've got nothing but respect for Graham Henry and I'm looking forward to competing with him this time.'

Behind the organisational supremo is a family man. Given the time that Clive spends on rugby, I wonder whether his family life suffers. It's a problem not unique to Clive of course, although in Graham Henry's case his children had grown up.

'I'm lucky, I've got three great kids who are very helpful, along with my wife. I've done this job so long with England that we talk about it and the upsides far outweigh the downsides.

'The downsides are that you lose some games and you get some nonsense in the press now and again. The upsides are that the kids will all be out there [in New Zealand] for the Test matches at the end of exams. I mean how many kids do that or have Jonny Wilkinson come round for tea?'

I wonder what makes Clive tick. He's a man with an enormous amount of talent but the public doesn't really know what motivates him. Certainly the New Zealand public sees a bloke who reflects all that they perceive as being bad about the English character. So I ask him the question.

'I just feel really lucky. In terms of sport, because the game has gone professional and we've all worked in normal jobs, I just regard myself as so lucky to be earning my living involved in sport. I would have loved to have been a professional player.

'Some people talk about the good old days but it's absolute nonsense. I would have loved to have been a professional rugby player or sportsman in any sport. That wasn't to be because the game I chose was amateur. So now to see the game go professional and be able to get a job as a professional coach makes you enjoy every day.'

BILL FROM LANCASHIRE

Thursday, 21 October 2004

When I look at Bill Beaumont, I can't believe that this man won 34 caps for England. All the signs are there, though: the cauliflower ears, the broad shoulders, the rugby-speak that he utters.

The thing is, the man's tiny – in the rugby world at least. He must be around 6 ft 3 in. tall but I would fancy my chances of winning a clean lineout ball.

Like any rugby fan, I know about Bill's career. He'd come out to New Zealand as a replacement with the 1977 Lions, playing in three Tests. He'd led England to Grand Slam glory in 1980 then captained the 1980 Lions in South Africa and by all accounts had done a good job.

His autobiography had painted a picture of a sporting icon. Although he was a talented international and a grand captain, I doubted whether he was in the same league as Martin Johnson as a lock or Fran Cotton as a forward. Could his popularity be because of his role for 13 years as one of the team captains on the BBC's *A Question of Sport*.

Bill missed out on the manager's job for the 1997 Lions tour to Fran Cotton. Now united with Clive Woodward, he's got his opportunity in New Zealand. Although the tour manager's role was important, Louise Ramsay was doing the real preparation work.

Since his playing days ended, Bill's had an impressive career in rugby administration, including being a director for the European Rugby Cup and being on the RFU management board in England. He is also currently an English representative to the IRB.

He's a people's person, sure enough. The journalists feel comfortable with him and treat him like a mate they'd have a pint with down at the pub. For Bill it must feel like a million years since the 1977 tour.

'Very long way,' he says. 'Happy memories for me though. I came out as a replacement and ended up playing in three Tests. You never forget those things.'

Bill's been back to New Zealand five or six times since the 1977 tour and feels a good deal of respect for rugby there and for the honesty within New Zealand rugby.

'They want you to enjoy the place, they are a proud nation, but we know when we get off the plane they want to beat you. We respect that.'

Bill is enjoying being tour manager. It was something that he thought he'd never get to do when he was a player. Especially when he wrote a book and was professionalised.

His job is to offer a framework and advice and to not necessarily become involved in the day-to-day running of the team. Somebody who is an independent, alternative voice. He hopes that he will also be able to free up the coaching squad to do what they do best – coach.

He's also got an important role in promoting the Lions within New Zealand and the game of rugby generally. Given the prestige of the man and his iconic status, he's suitably qualified.

His job is also about ensuring the squad gets out and mixes with the New Zealanders. Bill says he's been on tours that have been too insular and that doesn't increase the squad's chance of a series victory.

'If you look back, probably the most popular touring team to go to New Zealand were the 1971 Lions, who were of course successful. They won but because they were playing an exciting brand of rugby they excited the New Zealand public.

'You had your heroes like Gareth Edwards, Gerald Davies and Barry John, and you had lots of kids that wanted to be like them and play rugby. I remember talking with John Kirwan who said that his father took him to watch those guys play and it excited him.'

The New Zealand rugby public is knowledgeable, Bill tells me, and does respect good rugby and the traditions of the game. 'If someone plays some good rugby and beats them they will hold their hand up and acknowledge that. I hope we're the same.'

Bill is well aware that rugby is far more important than just the on-the-field results. It's about promoting the game as a worthwhile endeavour and ensuring that the grand traditions established by previous Lions squads are maintained.

Talk to any former Lion like Bill and they talk about the experience being the pinnacle. While playing for your country is always special, playing for the Lions is recognition that you're amongst the best players in Britain and Ireland.

Given the size of the squad the Lions are taking to New Zealand, I wonder whether such exclusivity remains. Still, the Lions of Bill's generation remain a select group. The camaraderie, with his teammates and even his opponents, remains as strong as ever.

'I see a lot of the lads around the traps. In terms of the All Blacks, I saw Andy Haden at the World Cup in 2003, while I saw Graham Mourie when I was down in New Zealand. These are guys I feel comfortable with. That's rugby. Hopefully they feel as comfortable in my company as I feel in theirs.'

On that subject, there's a touching story told in his autobiography of Bill going to see his former Lions teammate Gordon Brown before the Scottish lock died of cancer. In Glasgow to speak at a function, Bill ducked out to visit his mate at the hospital.

'Gordon was lying there on the bed with tubes everywhere and I didn't know what to say,' Bill wrote, 'so we had bit of a hug and then started to chat about the good times we had enjoyed together and the scrapes we had got ourselves into.'

'Reluctantly, I had to drag myself away, indicating that I was speaking at the dinner. I knew he was dying, he knew it too, and we were aware as I left that we would never see each other again.'

I wonder whether any of the 2005 Lions will strike up friendships of similar magnitude?

Bill's trying to combine his commitments as tour manager with his role as the head of his family's textile business. He admits that it doesn't leave him time to do much else.

I get the impression that this big-hearted Lion of Lancashire and England wouldn't have it any other way. Rugby is in Bill's blood and, without question, so are the Lions.

* * *

THE LAST OF THE HAPPY AMATEURS?

Although the 1993 All Blacks did not necessarily reflect the nation's cultural make-up, they were becoming more symbolic of New Zealand's cultural diversity. Polynesians especially were becoming more prominent in the All Blacks.

For example, in the All Black starting XV in the first Test in 1983, there were twelve Pakehas, two Maori and one Fijian New Zealander. In the All Black starting XV in the first Test in 1993, there were five Pakehas, four Maori and six Polynesians.

The 1993 Lions themselves were English dominated: 17 Englishmen, 6 Scotsmen, 5 Welshmen and 2 Irishmen selected in the original 30. The selection was as expected controversial, as Ireland had beaten England 17–3 in the last weekend of the Five Nations.

While the split between the four nations could have been debated, it is arguable with hindsight whether the selectors got the squad right. Leaving English prop Jeff Probyn out of the mix was probably a mistake, while choosing the Scottish front five proved an unmitigated disaster.

THE RIGHT CAPTAIN
One Scottish selection the Lions selectors got right was that of the captain, Gavin Hastings. Before the start of the Five Nations, the media were predicting Will Carling would be captain.

Carling, for all his success, would have gone down badly in New Zealand. Hastings had played club rugby in New Zealand in 1987 after the World Cup, toured the country with Scotland in 1990 and was universally liked by New Zealanders. Carling, on the other hand, had little experience of New Zealand.

267

I meet Gavin in downtown Cardiff of all places in late 2004. He's promoting Eden Park, a line of clothing established by the stylish French centre Frank Mensel. He's incredibly smooth, is Gavin. If I could choose to be like any rugby player, then Gavin would be near the top of my list.

'Leading the 1993 Lions was the greatest honour in my career,' he tells me. 'You go down to a place like New Zealand and you realise that the Lions are revered and held in high regard.

'Until you go on tour with the Lions, you don't realise how massive it is. It's a touring side and it means that the rugby public of this country don't know what it's like or the depth of interest.'

Like any kid fascinated with rugby, Gavin grew up with the stories of the successful 1971 side and Willie John McBride's squad in South Africa in 1974. Touring New Zealand as a Lion was always a goal, captaining the Lions something beyond his imagination.

'It was the right decision,' he says of his appointment. 'I was very honoured and it all happened in a short space of time. I only became Scotland captain at the start of that Five Nations year and so six months later I was the Lions captain.'

The Lions began with wins against North Auckland, North Harbour, the New Zealand Maori and Canterbury. Against the Maori, they had shown plenty of character to come from behind, while Jeremy Guscott had shown his class against Canterbury.

Then an incident occurred which caused a rift between the players and the administrative officials. English lock Wade Dooley was not allowed to return to the touring party as a player after the sudden death of his father.

While Martin Johnson was flown out as a replacement, it was intended that Dooley would return after the funeral. However, after the Lions had lost 37–24 to Otago, the squad discovered that even though the NZRFU had allowed Dooley to return, IRB regulations and the tour agreement prevented it.

It seems remarkable but the administrators claimed that rules were rules and must be adhered to. Although Dooley was invited to rejoin the tour as a guest rather than as a player, he, not surprisingly, turned down that offer.

Having been beaten by Otago, the Lions went into the first Test as underdogs. On paper at least they had a strong team, with Nick Popperwell, Ben Clarke, Dean Richards and Martin Bayfield in the pack and Guscott, Ieuan Evans and Gavin in the back line.

The All Blacks, on the other hand, had an eclectic mix of talents. The previous season they had been beaten 2–1 in a series in Australia but they *had beaten the Springboks in their reintroduction to Test rugby. Craig Dowd was playing in his first Test against the Lions, while Sean Fitzpatrick was captaining the All Blacks again.*

The first Test was a game the home side were lucky to win. All Black centre Frank Bunce scored a try in the first two minutes, although it looked likely that Evans also had his hands on the ball. Still, Gavin kicked two penalties to give the Lions a deserved lead.

Grant Fox then kicked two penalties for New Zealand, before Gavin added his third penalty to narrow New Zealand's lead to 11–9 at half-time.

The second half belonged to the Lions – almost. Gavin and Fox kicked five penalties in the first thirty-five minutes of the half, indicating the tenseness of the occasion and the fact that both defences were well organised.

With minutes remaining, the Lions led 18–17. They had deserved their lead and had generally played the better rugby. With only a minute to go, the All Blacks were awarded a penalty after it was adjudged that Dean Richards was offside. Whether it was a legitimate penalty or not, referee Brian Kinsey gave it.

Grant Fox stepped up and, as cool as a Kiwi cucumber, kicked the goal to give New Zealand the lead and, effectively, the win. It was heartbreaking for the Lions and they justifiably felt upset at what had occurred.

'Every now and again you think how did the referee give that decision?' Gavin recalls. 'I don't think that decision can be justified even now. It happened twice in my career where the referee made a decision that seemed incredible and it seemed that it cost the team that was I captaining the match.

'I feel confident that if we had won that first match we would have won the series. Twelve years on, I'm not going to be accused of sour grapes but the weight of history might have been different but for the referee . . . it seemed a ridiculous decision then and even more of a ridiculous decision now.'

The Lions licked their wounds with a win against Taranaki followed up by disappointing losses to Auckland and Hawke's Bay. Given their record and Gavin's hamstring injury in the lead-up to the Test, there was no doubting the Lions were the underdogs going into the second Test.

'I remember training before that game had been an absolute shambles compared to the first Test,' Gavin says. 'I was really unsure about my fitness but the physio kept saying I would be all right. I was not comfortable or confident. I remember Geech [Ian McGeechan] saying that he didn't

269

care if I came off after a minute and that I was leading the team and so that was a boost of confidence from the coach.'

The decision looked to have backfired early in the match when Gavin dropped a high ball in the Wellington sun and Eroni Clarke scored. Still, Gavin kicked two penalties and Rob Andrew dropped a goal to give the visitors a 9–7 lead at half-time.

The second half belonged to the Lions. Gavin kicked another penalty before the Lions scored the try of the series. Dewi Morris and Jeremy Guscott made breaks, before the ball was fed to Leicester RAF flyer Rory Underwood, who sprinted 50 metres to score. It was a terrific try.

Gavin kicked another penalty and the Lions ended up 20–7 winners. They had fully deserved their win, and it had in some respects made amends for the disappointment of the first Test.

'To this day it's still the greatest Test victory by the Lions in New Zealand, which is extraordinary because it wasn't that big a margin,' Gavin says. 'It just shows how tough it is to win Test match rugby in New Zealand.'

Gavin spoke to All Black captain Sean Fitzpatrick after the game. Fitzpatrick told him the home side would suffer a barrage of grief in the press and that the public would be unrelenting. How right he was.

THE GREAT AND LATE ALL BLACK

I agree to meet Sean Fitzpatrick at 4.30 one Thursday afternoon in October 2004 in the foyer of the St Andrews Hotel, St Andrews, Scotland, of all places.

As a celebrity, he's playing in the Pro-Am at the Dunhill Cup. I'm in St Andrews to take a look around and to interview the former All Black captain.

The allotted time comes and Sean's nowhere to be seen. I presume he's still on the course. So I sit in the plush foyer and watch as the likes of Samuel L. Jackson, Michael Douglas and Kevin Costner sign off after finishing their rounds. It all seems surreal.

With my tape recorder and notebook at my side, the hotel staff must think of me as a tabloid journalist and as the minutes tick by they treat me accordingly. I'm not enjoying it much either but seeing J.P. McManus, Michael Vaughan and Ernie Els is certainly somewhat different.

I eventually find Sean at the 19th hole at about 6.30 p.m. He's talking to some of his old rugby cobbers. I'm flustered. He apologises profusely and after a few minutes we go to a quiet corner of the hotel and talk.

Sean is one of the great All Blacks. He was in the side from 1986 to

1997 and was captain from 1992 to his retirement. He was noted for his outstanding ability and for his tenacity and guile. He was a champion.

In 1993, he was still 'learning the ropes' as captain. 'It was a watershed, really. People ask me what was the best game of my life but as All Blacks we inherently remember our worst games rather than our best games and to me Athletic Park in 1993, knocking the ball on halfway and Rory Underwood scoring, was the worst game of my life.

'I remember saying to Gavin after that match, "You watch the public turn on us, especially me." That was probably the worst week of my life in terms of captaining the All Blacks. I expected it but maybe not to that same degree.'

There was an anti-Laurie Mains (the All Black coach) campaign to begin with, most of which was originating out of Auckland. Many New Zealanders thought the All Blacks would lose the third Test.

'I remember talking with [New Zealand prime minister of the time] Jim Bolger about it and he said, "Sean, when the All Blacks win I would love to be All Black captain, when the All Blacks lose I would much rather be the prime minister of New Zealand."

'That sums up the whole psyche of New Zealand: there are four million stakeholders in the All Blacks. We've got to win. When the cricketers or netballers come second, the nation is pretty happy. When we [the All Blacks] come second, it's a national disaster.'

The Lions' midweek team were thrashed 38–10 by Waikato between the second and third Tests. There have been suggestions that the midweek Lions had come off tour before the match. Whatever the case, they let themselves and their teammates down.

A wounded All Black is a dangerous creature. Even when the Lions led 10–0 early in the third Test – thanks to a penalty by Gavin and a converted Scott Gibbs try – there was confidence in the All Blacks.

'The whole time I never thought we would lose the game,' Sean says. 'I was totally confident that we had prepared well, the guys were focused and that we would win the deciding match.'

Tries by Frank Bunce and Sean, both converted by Grant Fox, gave the All Blacks a 14–10 lead at the interval. Still, after being behind so early in the match, the tide had clearly turned and it was all black.

Two penalties by Fox and one by Gavin kept things tight before half-back Jon Preston scored the decisive try to take New Zealand out of sight. Fox kicked another penalty to round out the scoring and make the final score 30–13 to the All Blacks. They had deserved their win.

As the game meandered to a conclusion, the reality sunk in for Gavin that the Lions were not going to win.

271

'It was so different to the first Test, when we were winning the game and we had it taken away right at the death. You kind of prepare yourself in the last ten minutes knowing that you're not going to win the match because the whole game has gone against you, apart from the first ten minutes.'

The All Blacks had prepared badly before the Wellington Test and taken their medicine. They had put that right before the third Test and come away with the victory. Sean says the victory shut up the critics for a time and helped him grow as a captain.

'To be honest, it wasn't a fun series. In the press conference after the third Test, I said it was probably the most boring series I had been involved with.

'They were very defensively orientated and negative in killing the ball and it wasn't a fun series to play in. Then when we toured England and Scotland later that year the media were into me from the word go.'

Gavin knew the All Blacks would come back after Wellington and that Auckland would be different.

'The British journalists were naive in thinking that we had the series in the bag after the second Test,' he recalls. 'I kept trying to tell the guys, "If you think the last two weeks have been tough, wait till Saturday." The All Blacks changed their gameplan and won.'

Despite the result, Gavin has fond memories of the tour. The Test teams were evenly matched and had the Lions believed in themselves in the first Test, the series result might have been different, he feels.

BACK WHEN WE WERE AT UNIVERSITY

It was appropriate that Gavin and Sean were opposing captains in 1993. Both were outstanding players and magnificent men. They had played together for Auckland University in 1987 and were friends off the field. Had it not been for rugby they probably would not have crossed paths.

Gavin went on captaining Scotland, retiring after the 1995 World Cup in South Africa. Having gone on two Lions tours, captained Scotland successfully, been a Cambridge blue and been without question one of the great all-round full-backs, he not surprisingly retired with few regrets.

Modern rugby doesn't excite Gavin. He enjoys the World Cup and still loves the concept of the Lions but: 'The average game doesn't hold me in awe or in expectancy,' he admits. 'That's because there has to be something won or lost. The World Cup has that, the Six Nations yes, but the average game of rugby doesn't do much for me.

'You know I can honestly say hand on heart that I was never paid to play rugby. I retired three months before the start of the professional game. I've got friends all over the world that I played rugby with and against and I know that I can go and stay with them whenever. I'm very proud of that.'

Gavin's priorities are now elsewhere. Four months after finishing with rugby he set up his own business. He's now happily married with two children and these days golf is his passion. Getting the balance right is, he says, the key to a successful and happy life.

'You know it [rugby] was a part of my life that finished a long time ago. It gave me an opportunity to travel the world, to meet some great people, to play a game that I was and am passionate about. It also allowed me the confidence to go and face new challenges and it made me realise that you have got to go out and make your way in the world.

'The bottom line is if people ask am I happy, well yes I am happy. I am content. I have a good life but I don't get complacent in any way. I'm still very, very driven towards achieving the goals that I set myself.'

As I mentioned, Sean went on to play and captain the All Blacks until late in 1997, when injury ended his career. In all, he played 92 Tests (an All Black record), was arguably the best hooker in the history of the game and set the benchmark for toughness. He also played almost two full seasons of professional rugby.

The friends Sean has now are the blokes that he played with in the amateur era. 'We lived with each other, the girls were friends, we were close and that showed. These days, the players see each other from nine to five at training and figure that's enough.

'When I was managing the [Auckland] Blues, I found it very difficult to get the families together. "Why do we want to have dinner together on Wednesday night? I would rather be home doing my own thing," they would say, which in our day wasn't the case.'

Sean accepts the changes that have taken place in rugby since 1993. He accepts that it has made the game a more attractive spectacle and that it's easy to criticise from the outside looking in. Still, he says, taking the All Blacks out of the NPC would be a huge mistake.

'We need All Blacks playing NPC more than All Blacks playing Super 12. I can't believe they are going to take the All Blacks out of the NPC. Basically the All Blacks aren't playing NPC now.

'I think it's ludicrous for a reserve player to come back from All Black duty having played no games, to have two weeks off. I think we've got to be careful not to take those players out of the environment that's going to help our next crop of players.'

A global season is inevitable, Sean tells me, for the good of the game in New Zealand.

'We need to be involved in a global season, playing up here [in Europe]. You watch the club football up here and the intensity of the forward play is miles ahead of what we do. You speak to any New Zealand player who plays up here and they will tell you that the intensity is harder up here.'

Sean should know. He's spent the last two years in Britain doing television, public speaking and commercial work. He's New Zealand's answer to Will Carling and he's made the most of being iconic.

Before moving to Britain, he assisted in setting up the Players' Association in New Zealand and managed the Blues and the New Zealand Colts. He tells me that this is the first year since his retirement he hasn't been contracted to the NZRFU.

Sean and his family will eventually return to New Zealand. He'll then have a better perspective of New Zealand life and what he would like to contribute in future. There's no question that Sean will become the Colin Meads of his generation.

After I've finished my questions, Sean, his wife Bronwyn and I talk about what's happening back home. They are nice people, the Fitzpatricks, and on an afternoon of movie stars and golfing celebrities, I'm enjoying being with fellow New Zealanders.

After a quiet drink, Sean organises for a car to drop me at the train station as I'm going back to Edinburgh tonight. It's been a tiring day and I feel very much out of my depth in the home of golf. I yearn for home. Still, it's not a day I'll forget in a hurry.

PART FIVE
Lions Build-Up

Sport has an extraordinary effect on otherwise sane people. Critical faculties are brushed aside for the glory of the moment and the winning of the contest. Partly it is nationalistic fervour, partly glimpses of beauty offered upon a field. Partly it is the recollection of lost youth, partly the primeval urge of man against man.

Peter Roebuck (cricket writer)

THE EXCLUSIVE CLUB?

Sunday, 21 November 2004

One evening when I was 12, I witnessed what it meant to be an All Black. Craig Green (who was a talented midfielder and left-winger in the 1980s) lived along the road from me in Lincoln. A relative of mine kindly organised to take me to meet him.

It was a Thursday night before the great 1983 Canterbury side was to take on Wellington in a Ranfurly Shield challenge. As well as being a rugby player, Green was studying at the local college.

So here we were, my relative and me, on the doorstep of Green's flat. He'd the game on Saturday to think about, college exams to sit in the next month and now a 12 year old to make small talk with.

Although he must have hated it, he invited us in and chatted to us about rugby. Ironically, Green had been tapped on the shoulder that very day about whether he was available for his first All Black end-of-year tour.

You might expect that with everything happening in Green's life it would have made him somewhat too preoccupied to talk with me. But, no, he was gracious, polite and deeply embarrassed to be receiving such full-on attention.

Looking back now, I learnt that day that being an All Black was about far more than what you did on the field. It was also a way of acting in public, a way of behaving with fans and recognising where you were from. It was a privilege and a responsibility.

Undoubtedly, this required behaviour was due to the fact that being an All Black was something rare and something few rugby players achieved. It was an exclusive club where traditions were paramount.

Professionalism was inevitably going to place pressure on those traditions. Money dictated that. In a small country like New Zealand, professionalism was going to have a dramatic impact on the exclusivity of the All Blacks.

Since 1997, the All Blacks have visited Europe five times (including the 1999 World Cup hosted in Wales). The northern hemisphere tour has become a staple of the All Blacks' season, much the same as it has been for the Australians and South Africans.

The major reason why the NZRFU has been flogging the All Black horse has nothing to do with on-field activities. The reason is in fact financial.

New Zealand, like all major rugby countries, has to provide a certain number of Test matches every year to the broadcaster. To get some of the major northern hemisphere teams to tour New Zealand it must undertake reciprocal tours, whether the All Blacks themselves like them or not.

Around half of the NZRFU's income comes from television revenue. The NZRFU is therefore in many respects at the whim of broadcasters.

So after playing in Super 12, the home internationals and some of the NPC, the All Blacks head off on another rugby odyssey that frankly they do not need or want.

The situation came to a head in 2002 when a number of All Blacks chose not to tour at the end of the year. The official line was that they wanted to refresh ahead of the World Cup in 2003.

The result was that a depleted All Black team toured Europe. Although they did surprisingly well (beating Wales, drawing with France and narrowly losing to England), could it be said that they were the real All Blacks?

It could be argued that even from a financial perspective selecting a weakened All Black team does not make good business sense. It weakens the brand and ultimately the rich heritage of the All Blacks.

A further result has been that because of the number of tours to the northern hemisphere, the All Black coaches have had to compensate by taking larger squads and have included some players with promise but little else.

The All Blacks are not the exclusive club that they once were. Being an All Black now does not necessarily mean that you are the best in your position.

Although this policy often paid dividends (in the 2002 squad for example were Tony Woodcock, Kevin Mealamu and Keith Robinson), it cheapened the jersey.

After the 2004 NPC had been concluded, the All Black selectors named a squad for the end-of-year Tests that included, for the most part, the best players in New Zealand. The one notable exclusion was Justin Marshall. It would have been perhaps his last tour to the northern hemisphere.

The reason for Justin's non-selection was apparently to give the other half-backs (in particular Byron Kelleher) a chance to stake their claim and to rest him. The decision would have been sound if Justin had been under-performing. The reality was that Justin had played outstandingly in the NPC. He did not deserve such shoddy treatment.

On the plus side of the tour selection was the return to the squad of Anton Oliver. The fairy tale had come true after he had had a commanding NPC with a disappointing Otago side.

I had the opportunity to follow the All Blacks on their end-of-year European jaunt in 2004. The thought of seeing the All Blacks play in Rome, Cardiff, Paris and London was deeply attractive.

Yet my desire was tempered by the fact that money, and not rugby, motivated the administrators that organised All Black tours to Europe these days. This was not touring, this was fly in, fly out sport.

Where were the great matches against Newport, Cardiff and the various French selections? Where was the opportunity for the All Blacks to meet the locals in their own communities and to promote the sport at the grass roots? No, this wasn't a tour, it was pay for play.

So I decided to go to Europe in October when the All Blacks and the provincial players were in the last throes of the NPC. As small as it was, I was making a statement of what I thought of what had happened to the All Blacks and their proud traditions.

Professionalism does not mean that you necessarily need to throw out amateur ideals. Tours can still take place. It only requires rugby's administrators to accept that you may have to take less from the sport's backers to get more in the long run.

THE BOY FROM SOUTHBRIDGE

November–December 2004

An 'experiment' on the end-of-year tour is the selection of Canterbury inside-back Daniel Carter as a first five-eight. Daniel has been an All Black since the start of the 2003 season, although has been played as a second five-eight in all 14 of his Tests.

Allowing Daniel to develop in the position meant leaving veterans Andrew Mehrtens and Carlos Spencer at home. The latter was injured and not considered, although the non-selection of Mehrtens signalled a clear changing of the guard.

Time, it has been said, waits for no man and this is Daniel's time. There's a lot to like about the way he plays: he's a magnificent runner, kicks superbly, is a fine defender and, perhaps most importantly, appears to have an even temperament.

The only criticism of his move to the number 10 has been that he's too quiet to run a back line. Wayne Smith figures that he will develop this skill and there is no question that if he does, he will be one of the most complete players in world rugby.

Daniel is named in the number 10 jersey for the Test against Italy in the first match of the tour. 'There was a bit of pressure, mainly because it was a year and a half since I played there,' he tells me at Rugby Park in Christchurch after the tour has finished. 'I was also excited about the challenge. That was where I played in the lead-up to my professional career and it was just a matter of shaking off the cobwebs and getting into my work. I was pleased with the way the match turned out.'

He scores a try and kicks seven conversions against the Italians. The trial in the Roman cauldron pays rich dividends. A better test for the boy from Southbridge was to come against the Welsh in Cardiff.

'It was an extremely tough game,' he says of New Zealand's 26–25 victory, 'and we were extremely pleased to come away with a result. It was a hard-fought battle and to come away with a win against a quality side like the Welsh was pleasing.'

That aside, the All Blacks play virtually a second-string side in the Welsh Test. It's difficult to imagine the All Blacks of yesteryear running out their second-stringers against the Welsh but that's the sad reality of professional rugby.

Regardless of how you look at it, playing a second-string All Black side in a Test against a top ten nation in the world is insulting to both the opposition and the history of All Black rugby. To say otherwise is to cheapen one of the traditional rivalries in rugby.

Apart from the win, the most pleasing thing from an All Black point of view is that for the first time Richard McCaw captains the All Blacks.

After the Test the players actually had a rare chance to dine together. 'It wasn't that long but we had a chat to the odd guy,'

Daniel says. 'They were good jokers and they were a bit like us in the sense that they play hard on the field and then they relax when the game's over.'

Two wins from two Tests, the All Blacks move on to Paris to tackle the French. It is the defining Test of the tour. The home side are erratic, the All Blacks are sublime and run out convincing 45–6 winners.

'Our overall performance was really satisfying [that day]. It had been a long year and we had been working on a lot of things. A lot of hard work had been put in by the team and on that day it paid off.'

The critics rightly label this as the All Blacks' best overall performance of the season. With Anton Oliver and Richard McCaw leading the way, the warning signals had been well and truly sent out to Clive Woodward and the future Lions.

The win in Paris is the end of Daniel's season. The All Blacks, on the other hand, have one match left: a tie against the Barbarians in London.

Perhaps unwittingly, the Barbarians have come to symbolise the corporate and individual greed that has become so common in international rugby.

While the All Blacks beat the club 47–19, there is no one from the home unions in the Barbarians' line-up at any stage during the match. The closest they get is an Italian, who comes on as a substitute.

With British players contracted to clubs and not national unions, the Barbarians are made up of Australians, South Africans, Fijians and New Zealanders in search of a quick pay-day.

Ridiculously, Justin Marshall and Xavier Rush, who earlier that season played for the All Blacks, have flown to London to play for the Barbarians against the All Blacks! Justin's situation is made the more absurd by the fact he's been told to rest by the All Black selectors.

There is also controversy over the gate-take in this match. The NZRFU are given a cut of the gate-take and all proceeds from selling the television rights in New Zealand. This is contrary to the traditional stance taken by the northern hemisphere unions in IRB-sanctioned games.

The Barbarians didn't need to become the joke they have become. The fact that there are no British players in the British Barbarians makes a mockery of the proud 113-year institution and should, at the very least, lead to urgent reform by the club itself. Rugby and its traditions deserve better.

While the All Blacks were playing the Barbarians, Clive Woodward was using state-of-the-art technology called ProZone to track them individually on the field.

The high-tech system enabled Clive to look at how each All Black played – including examining a vapour-like trail showing where the player ran, how far and how fast.

The All Blacks suspected the system was installed at the Stade de France in Paris and was used to dissect their win against the French. Anything, it appeared, to give Clive an extra edge.

Daniel, on the other hand, is thinking of summer and the off-season. He is, it could be said, a blend of the best of amateur and professional. He grew up playing all sports in the tiny village of Southbridge, about an hour outside Christchurch.

'I started playing sport because I enjoyed it and that's why I still play now. If I stopped enjoying playing, I would give up. That's what it's all about: having fun, getting out there with your mates and throwing the ball around.'

I remember reporting on Daniel as a kid, although as a promising cricketer and not as a rugby player. If he had applied his talents there, he could have played for his country in that sport as well.

'I wouldn't go that far,' Daniel laughs. 'I played for the first XI at school and a little bit of representative stuff as well but I had to put that aside when I made the Crusaders and things like that.'

He doesn't regret putting cricket – or other activities – to one side. 'I'm living a dream right now and although I've had to make sacrifices, at the end of the day it's worth it because I'm doing what I love. I still get the odd chance to chuck the pads back on.'

Although he attended his local high school, Ellesmere College, for the bulk of his high school years, rugby opportunities saw him come into the city and play for the first XV at Christchurch Boys' High School.

Following in the traditions of Andrew Mehrtens and Aaron Mauger, Daniel wore his school's number 10 with pride. When he was at Boys' High, there was a promotional video made at the school. The instructors were Mehrtens and Justin Marshall. One of the boys being instructed was one Daniel Carter.

Like Mehrtens, Daniel shone more after he left school. He made the New Zealand Colts easily enough, while his progress throughout 2003 and 2004 stamped him as one of the best inside-backs in the world. He had that feature possessed by only the best – plenty of time.

While he was excelling on the field, off the field he was becoming one of the new faces of New Zealand rugby. Like Richard McCaw, he was loved by women of all ages, and as a result, he was doing immense good for the game's marketability.

'[Being public property] can be quite challenging at first but it is something that grows on you and you get used to it as you spend more time playing professional rugby.

'They [the media and sponsors] are obligations that you have to accept and they help out in their different ways and they are all part of it. I don't see it as a hassle or a pressure.'

With Daniel, however, the hero-worship has been taken to the extreme, helped no end by the fact that he's now the kicker and pivot.

'It can be quite weird at times. It certainly was when I started getting recognised on the street and people were asking for autographs and saying hello. It has grown on me and I've got used to it. It's not a big deal: you just say "G'day" and keep a smile on your face. It doesn't take a lot of time.'

With Richard McCaw, Carl Hayman and Chris Jack, Daniel has become one of the most valuable All Blacks in their quest to beat the Lions. I ask Daniel about the Lions, fully realising that his generation would not recall too much.

'I remember them coming here in 1993, when we beat them 2–1 in the series. It doesn't come around much, maybe once in your career, and to be a part of it would be very special.'

With Jonny Wilkinson likely to tour, the pressure is mounting on Daniel. That battle in many respects could be series defining.

'I know the pressure and expectation of the public is building up. But if you let that get to you then you're not going to perform and you're going to lose your focus.

'I would be joking, though, if I said that I don't feel it at all but I have to push that aside and concentrate on what I'm doing at the moment and not look too far ahead.'

The commentators were already talking about the Carter versus Wilkinson battle, irrespective of the forward packs in front of them. Daniel tells me he hasn't been following the 'Wilkinson saga' too much.

'If he's not here, they have quality five-eights to fill his shoes. [In saying that] he's a world-class player. He's been unlucky with injuries lately but personally I would like to see him here. You always like to compete against the best and he is and so we will just have to wait and see.'

Daniel and Jonny have met. They got on well. The battle would not be personal. Daniel hopes they could become friends later in life. The contest would end when they left the field, regardless of who won.

Rugby players at the elite level tend to live in the here and now. Despite the building hype in New Zealand, the Lions are not on the immediate agenda for Daniel and his mates. When he does think ahead, he thinks of what he needs to do to become a great All Black.

'Most guys are motivated by the end result. They strive to be an All Black or a Crusader. You could say I've done all that. I'm not just happy with that. Now that I'm an All Black, I want to be a great All Black.

'To do that I've got to spend time in the jersey and that means being the best at your game for a number of years. Hopefully if I can do the small things right I can hold on to the jersey for years to come.'

Whether he does that, Daniel has already proven himself to be potentially one of New Zealand's finest backs ever. Marketing and hype are for promoters. True talent passes the test of time and I get the feeling that time will measure favourably Daniel's immense talent.

MAKING THE GRADE

February–March 2005

Clive Woodward made it clear that Six Nations form would be the indicator as to who would be a 2005 Lion. His line was that he would have to have good reason to go outside those that made themselves available for their countries.

'I don't think you can ever say never but I would have to have a compelling reason to pick any player who is not available to international rugby,' Clive said. 'The key thing that I want to stress is that I intend to use the Six Nations and the players who are available to international rugby as the key benchmark.'

The Six Nations (or its predecessor the Five Nations) has traditionally provided Lions selectors with the most obvious indicator as to who can cut it on a Lions tour.

Often, however, Six Nations form painted a flattering picture. Playing in front of a partisan crowd with your fellow countrymen is a good deal different from playing for the Lions in New Zealand, South Africa or Australia.

The challenges of touring with the Lions are unique. Some players thrive on it, others find it more difficult. Merely picking players on what they did when representing their countries was short-sighted. As a result, selection was often hit and miss.

Yet in the professional age, Lions selectors have been less swayed by what the individual has done for their country. They see the bigger picture and choose players who they think can cope with the pressures of touring and the physical and tactical challenges ahead.

In 1997, for example, the Lions selectors made a number of bold selections based on the correct formula. As a result, a number of returning league converts such as Alan Tait, John Bentley, Allan Bateman, Scott Gibbs and Scott Quinnell made huge contributions to the Lions series victory on and off the field.

In 2001, the Lions selectors did not show the same vision. Their selections were conservative, uninspired and perhaps too Welsh-based. As a result, the mix was wrong and players such as Gregor Townsend and (initially) Scott Gibbs were left at home.

It has also been said that Lions squad selections are political affairs and trade-offs based on rugby opportunism. In 1993, for example, it was alleged English prop Jeff Probyn was not selected for the Lions because there were 17 Englishmen in the squad already.

The Lions selectors also had to overcome the national stereotypes that often marked selection. The Welsh, for example, were regarded by some as being poor travellers who got homesick and tendered to hang around together. These stereotypes often prevented the strongest Lions squad from being chosen.

Clive Woodward was at pains to point out that half the battle for him was in the selection. Get that right, he figured, and he was halfway to achieving his goal of a series win in New Zealand.

In an attempt to get to know the players from Wales, Scotland and Ireland, Clive spent time with each nation (along with the Italians) in the autumn Tests.

Although he was working on his gameplan to beat the All Blacks, he was also developing relationships that he hoped would pay dividends the following year. In many respects, Clive was transforming himself from England coach to coach of the Lions.

Working out a gameplan to beat the All Blacks is one thing, finding the right players to do it is another. The answers would be clearer to Clive and the general rugby public after the 2005 Six Nations.

My focus during this Six Nations was on the individuals I was following. I knew that Simon Taylor, Brian O'Driscoll, Martyn Williams and Lawrence Dallaglio all had reasonable chances of making the Lions tour of New Zealand.

When I'd spoken to them in the northern autumn of 2004, they had all talked passionately about the Six Nations. It was a huge test for a northern rugby player and the prize at the end of it for the successful was a trip to New Zealand in the northern summer.

Lawrence Dallaglio was in perhaps the most interesting position. When we spoke, he had already announced his retirement from England duties. His focus, he said, would now be on Wasps.

Just where this put Lawrence as regards the Lions was still anyone's guess. I suspected that Clive would struggle to leave such an experienced campaigner at home. At the very worst, Lawrence would be a fine captain of the midweek side.

In the months after we spoke, Lawrence made mutterings in the media that if chosen he would be a worthy selection. 'Put it this way, I wouldn't let anyone down, I can assure you of that. I know what it takes and I know what I have to offer,' he said.

He also commented that he would be fresher than the internationals. 'Well, I'll be in good shape and fresh without another ten Tests on the clock, won't I?'

Lawrence was, however, realistic enough to know that his fate was not in his own hands and that he would have to rely on his past achievements to gain selection.

So while the England side struggled to gain any consistency in the Six Nations, Lawrence watched on from his west London home, knowing that he had a decent chance of being on the plane to New Zealand.

Meanwhile, Scotland's Simon Taylor was on the comeback from injury. In late 2004, Clive Woodward had publicly stated his admiration for the loose forward and more or less guaranteed him a spot in the squad if he was fit.

After missing the early rounds of the Six Nations, Simon made his first Celtic League appearance for Edinburgh in a year on 19 February 2005.

He scored a try and put in a sound performance in Edinburgh's 41–33 win over Leinster. Simon was back. Given Scotland's woeful season, Simon was not surprisingly rushed back into the Scottish squad for the Italian match. Selection for the Lions was a formality.

'Guys that I've had to worry about in the past are now going to be my teammates,' he said after his selection, 'which is going to be a different feeling. It will be nice not to be on the receiving end of what they can do.'

While Simon's season had been dominated by injury, Brian O'Driscoll continued on his merry way. If he wasn't the best player in the world, he was up there with the best.

Before the Six Nations, he'd reiterated the line that there was nothing to stop the Irish from winning their first Grand Slam since 1948. There was no pressure, he claimed, despite the fact that the bands were drumming for Brian to be made Lions captain.

When we spoke in October, the Irish captain was a contender for the job, although he was one of many. As the Six Nations wore on, he quickly became the hot favourite as England especially struggled to make any traction.

The Irish had a bizarre Six Nations: wins in the first three rounds (including against England) before losses to France in Dublin and Wales in Cardiff signalled the end of a disappointing campaign.

It wasn't so much that the Irish did not live up to expectations, it was more that their pack failed to dominate for the full 80 minutes in any international. They had peaked the season before.

Brian was his normal magnificent self in the midfield, although he'd injured himself against the Italians in the first round and had missed the Scottish international as a result. His try against England was typical O'Driscoll and was reflective of his truly amazing career.

At the end of the Six Nations, I was convinced that Brian would captain the Lions to New Zealand. His only serious contender appeared to be another Irishman, lock Paul O'Connell.

Brian, though, was a certainty for the Test team, had been on a Lions tour before, was universally liked in New Zealand and had the advantage of not being an Englishman in an English-coached and English-managed side.

When I'd spoken with Martyn Williams in a cold dingy corridor in October, I wasn't confident that he would be on the plane to New Zealand. My thinking was sound: he hadn't been a huge success in Australia with the Lions in 2001 and there was no guarantee that he would even be in the Welsh side.

Yet Martyn belittled my lack of faith by starring in the Six Nations and was rightly named RBS Player of the Championship.

The Welsh were at 40/1 odds to win the Championship but defied everyone by upsetting England in the first round, France in the third round in Paris and then Ireland 32–20 in Cardiff in the finale.

For the first time in 28 years, the Welsh were the undisputed champions of Europe and Martyn was the star. Like every other rugby fan in the world, I was amazed by what had occurred.

Martyn had excelled and, it appeared to me, booked his ticket on a second Lions tour. He'd won his award after 23,000 fans had voted during the final week of the Six Nations. He'd polled 7,796 votes, over 5,000 more than the second-placed Brian O'Driscoll.

'It's a great honour to be named Player of the Championship, especially as this is voted for by rugby fans,' Martyn said. 'This award caps a tremendous Six Nations for Wales, and is as much a vote for my teammates as for me. When I got this award, I thought what about Gethin Jenkins, Shane Williams and Stephen Jones among others? They are all deserving winners of this award, and that's testament to the Wales side as a whole.'

Wales's win put the All Blacks' one-point win in late 2004 in perspective. I wondered what Graham Henry and Steve Hansen were thinking when they watched Wales win the title in Cardiff on 19 March.

The question was now how many Welsh lads would be on the plane to New Zealand? In a squad of 44, they could expect plenty.

While the Six Nations was coming to an end and attention moved to who would be in the Lions squad to tour, Craig Dowd was deciding his future.

As he'd hinted in October, Craig announced that he was going to hang up his boots at the end of the season. He was going to be part of a new coaching staff at Wasps headed by Ian McGeechan. Warren Gatland was on his way back to New Zealand to coach the Waikato NPC side.

Professional rugby was consistently changing but I am sure if you asked any Welshman on 19 March 2005, they would have told you that on that day they wished that time would stand still.

FINDING JACKO

Friday, 1 April 2005

The yearly ritual that is Super 12 has rolled around again like tooth plaque and yet my mind is on the Lions. I'm feeling the cold today but my heart is warmed by the realisation that this is Lions year.

I'm not alone, as there is a hush throughout New Zealand rugby whenever you mention them, sort of like a nation must feel when they are about to be invaded by a foreign enemy (which is probably not far from the truth).

As in any All Black team, there will be key individuals in the 2005 side. In the 1960s, it was Colin Meads, Ken Gray, Wilson Whinerary, Kel Tremain and, later, Brian Lochore.

In the 2005 All Blacks, I'm guessing that it will be Richard McCaw, Tana Umaga, Carl Hayman, Daniel Carter and a lanky lad from the Shirley club in Christchurch called Chris Jack.

You wouldn't think it, though, as we chat in the stand at Rugby Park in Christchurch. Chris is down-to-earth, friendly and, unlike so many other rugby players, talks with me rather than providing me with clichés.

Right now, though, he's the only lock New Zealand's got who is international class who is not injured or suspended. As a result, his value to the All Blacks cannot be overestimated. He, however, plays down his importance.

'New Zealand rugby is full of superstars being injured and someone coming through. It's always going to be like that. If I weren't in there, someone else would take the spot and probably do it just as good.

'There's a couple of other guys who are probably a whole lot higher [rated] than me, one of whom they are probably pretty worried about at the moment.'

He's talking about Richard McCaw, who has suffered another concussion, this time against the Bulls in South Africa a few weeks previously.

Chris had developed into a fine All Black. Yet while others had stolen the limelight, he'd gone about his business with little public profile. I wondered whether he was better off as a person as a result of this.

The previous Saturday, I'd seen Chris at a club match in Christchurch. Here was this lanky fellow standing with the builders, the freezing workers, the car salesmen and the accountants watching his club play.

The thing was that he looked far from uncomfortable.

He chatted to the spectators, winced like the rest of us when there was a big hit, enjoyed the innocence of the occasion and yet (unlike me) did not scoff down two sausages in bread (at NZ$2 for two, very reasonable).

'It's completely different,' he tells me when I ask him about comparisons between the club game on Saturday and the professional game he plays. 'It's a different mindset. It's almost apples and oranges. We train every day, we try and perfect what we do, we expect our skill level to be a lot higher, there's so many things that we have expectations on, especially how we want to play the game.'

Chris is four games away from earning his club blazer (fifty games) and he's determined to get there. 'It's been a bit frustrating not making it but I love going down and watching the guys and trying to help out when I can.

'I do find club rugby frustrating but then again I love my club. They don't see me too often but they are my mates from school and if I could spend some more time with them I would.'

Chris appears undeniably shy, yet not in an introverted, individualistic sort of way. Reserved, maybe. Going out in public must be a nightmare when you are an All Black and 6 ft 7 in. to boot.

'There's a lot of things that you have got to learn to deal with [as an All Black]. It's taken me a long time to learn how to handle people recognising me and things like that but if I didn't enjoy it [the rugby], I wouldn't do it.'

Another one of the few negatives of professional rugby, Chris tells me, is deciding what to do after the merry-go-round ends. I'd read somewhere that Chris wants to be a primary school teacher. I've only met him once but I know that he'd be really good at it.

A realist would suggest that he has years before that happens. As I glance across Rugby Park and spy on the promising young players going about their drills, I know that we are both thinking about the Lions.

As mentioned, professional rugby players live in the moment. They think about this week's game and not the game two months away. Yet we are both thinking about the Lions tour and the contest ahead.

'I went to a Lions game at Lancaster Park [as it was called then] in 1993 and all I can remember is watching them run out and seeing Dean Richards with his socks pulled down and his dirty boots and my dad commenting that I should never do that!

'I understood what it was about and how important it was but as a kid I can't really remember too much. I must have been 12 – I had other things to think about! My uncles played against them for Southland on an earlier tour.

'Because they [the Lions] haven't been here for so long, New Zealand has forgotten how important the series is. It's us against our heritage, I guess, for a lot of people here. We've got our own culture here now and we want to stand up and say, "Yeah, this is us."'

Chris has spoken with the Australians about the intensity involved in playing the Lions. He knows what the challenge will be like, along with the intensity that will be required to beat them.

'There is only one option for us,' he says quietly, thoughtfully. 'As All Blacks, we really want to stamp our mark on the series, [as much] for the coaches that we have at the moment.'

The pressure is certainly mounting. Not only does every second interview he does now have a Lions element to it but, like me, Chris can also sense the excitement in the rugby community.

'You're hearing about it, you're hearing about the tickets . . . I don't know about the pressure of it, it's more excitement, really.'

'You're not thinking about Danny Grewcock or Paul O'Connell then?' I ask.

'Not really, mate . . . I rate O'Connell highly, though. I've played against him once and found him difficult to combat.'

Chris is at the stage of his career when he could move from being a good All Black to a great one. The tradition is that when you first wear the black jersey, your goal is to be a good All Black and then a great All Black. He is without question world class right now.

'As a player you just try and reach your potential and hopefully make the team. People have likened me to a lot of ex-All Blacks but at the moment I'm just doing the best I can and if that's good enough to play for the All Blacks, then I'm happy.'

I get the feeling that the Lions tour will be the stage where Chris steps up and takes his place alongside Meads, White, Whiting and

Haden. As we finish talking, I can't help thinking that there are a lot of old-fashioned values in Chris Jack. As a result, there is a lot to like about him.

CHOOSING THE LIONS

April 2005

In mid-April 2005, as Bill Beaumont announces the 44-man squad to tour New Zealand, I'm struggling to sleep in Christchurch. I have to work the next day but the lure of going online and finding out the lucky names is almost too much to resist. While the players selected are being informed of the good news, I'm going over in my own mind who will make it.

So as I toss and turn debating whether I should get up, I cannot stop thinking about how previous Lions were informed. I'm particularly thinking about how Jack Kyle's father found out about his son's selection from the *Belfast Telegraph* in 1950.

Where in the past those selected used to hear their selection on the news or from excited family and friends, these days the players get text messages. I wonder what's wrong with the simple courtesy of a phone call?

I resist getting up. I know that if I do I will spend the next two hours lamenting who didn't make it and who's a likely contender for the Test squad. I've rarely been so excited about the selection of any side.

When I do wake, groggy and tired, I dress quickly and check the news to see who's in. Brian O'Driscoll has been named as captain and the squad contains 20 Englishmen, 11 Welshmen, 10 Irishmen and 3 Scots.

They don't have enough space in the news to name the 44 players but they do point out that Jonny Wilkinson has not been named but that Clive Woodward is keeping the door open for him.

'I spoke to Jonny last Friday and he supports what we are doing here,' Clive says. 'It would be wrong of me to pick a player who clearly hasn't played or got through 80 minutes of rugby for a long, long time.'

Confirming the need for stars in sports, Wilkinson's omission for now is the story and will be the story in the weeks ahead. No disrespect to Wilkinson but my mind is on the players whom I've been following.

I quickly log onto the Internet and find that Lawrence, Simon, Brian and Martyn have all made the squad. I'm ecstatic for them all and for more than a moment I reflect on last October when we spoke and the hopes and aspirations that they had shared with me.

When I'd heard that there were only three Scotsmen in the squad, I'd feared for Simon's chances. After all, there were a number of contenders from Scotland. Yet Simon had thankfully made it.

Brian's selection as captain was expected. He says all the right things about what an honour it is and how the Lions have a great chance to win in New Zealand. For one of rugby's superstars, he looks surprisingly overwhelmed by the amount of attention. Even as Irish captain, he hasn't had to deal with this level of interest before.

I think back to that cheeky grin that he'd given me last October when I'd put it to him that he'd be a grand choice as captain. Thinking back, you could see that his ambition this season has been to be named captain of the Lions to New Zealand.

The facial hair had gone and there was no dyed hair now. His individuality had been replaced with conformity. It saddens me that any individual has to change his ways to reach his goals but that's life I guess and for Brian at least, the policy had paid dividends.

After his outstanding Six Nations, Martyn's selection for the Lions was almost guaranteed. I think back to that wet night in Limerick when we'd spoken in the corridors of Thomond Park. His wet shivering figure had not inspired any great hope in me that he would make it to New Zealand with the Lions. He is a success and I admire him for it.

As I'd thought, Clive couldn't leave Lawrence at home to bask in Chelsea's success in the Premiership. Regardless of whether he made the Test team, he would be a vital cog in the 2005 Lions. Looking back now, there never seemed any doubt that Lawrence would be in New Zealand. His motivation to avenge England's 2004 defeats would be profound.

The squad itself looks well selected and comprehensive. The Blackrock club in Ireland has two representatives named (Brian and hooker Shane Byrne), while as expected Ulster is not represented.

London Wasps in England has Lawrence, veteran half-back Matt Dawson and wing/full-back Josh Lewsey in the squad (Simon Shaw is named as a replacement later). Simon is Edinburgh's only representative, while Cardiff has prop Gethin Jenkins, Martyn, and centre Tom Shanklin named.

Although there are unlucky players – Scots Tom Smith, Jon White and Chris Paterson, Irishman Johnny O'Connor, Englishmen Mark Cuerto and Welshman Mefin Davies the most obvious – it is difficult to argue with the selection given the amount of information available to the selectors.

It is obvious that these are the modern Lions. Proof of this is the fact that Clive has left the door open for Wilkinson, prop Phil Vickery and centre Mike Tindall. All three would have been in the original squad and still have an opportunity to make it if they are able to prove their fitness.

Wilkinson's story is not surprisingly the most followed. It amazes me that any back receives more attention than any forward. After all, without the ball the backs are like captured chess pieces. Also, forwards win series, not backs and I figure that will be the case in New Zealand in 2005.

'All I can do is to get fit and say, "Look, I feel I'm able to play this weekend, what do you want me to do?"' Wilkinson told the media. 'My priority is to get back fit and play for whoever asks me to play.'

Most rugby fans – including Graham Henry – expect Wilkinson to be in New Zealand with the Lions. If he gets through a few games for his club side Newcastle, he will be on the plane.

I suspect that Wilkinson's presence in New Zealand will be as important psychologically for the Lions as it is in a playing sense. A Lions squad with Wilkinson has a firmer look about it, regardless of his lack of recent match play.

As the tour looms, it is still not certain just how many Lions will be in New Zealand. Although I hate comparing this trip with previous Lions tours, the contrast is inevitable. As Clive had told me in October, he will be throwing the kitchen sink at the challenge of beating the All Blacks in New Zealand.

THE COMMERCE OF
THE LIONS TOUR

I'm interested in rugby and people more than commerce and finance. Yet there is no denying that the 2005 Lions tour of New Zealand will be a huge commercial event that has massive ramifications for New Zealand and the sport of rugby in general.

The New Zealand public first became aware of the size of the event they would be hosting when it was announced that they would not necessarily be able to purchase tickets to see the Lions matches.

The NZRFU decided that the fairest way to determine who got to attend Lions matches was to have a ballot. Those who entered the ballot and were successful would have the opportunity to purchase tickets.

Although the ballot had inherent flaws (such as the possibility of on-selling tickets for an inflated price) the ballot was a sound way of ensuring equality.

Registration for the ballot closed the day before Christmas in 2004. Around 100,000 people registered for the 150,000 tickets available. The Tests were naturally over-subscribed with fans having virtually a one-in-three chance of success.

Fans were required to list in preferential order which Tests and provincial games they wanted to buy tickets for. The Tests and the Auckland, Wellington and New Zealand Maori matches were the most popular.

I went into the ballot. I filled in my details on the Internet and listed the games (including the three Tests and the Otago, Southland and Auckland matches) that I wanted to attend.

There were other ways to attend the games – including hospitality packages and season passes – although the ballot was going to be the cheapest method if you were successful.

When the ballot was drawn, I waited by the phone like a child at Christmas time in nauseating expectation. Would I be successful and get to share my home ground with thousands of Lions supporters?

Like a jilted lover, I wait but the call never comes. While the media were quick to find some of those who had been successful, I cry into my Steinlarger at the thought that I won't be there.

Then one afternoon (just after lunch) the call comes. 'Is that Mr Nicholls? This is the New Zealand Rugby Football Union calling . . . '

Yes! I have made the ballot! I think.

'We would like to invite you to purchase Lions tickets for their match against Otago . . . '

'Otago?' I ask. You could sense the disappointment in my voice. I feel like the kid who wants a bike for his birthday and ends up getting clothes.

'Yes, Otago in Dunedin on June 18,' the female voice down the end of the line says. She must have been used to such disappointment.

So I purchase the tickets, despite Dunedin being a good five-hour drive away. If I don't want to head south, I will find someone who wants them.

With no Test tickets, I consider my options. I decide to go down the Lions Hospitality avenue. Before I ring the company, I stop and think back to a photo that I'd seen of fans lining up at Eden Park in Auckland before the fourth Test of the 1959 series. How times have changed. I shake my head and try to stay positive.

So I make the call. Karen is on the other end. She tells me there is a range of options. At the lower end, there is the Pub 'n' Pint option, which costs NZ$330 (plus Goods and Services Tax) and at the top end there's the Platinum option which costs NZ$1,150 (plus GST). Lions Hospitality 2005 will apparently host up to 50,000 people during the 11-match tour.

I ask what the Pub 'n' Pint option gives me and Karen informs me that it gives me corporate hospitality in a pub in Christchurch before the match and, most importantly, a ticket in the less than glamorous DB Stand.

I eventually decide to purchase some corporate hospitality and rest in the knowledge that at the very least I will be going to the first Test in Christchurch. So I send up my credit card details and proof of nationality (the tickets are only for New Zealanders).

Ironically, by May not all the tickets for the games have been sold. Consequently, 46,000 tickets go on sale on 3 May. The tickets are sold at about 13 a minute on the day, although they go more slowly for the Otago, Southland and Taranaki matches.

It is estimated that there will be between 15,000 and 25,000 Lions supporters coming to New Zealand, not all of whom will have tickets for the matches. The reality is, however, that New Zealand's stadiums will be packed with visiting supporters.

Reports suggest that about 9,000 Lions supporters have paid an average of £5,000 for organised package tours to New Zealand.

Nine venues for the traditional post-match 'beer and analysis' have been organised throughout New Zealand, while the Barmy Army have commissioned a 12-metre touring HQ, equipped with a stage called the Big Red Box.

Freddie Parker, the Barmy Army's optimistic project manager, says that there will be a host of activities throughout the tour, including several world record attempts.

'We're the most passionate fans in the world,' Parker believes. 'We think we have to get behind our teams to help them win. I just can't see the Kiwis challenging us. As a nation, we're the world champions in support.'

The Barmy Army have already got their songs together and Parker is confident that the Lions will at least win the singing, if not the rugby.

I have a sneaking suspicion that the Lions will feel on occasions like they are playing at home, such is the support they are going to receive. I lament the fact that a tour of New Zealand has become more like an internal tour in a New Zealand setting.

'Everybody seems to want to know numbers. Look what happened in Australia for the last Lions tour – 30,000 turned up for the last five games. Why would it be any different here?' Parker asks.

Both Clive Woodward and Graham Henry have recognised the importance of support at the grounds. Graham has said that any New Zealander who sells their ticket to a Lions supporter is certainly not helping the All Blacks' cause.

'This is the biggest sporting event in the whole of British sport this year and it's going to be massive in terms of what's coming down,' Clive said in January in New Zealand during a fact-finding mission.

Still, the tour will be a financial windfall for New Zealand. It is estimated that Lions supporters will eat a million meals, play more than 20,000 rounds of charity golf in the different venues and spend up to NZ$150 million during the six-week tour.

Estimates are that they'll travel in 1,150 campervans, one cruise ship and the equivalent of 58 extra domestic jet flights. Several Cook Strait ferry freight sailings (between the North and South Islands) have been devoted to clearing the expected backlog of rental vans.

Meanwhile, there will be 20,000 Tourism New Zealand postcards given out, half a million beers served at Lions Hospitality functions and one million promotional cardboard cups on Air New Zealand flights during the tour.

In Christchurch, they are talking about erecting tent villages in some of the local parks to house Lions supporters. Sports marketing teams from the Christchurch City Council are meanwhile working on events to create an exciting atmosphere around the tour.

Local rugby clubs are arranging special events that will be on offer to Lions supporters, such as hosting hangis, Golden Oldies tournaments and farm visits.

Pubs and clubs in the host cities and towns are already preparing themselves.

'We've secured our supplies and we won't be the pub with no beer. An ounce of planning is worth a pound of results,' Steve Holmes, general manager for The Tap Room and The Holy Grail pubs in Christchurch, said. 'We see this as a huge event, probably something that New Zealand and Christchurch has never seen before. It's going to be bigger than *Ben-Hur*.'

The brothels are also gearing up. Monique, from Christchurch's Capri Gentlemen's Club, says there will definitely be a special rugby-themed evening during the Test match week. 'With all the overseas boys and the local guys, it will be a big one.'

In Auckland, the planning is even more intense. Lion Breweries is working with the Barmy Army to set up nine regional outposts and a main Auckland headquarters for the tour, mostly for supporters who will turn up without game tickets.

A village with five bars and room for 4,000 patrons is being negotiated including, would you believe, a 'choir practice' area. Amazingly, some 75,000 copies of 'Barmy Army Harmonies' will be distributed to supporters throughout the country.

Giant-screen alcohol-free viewing areas are being planned in the Test venues, while Air New Zealand is laying on seven extra flights to leave the capital after the second Test on 2 July, taking fans back to hotels in Christchurch, Auckland and Blenheim.

The last plane is scheduled to leave at 11.30 p.m. but Wellington Airport has been granted a one-hour extension to its usual midnight curfew to allow for the game going into extra time.

It's arguably the biggest sporting event that New Zealand has ever hosted, even eclipsing the America's Cup yachting. As Graham Henry pointed out a few months earlier, this is a test of whether New Zealand can host a major sporting event.

I wonder whether the country has the infrastructure and facilities to cope. I also wonder whether the nation has the ability to embrace the concept that, rightly or wrongly, the Lions series is more than just about a rugby tour.

To be honest, the whole thing scares me. I'm not sure whether it's the thought of the All Blacks losing, the sheer scale of the Lions and their supporters, or the comparisons that I'm bound to make with previous Lions tours. Whatever I'm afraid of, I'm looking forward to the rugby but not necessarily the event.

As Craig Dowd told me back in October in London, rugby players are just blokes from different places that pull on their boots each Saturday. If we keep remembering that during this tour, we'll be OK. If we get lost in the periphery, then the grand traditions of the previous tours will be lost for ever. Let the rugby begin.

PART SIX

The Tour to End All Tours

This is the beauty of the game: a bunch of players, sticking together, knowing, deep down, what they are capable of.

John Ryan, *Daily Telegraph*

THE AGE-OLD NOTION
OF THE TOUR

Friday, 27 May 2005

A rugby tour, someone once wrote, is an adventure into the unknown for tourist and host alike.

In many respects, that's how the New Zealand rugby public and the 2005 Lions are feeling when the tourists touch down in Auckland from Sydney.

The welcome is not quite as large or as grand as on many earlier tours, although it is enthusiastic nonetheless.

Around 100 supporters are waiting at Auckland Airport, their enthusiasm whipped into life by the Lions' very own TV crew.

'Lions, Lions, Lions,' they yell lustily when the 75-strong party arrives at Gate 10, jet-lagged but happy to be, at last, in New Zealand.

There is no six-week boat trip across the world for these Lions: they have flown business class with British Airways to Sydney and then picked up their own private jet to transport them to and around New Zealand over the next six weeks.

As the players and the management file through an arch of black and red balloons, journalists, security, police and airport staff watch curiously.

Led by Clive Woodward and tour captain Brian O'Driscoll, the Lions look all smiles. Their expectation is plausible – the tour has begun and all the planning can now, at last, be put into action.

Naturally it is Jonny Wilkinson whom the crowd wants to see the most. The rumour is that the Lions management had had to book his reputation a seat of its own, such was his status in the game.

Wilkinson had started for the 2005 Lions in their scratchy 25–25 draw with Argentina in Cardiff first up. He looked slightly rusty still, although his magic touch (and his quality goal kicking) was still there.

On their arrival, the Lions exude confidence. From the way they walk through the terminal, to the looks of quiet determination on their faces, this tour is clearly business and they appear ready for the challenge.

Such a view is reinforced at the first press conference of the tour at the ultra-plush Hilton Hotel in Auckland, where the party is based.

'We come here with enormous respect for New Zealand, New Zealand rugby, New Zealand players and all the New Zealand coaching staff but we have no fear of them,' Clive Woodward states.

His view is reinforced by Brian O'Driscoll: 'We will respect all of our opponents but we will not fear them. We realise if we train well, prepare well and play well, we can win.'

It is obvious that the answers have been prepared with thorough precision. There is no spontaneity, no sense of realness or sincerity. Naturally, the media lap it all up and fuel the fire by reporting it.

Clive has other lines, some of which he has been espousing for weeks: 'I make no apology for saying this is the best prepared Lions tour in history and this squad have the making of a great Lions Test side. But nobody is underestimating the scale of the challenge ahead.'

Already, Clive is setting the tone for the tour: controlling as much as he can, getting his message across, while putting out positive vibes to all.

Things are a good deal more relaxed in Rotorua, although no less passionate, ahead of the Lions' first match of the tour next weekend.

A day before the Lions' official welcome to Rotorua, flags and banners are flying on lamp-posts and power poles, while there is a growing sense of expectation about the visit.

A host of events are being planned for the weekend of the game, including a Lions breakfast, a Lions pool party, an 'Undie 500' street race, rugby matches between Lions fans and locals and markets selling local arts and crafts.

The excitement is not unique to Rotorua: the New Zealand rugby fraternity is looking forward to this tour with an eagerness that is almost unprecedented in modern New Zealand sport.

The New Zealand rugby community you see has not hosted a major rugby tour since 1994, when the Springboks visited, and the absence has been noted.

Professional rugby and the demands of broadcasters had largely focused on Tests and not traditional tours that used to be such a feature of the rugby calendar.

The Lions on this tour will not visit the majority of the provinces like they used to, although they will still visit some provinces, the importance of which cannot be underestimated.

As Clive Woodward had told me back in October, the size of the touring party meant that his players could do the civic duties and could mix and mingle with the local communities.

The Lions tour, with the mass expectation and the legions of supporters heading south, is the closest thing New Zealand rugby fans have to reclaiming the great old days of New Zealand rugby.

You see, this is a nation that lost the co-hosting rights to the 2003 World Cup. This is a nation that has not won the World Cup since 1987. This is a nation that sees rugby as an extension of its national identity.

The excitement is plausible, helped no end by the months of expectation, build-up and all the hoopla over the commercial considerations concerned with perhaps the biggest rugby tour of all time.

It is an excitement fuelled by an absence of 12 years, in some ways England's World Cup win in 2003, but mostly the thrill of a team touring.

A generation of New Zealanders grew up with the likes of Mike Gibson, Willie John McBride, Barry John, Andy Irvine and Ollie Campbell visiting.

A generation of New Zealanders grew up with the nervous expectation of a bunch of Lions attempting to beat the best the All Blacks could offer.

A new nation grew up with teams from Britain and Ireland, South Africa, France and Australia visiting and bringing with them their own sense of international perspective.

To generations of New Zealanders, as I discovered in 1993 during the last Lions tour, these rugby players were not merely sportsmen but, if you like, windows to the outside world.

They were symbols of opportunity and freedom. In the Lions' case especially, they reflected the Old World, the colonial world and, with respect to European New Zealanders, some degree of ancestry.

This is the environment that Clive Woodward and Brian O'Driscoll and their Lions have entered into and which, they correctly say, is the most intimidating rugby environment on earth.

THE CRUEL FATE OF RUGBY

Saturday, 4 June 2005

In rugby, as with any sport, years of preparation, build-up and expectation can be extinguished in one simple moment.

A rugby career can be fleeting and yet the very nature of the sport means that the participants are required to go full throttle at each other and, in the process, maximise their chances of injury.

Lawrence Dallaglio, outside Brian O'Driscoll arguably the most important player in the Lions touring party, storms onto the pitch at the Rotorua Stadium for the first match of the tour and it is clear that he means business.

Even from a distance, Lawrence has that same sort of hugeness that I'd witnessed first hand back at Wasps' training facility in October: he appears the closest thing the Lions have to an action hero lookalike.

Clive Woodward is in the same mood, albeit at a managerial level. The side he chooses to take on Bay of Plenty has a Test look: Brian, Lawrence and Martyn Williams are all included, a sign of how important it is to get the tour off to a good start.

If there is any doubt that the spirit of rugby has been totally lost in the professional game it is dispelled in that simple moment when Ronan O'Gara kicks off and the 2005 Lions tour is under way.

In front of 33,000 hearty souls, the atmosphere has that rich intensity that is often missing in professional rugby. It is clear that this match has a meaning, a sense of history and perspective. Quite simply, it matters.

Everywhere you look in Rotorua there are reminders that the Lions are in town – even when mobile phone coverage goes down this weekend, the message reads proudly across the screen 'Go the Bay'.

The Lions start the tour with a reckless rage that must only come from weeks of preparation. The Lions lead by 17–0 after 15 minutes, thanks to three superbly taken tries, one after an outstanding cross-kick by O'Gara.

The speed at which the tries are scored hushes the crowd quicker than if the ground announcer had cried, 'There's free beer at the bar down the road.'

Lawrence is dominating, his freshness obvious, his enthusiasm infectious. He looks like the world-class back-rower that he is. Then comes disaster for him.

After 20 minutes, he appears to slip and fall awkwardly when attempting to make a tackle. The result is a broken ankle.

Lying on the turf alone, Lawrence must know his tour is over. As he waits for the stretcher, the months and perhaps years that he has been dreaming of this tour flash through his mind. His pain is total.

'Clearly, he's out for the rest of the trip,' Clive Woodward says after the game. 'I'm shattered for him, he's been looking forward to this tour for a long time and he was in great physical shape. I'm gutted for him and his injury has taken the shine off a great game of rugby.'

Clive says that Lawrence will be missed on and off the field. 'He's a world-class player and he will be sorely missed but that's also why we have 45 players on this tour, because of these things.'

Lawrence is naturally distraught but equally as philosophical about his fate. 'I am obviously very, very disappointed that my Lions tour should end in the first match with an injury that puts me out of the whole trip,' he says from his hospital bed. 'But I've been around long enough to know that injuries are part of the game and no matter how difficult it is, you have to be philosophical.

'I now just have to prepare myself mentally for the long process of recovery. For me, the tour is over but for the other players they have a great challenge ahead of them and they know they have my full support.'

It is hard to know whether the Lions stumbling for the rest of the match is a result of Lawrence's injury: regardless, they go on to win 34–20.

Martyn Williams has a strong first game and has put his hand up to wear the Test number 7 in Christchurch.

Brian O'Driscoll, on the other hand, is quiet throughout the match, not helped any by the swarming home defence that has clearly marked him as the Lions' most lethal attacking weapon.

Bay of Plenty, a side made up of six professionals and sixteen amateurs, have pushed the Lions and shown the spirit of gladiators. For these players, playing the Lions is the match of a lifetime and they have savoured every moment of being on the world stage.

At least Lawrence made it onto the field. The same cannot be said for Simon Taylor, arguably the unluckiest Lion in the history of the institution, and one of rugby's nicest guys.

When Simon had returned to play for Edinburgh and Scotland in the last northern season, after a serious knee injury, his form suggested that he had a good chance of pressing for a Test spot on this tour.

Ironically, after Lawrence's injury, Simon's chances have risen still more. Yet a long-standing hamstring injury is causing him problems. He wasn't available for the Bay of Plenty match, while he appears unlikely to play against Taranaki in the next match of the tour.

Lawrence's injury, especially, robs the Lions of one of their most charismatic characters and leaders. He is the type of player whom individuals follow. His loss appears a massive blow to a side finding its feet.

What his injury also shows is that regardless of how much training you do, you can have your dreams shattered in a moment of bad luck. It's as if rugby is a metaphor for life and it can be equally as brutal.

RUGBY IN THE HEART OF THE PROVINCES

LIONS V. TARANAKI, NEW ZEALAND MAORI AND WELLINGTON

While the Lions have done well to win their first match, their performance has given the other provinces hope that they are beatable. Although talented, they are not the superheroes they were portrayed as being before the tour began.

Playing the Lions is not only a rare experience for the provincial players, it is an opportunity to be a part of a big community occasion. For some, the lure is so strong that they even delay retirement for it.

Gordon Slater is a farmer. An All Black prop in 1997 and 2000, he was close to retiring from first-class rugby at the end of last season. So there he was on the farm one day last year thinking.

He'd done almost everything that was possible to do in rugby – he'd played Tests for the All Blacks, Super 12 rugby for the Hurricanes, and well over 100 games for his province of Taranaki. He'd even played for Taranaki against the Lions in 1993.

Yet he had this burning desire to lace up his boots again in order to be part of the 2005 Lions tour of New Zealand. It wasn't just the thrill of packing down in numerous scrums in the course of 80 minutes that motivated him.

It wasn't just the craic that the Taranaki boys would, hopefully, share with the Lions after the match in New Plymouth. No, Gordon thought, it was the thrill of being part of something that was bigger than rugby. It was a community event and he wanted in.

'I was thinking about giving it away but the opportunity to play against the Lions and help out Taranaki was a real factor in my decision to give it another year.

'It's wonderful how the whole province, the whole country in fact, has got into this tour. There are so many Lions supporters around and there is a terrific atmosphere.'

So here he is, one Gordon Slater, propping the scrum for Taranaki, some 12 years after he had last appeared against the Lions, and doing a fine job.

After the match, Gordon says there wasn't much difference between the 1993 Lions and their 2005 counterparts – either on or off the field.

'We are obviously playing in the professional era now and so that's changed but an international side is an international side and in that sense they [the Lions] are always tough to play against.

'Off the field, we managed to mingle with the Lions and some of the lads met up with them in town afterwards and so in that sense not a lot has changed. It was really good for the boys to do this and a real highlight of the occasion.

'What has obviously changed is the number of Lions supporters around town both before and after the match. There are a lot more than what there were back in 1993.'

Gordon's story symbolises why the New Zealand public are embracing the Lions so passionately: they want to be part of the occasion, part of the hype, part of the history. The Lions are bringing the New Zealand public together.

What is dividing the New Zealand public, on the other hand, is who should be the All Black half-back. After being ambivalent about playing against the Lions, Justin Marshall is now the ultimate team player and will accept it if he's on the bench for the series.

He'd had a terrific Super 12 with the championship-winning Crusaders and had been the form number 9. He is the best half-back in New Zealand and yet Byron Kelleher had been the half when the All Blacks dismantled France in Paris last year.

The 'Marshall Drama' has been worth watching and is the closest thing New Zealand rugby has had this season to its very own soap opera. His relationship with the All Black selectors has been like a courtship.

After not being selected for the end-of-year tour last season, there was ill feeling between Justin and the selectors. Justin initially played hard to get this season, suggesting that he had mixed feelings about whether he played against the Lions or not. Since signing for the Leeds club at the end of last year, his mindset had not surprisingly moved elsewhere.

He initially made himself unavailable, before being talked around by Anton Oliver. Eventually Justin called Graham Henry and told him he'd changed his mind. The All Black selectors are now, finally, enjoying having their best half-back on board to play against the Lions.

After Justin and the All Black selectors have kissed and made up, the loving quotes coming from both parties are touching, if not a little ironic given their recent relationship.

The issue is now who will wear the number 9 for the first Test at Jade Stadium. Most commentators are picking Byron Kelleher, although I have a sneaking suspicion that it will be Justin.

While the mind games are occurring ahead of the All Blacks getting together, the Lions continue on their winning way, beating Taranaki in the second match of the tour, 36–14.

A clear pattern is emerging after the first two matches: the local sides are hanging in there in the first half, before the greater professionalism of the Lions tells and they pull away in the second half.

Along with winning the first two matches of the tour, the Lions are doing everything right off the field. They are visiting schools, hospitals and many other community services and bringing with them enough goodwill to last several Christmases.

The Maori are the first real test for the Lions. With ten All Blacks in the starting XV, a good performance against the Maori will see the Lions go into the first Test as favourites.

The Maori beat the Lions 19–13 and it is obvious that the victors want the win more than the tourists do. You can see it in their body language and in the way they throw themselves into tackles.

The Maori show on this occasion that rugby, whether professional or amateur, can be a game played with a passion that is only a part of the most dramatic art, the most dramatic intention. They have raised the bar for this tour and the question is now whether the Lions are able to reach the same heights.

The news gets worse for the Lions with Simon Taylor now out of the tour, his hamstring injury still a concern. For Simon, who has been on two Lions tours and has yet to start, the news is heartbreaking.

The medics had thought the injury, which had flared up again before the Argentina match, would have come right in ten to twelve days. Yet Simon is still feeling discomfort and so he will not be available to play before the first Test. Hence, he is going home.

'Simon is hugely disappointed,' Clive Woodward says on making the announcement, '[and] there is not a lot you can say to him. It has been tough. Simon is a class player and I feel for him but he has the character to come back from this and we wish him well in his recovery.'

Clive Woodward now changes the focus somewhat by stating that his squad is here to win the Tests and that he remains more confident than ever that he has a Test-winning team in his ranks.

Yet the change in focus within the Lions camp is obvious after the loss. The intensity has increased, the mood is more sober, more business-like. The sincerity that was so obvious early in the tour has lessened.

Befitting the business-like nature of this tour, the Lions set up camp next in Christchurch, the first Test venue, rather than Wellington, the nation's capital and the venue of the next game.

The squad for the Wellington game flies north for the match the day before, staying at the InterContinental Hotel in the downtown area of the city. Such is the increase in intensity that the Lions are developing something of a siege mentality to anything and anyone outside of their inner circle.

Other guests at the hotel get a surprise when they receive a memo from hotel management advising them about the Lions. It reads: 'During your stay with us you may recognise a team of very well-known people, who have chosen this hotel for the same reasons as you – excellent location, excellent service and attention to detail. We ask that you help us maintain this atmosphere for all our guests by resisting the temptation to ask for autographs or photographs while this team is staying with us.'

Paying guests at this exclusive, upmarket hotel are also not able to get through the lobby or order a drink at the bar without being subjected to some third-degree treatment from the staff.

Such exclusivity is yet another example of the Lions (whether it is their intention or not) shutting themselves off from the nation they are touring and, it must be said, from reality.

Already they have shown their intention in this regard. The security around Jonny Wilkinson throughout the tour is but one example of a party not adequately gauging the environment. Another has been the obvious security in attendance throughout the tour and the so-called ringing-off of some of the training fields ahead of tour matches. Journalists are now talking of a siege mentality and there is plenty of evidence to reinforce this view.

On the other side of the fence, it is disappointing that the All Black selectors have elected to not release the bulk of their squad for the series in order for them to play for their provinces against the Lions.

As a result, there is no Umaga, Collins, Smith or So'oialo playing for Wellington, while there will be no Hayman or Ryan in the Otago pack at the weekend.

Such a policy is wise in an All Black preparation sense. After all, it could be argued that the All Blacks should have been in camp some three or four weeks before the first Test in Christchurch.

Yet Bill Beaumont is right to criticise it. Simply, it takes away some of the romance, some of the special ethos of past Lions tours in New Zealand, when internationals often used to play for their provinces against the touring side, sometimes straight after a Test.

Wellington could have used their internationals: they go down 23–6 in a largely forgettable game played in wet conditions. The Lions, playing their near-Test-strength side, are little better but deserve their win.

Jonny Wilkinson, Jason Robinson and Gareth Thomas get their

first starts for the Lions in New Zealand, with only Thomas showing any real sign of form.

Clive Woodward is being criticised for his selection. It appears that this will be the only opportunity that the bulk of his Test squad will get to play together. Most commentators are suggesting that Clive needs to bite the bullet and pick his Test team to play Otago next.

Yet he doesn't. His team to take on Otago has a second-string look to it and it appears that his Test team is being kept in cotton wool ahead of the first Test. Ironically, that is something that Clive has in common with the All Black management.

ROMANCE IN A DUNEDIN WINTER

Friday, 17 June to Sunday, 19 June 2005

For me, the realisation that this Lions tour is truly on takes place at the lush surrounds of the Kentucky Fried Chicken outlet in Main Street, Timaru.

There, some dozen Lions fans – all wearing Lions jerseys – line up with Steph and me for our fast-food fix masquerading as dinner.

They are a rowdy bunch, some having had their fair share of alcoholic beverages already. Like us, they are on their way to Dunedin for the Lions match with Otago at Carisbrook tomorrow. They are in good spirits though, and their behaviour isn't what you would call out of line.

As Steph and I chomp away on our fried chicken and coleslaw, we eavesdrop on what the Lions supporters are saying. They appear not to be concentrating on the rugby as much as having a good time. It is refreshing and hopefully a sign of things to come.

The road south to Dunedin is surprisingly light on traffic. Most of the Lions supporters appear to have come down earlier in the week to enjoy the festivities.

When we arrive in the cold, dark southern city just after eleven, we pass the campervans belonging to the Lions supporters who have been situated in the car park of the railway station. From the lack of lights switched on, it appears that everyone is at the pub.

Our bed and breakfast, based on the Otago Peninsula, is cosy. Our proprietors are Bill and Jill, a middle-aged couple who appear happy to have us.

'So you've come for the rugby have you?' Jill greets us on our arrival.

When I confirm, she says, 'Well, what do you know, we've got two Welshmen staying with us as well and they are also here for the rugby.'

'I'm writing a book culminating with the Lions tour,' I say politely.

'Well, what do you know, our Welsh visitors are producing a documentary about the Lions tour,' Jill says proudly. It's going to be a fun couple of nights.

We didn't meet our Welsh housemates that evening. At about midnight, the lads return after a few drinks. They stumble up the stairs, talking in their Welsh brogue about tomorrow's game. I feel like we are being invaded by Gareth, Barry and J.P.R.

As Steph and I lie in bed, we hear cruel sounds from the bathroom next door. As they were here first, our Welsh friends have got the en suite bedroom. The sounds are primitive, basic and amazingly rugby-like.

We meet our Welsh friends the following morning; Barrie and B.J. are, after all that expectation, father and son. They are Welsh, sure enough, but the family has been living in Auckland for the last 15 years.

Barrie and B.J. are following the Lions around New Zealand religiously. They are passionate supporters and over bacon, eggs, black pudding and heaps of toast, they tell us their stories.

'We try and get to the World Cups and we followed the Lions in Australia in 2001,' Barrie says proudly.

'It must cost you a small fortune?' I ask sincerely.

'Ah, it's only money,' Barrie says in his rough Welsh accent, 'and besides, what else would I be doing with it,' he chuckles loudly, as if we were in a pub somewhere sharing war stories.

B.J. looks a lot like the director of the *Lord of the Rings* trilogy, Peter Jackson. I suspect that it was him who was making the animal-like noises last night.

Barrie and B.J. are opinionated: they are 'dirty' over the fact that Clive Woodward is likely to pick many of his favourite Englishmen for the first Test next weekend.

'You would have to pick Henson wouldn't you?' B.J. says, tucking into another helping of bacon and extra pieces of toast.

'And what about this new lad Ryan Jones?' Barrie asks passionately. 'Surely he should have been in the original touring party?'

I don't want to debate with these big lads, as they are passionate Lions supporters. Steph has remained remarkably quiet and to this point I have ignored her none-too-subtle digs that it's time to finish breakfast (and talking rugby) and start exploring Dunedin. 'So who do you think will win next weekend?' Barrie asks me rhetorically. It is a pleasant interlude from his extended essay on the beauty of Welsh rugby.

'Well, I don't know,' I say honestly. 'The Lions haven't shown anything to suggest they are favourites. They may be keeping something up their collective sleeves but I would be worried as Clive doesn't seem to have played his top team too much.'

Barrie is having none of it. 'England won the World Cup in 2003, Wales are Grand Slam champions,' he says as if he himself was propping the Welsh scrum on the latter occasion. 'We must be favourites!'

I shrug my shoulders and now understand that regardless of what I say, Barrie and B.J. are united in their belief in the Lions. I admire that but it is beyond the notion of reason and so Steph and I head out.

When we arrive downtown, we find that Dunedin is in party mode. A university hub, the locals and the legion of youthful Lions supporters have made the city full of energy and expectation.

The centre of the city, the Octagon, is especially full of Lions supporters. A large 'Champions of the World' truck sits in the middle, Lions fans purchasing jerseys and memorabilia from it. It amazes me that you can buy the match programme so far in advance of the match.

A country band is playing in the Octagon, while workmen are erecting a large black screen so that the game can be broadcast to the city this evening.

Lions supporters outnumber the home supporters and regardless of what pub or café we go into, there are Lions supporters everywhere like a plague.

Somewhat surprisingly, the visitors are younger. It could be that the tour parties will arrive next week before the first Test, yet as a result we feel particularly ancient.

What is disappointing, however, is the Barmy Army base, also situated at the railway station. The big red bus, as it has been termed by the optimistic Freddie Parker, looks like a mobile shop selling memorabilia.

There are people milling around but it would be fair to say that it is not doing a roaring trade. In fact, the bar where the Barmy Army is supposedly based is empty when we take a peep in mid-afternoon.

It is fast becoming apparent that the Barmy Army invasion, as Parker had built up so enthusiastically pre-tour, was more marketing hype than substance.

Several fans we spoke to today said not only did they not want to be associated with something that is essentially an English cricketing invention but they also did not want to support Parker's pocket.

We park the car close to the ground some two and a half hours before the game and decide to go for a walk to find food and soak up the atmosphere.

When we get to the ground, we find we are on the terrace and not in the stands. I apologise to Steph as we quickly find a good position. As we stand and wait, the number of supporters grows and the tension mounts.

It is clear that many of the Lions supporters here tonight are already living in New Zealand and Australia. They are proud fans, sure enough, but they haven't spent thousands of pounds to get here.

The weather is cold but the heat of the supporters on the terrace keeps us warm and we are happy. The game itself takes on a similar pattern to other matches on tour: the home side is competitive early on before the Lions pull away to win 30–19.

After the match, and despite the result, there is little aggro and everyone seems to have had a great time. The streets are littered with fans, while downtown Dunedin is a hive of activity. Ironically, although there is enough beer in this town to sink a ship, you could go thirsty as you may struggle to get to the bar.

After having a quick walk through the centre of the city and lapping up the atmosphere, Steph and I take the easy option and head to the seaside suburb of St Kilda where we find a pizza place. We sit and drink rum and Coke and go over the game, both of us looking forward to next weekend, in all honesty perhaps me more than Steph.

This evening has once again shown me that regardless of what happens on the field, rugby is far more than about winning or losing. It's about meeting the Barries and the B.J.s and about sharing an experience with someone you love. Simply, it's about being part of something bigger.

The following morning, before we begin our long journey home, Barrie interviews me for the informal documentary he is making on the tour.

I am not sure whether it will ever screen in Wales. I wax on about the tour and about this Lions team. What I don't say is that I am now feeling a clear connection between previous Lions tours and this one. The connection is real and I could not be happier.

THE BUSINESS OF THE LIONS

Tuesday, 21 June 2005

After Dunedin, the focus moves to the first Test. It's announced that Anton Oliver will not be playing in Christchurch because of injury. He'd injured a calf muscle while playing for the Highlanders against the Crusaders during the Super 12 earlier in the season and he hasn't recovered in time.

I really feel for Anton. When I'd interviewed him last season, he'd told me quietly that playing against the Lions would be a dream, one that he ought not to contemplate as at that stage he was out of the All Black frame. Yet he had been outstanding in the NPC, been selected for the end-of-year tour to Europe and had shone against France. He was a certainty for the Lions series, and I felt enormously frustrated for him.

As I'd predicted, the All Black selectors have gone for a horses-for-courses approach to their first Test selection. Justin Marshall will wear the number 9, while also named in the starting line-up are, less surprisingly, Daniel Carter, Chris Jack and Richard McCaw. I feel delighted for each of them, having understood how important this series was to them.

After Dunedin, the Lions return to Christchurch to prepare for the first Test. As against Wellington and Otago, those selected for the Southland match midweek will go down to Invercargill separately, while on this occasion they will return to Christchurch the same night on their jet.

With the Lions camped in Christchurch, I get some idea of the extent of their operation and the lengths to which money is being spent to ensure that the players receive first-class treatment.

Take their transportation for example. The Lions flew British Airways to Sydney and then picked up their privately chartered jet to fly to Auckland. Amazingly, the plane is on demand throughout the tour.

The plane has this week been sent back to Christchurch to pick up three members of the touring party, before returning again to Invercargill. What the cost is of hiring such a plane remains undisclosed, although it would be in the millions of dollars.

The Lions have two large buses at their disposal throughout the tour, various Land-Rovers to transport the Lions and their partners, while Clive Woodward has a Jaguar available for him to use in the three main centres. Clive has used this vehicle only a few times while in Christchurch, and only for short periods.

The players are also delighted (for the most part) about the arrival of their partners this week. Given that each of the touring party has his own room, having partners to visit is practical, although somewhat against the traditional ethos of touring. Still, this calming influence could be part of the reason why there has not been any trouble off the field so far.

Although there are conflicting reports about whether the Lions players are enjoying this level of professionalism and pampering, there is no question that in many respects it has encouraged something of a closed-in mentality within the larger squad.

There are numerous examples of this. The Lions are training for the Test at Christ's College, a private boys' school about half a mile from where they are staying but rather than walk to the school, the Lions are bussed there and bussed back to the hotel afterwards for security reasons.

After player autographs appeared on the New Zealand website www.trademe.co.nz early in the tour, the party has decided to be selective about whom they give autographs to. Likewise, some of the party won't sign autographs at all.

Jonny Wilkinson is particularly under pressure regarding autographs and such like. He will sign on occasions, although several voluntary organisations in Christchurch haven't been granted the privilege of his signature on balls they provided him with.

Undoubtedly, there are reasons for this siege mentality. The British press, seemingly everywhere at the Lions' hotel, are always on the lookout for a quote, or some insightful knowledge. In the professional age, the Lions squad is used to this.

It must also be said that the Lions are from an environment where security is more prevalent. As a result, there are two senior New Zealand police officials travelling with them, while the Lions also brought their own security with them on tour.

Yet when you add this to the fact that the Lions are travelling essentially by themselves, as well as the fact that they have cancelled a number of public engagements (as happened in Dunedin), you start to get a picture of a team devoid of reality.

After a gruelling 11-month season, it is, however, not difficult to understand the reason for Clive's approach.

The response of the Lions' management when asked by journalists whether their approach is over the top is to suggest that they can afford it, so why not?

Yet this approach is not only isolating the Lions from their hosts but also surely affecting the squad's ability to bond as a unit.

One of the beauties of touring is rooming with another member of the squad, maybe from another country, and connecting as people. Undoubtedly, this translates into greater communication on the field and a better sense of the notion of the team.

This deficit is appearing in numerous ways, some of which are relatively simple. The Lions players and management have throughout this tour tried to meet once a week separately as a group. In Christchurch, the players decided to eat out at a small restaurant. Such is the size of the party, the restaurant couldn't cope and so some of the players were distributed to other restaurants in town.

It appears so far on this tour that many of the Lions squad don't know each other off the field and they are currently playing like it on the paddock. Professionalism, for all it's worth, appears to be having a significant cost to the Lions' results.

Money appears to be no object (the management, for example, have this week had their weekly bonding dinner at a very expensive restaurant), yet it appears to me that what makes sides great cannot be bought by money alone. It is all a far cry from previous Lions tours.

The Lions jet in to Invercargill and come away with a scratchy 26–16 win. Their hosts have come to the party and played as though their lives have depended on it. It is telling that a group of seasoned internationals can only narrowly beat a team made up largely of amateurs.

MORE THAN RUGBY

Saturday, 25 June 2005

The atmosphere in Christchurch is everything that the locals were expecting and more. Yet as I found in Dunedin, the concept of the Barmy Army has been seriously over-played.

The vast majority of Lions supporters are, rather, a combination of the young enjoying travelling around New Zealand (and perhaps Australia as well) and the older fans on expensive tour packages.

They started arriving in Christchurch on the Tuesday before the first Test, increasing in number as the week has gone on. They are noticeable by their red, white and blue jackets, their 'tourist look' if you like.

The city that they find is one doing its best to make the week memorable. There are signs stating 'Lions Supporters make yourself one hundred per cent at home' in shops, All Black banners and advertising hoardings are everywhere, while marquees are being put up out the front of several bars around the city.

Not surprisingly, the atmosphere in the city reaches a peak on the eve of the Test. I venture into town and notice that the pubs have never been fuller. Everyone seems to be having a great time, while amazingly few fans seem to be talking about the rugby itself.

The morning of the match is overcast but fine. As I stated in the prologue of this book, I go into the centre of the city to partake in some of the hospitality and soak up some of the atmosphere. It feels like the way rugby should always be: civilised but enormous fun.

I'm at the pub to meet friends, but as I wait, I come across an older couple sitting quietly by themselves, sipping their drinks and looking quietly into the blue yonder. They smile when I walk over and sit down and then, slowly, we begin to talk.

Diane and Robert Lawrence are from Aberdare in South Wales and are in New Zealand on what they proudly describe as 'a trip of a lifetime'. They made the decision to come after watching the Lions in Australia in 2001.

The Lawrences are rugby fanatics. Supporters of Neath, they are now of course fans of the professional side the Ospreys (Neath-Swansea). I get the feeling they hanker for the days when it was just Neath.

'I remember when the All Blacks came in 1989,' Diane says proudly. 'They were lucky to get away with a win that day!' she says. 'The clubhouse was just packed with people, it was a great day.

'That All Blacks team was a great side. They had players like Buck Shelford and John Kirwan and we didn't think we had any chance of beating them. From memory, I don't think they lost a game on that tour.'

The Lawrences purchased a Gullivers tour package. What that got them was essentially match tickets, supporters' gear and various transfers to the matches. Unlike many other fans, the Lawrences are taking the motel option and are not in a campervan.

They arrived in New Zealand this week and are still feeling slightly jet-lagged. The journey took them what seemed like for ever and yet what they have found is a country that reminds them of Wales.

'The people here are rugby mad,' Diane says. 'They are very similar to people back home in that regard, while the land seems very similar to South Wales, very green.'

The Lawrences watched all the matches on tour before coming to New Zealand. Not surprisingly, they feel there should be more Welsh in the Test team and point to 'our Shane Williams, Gavin Henson and Rhys Jones' who should be in the Test XV.

Over the next two weeks, the Lawrences will travel throughout New Zealand. After this Test, they are heading north and exploring the wineries in the Marlborough region. They will also head to Palmerston North to watch the Manawatu match.

So what motivates these rugby people to travel halfway round the world to watch rugby? 'We've grown up with All Black rugby,' Robert tells me. 'New Zealand rugby is something that we always wanted to see and now it's great to be here and see it in the flesh, if you like.'

Regardless of who wins tonight, or in the second or third Tests for that matter, the tour for Diane and Robert won't be a disappointment. They tell me that rugby is far more important than who wins and loses on the field. As with me, rugby is in their blood.

Tonight, Diane and Robert and all the other Lions supporters sit at the ground and shout themselves hoarse. The Lions are competitive throughout but the All Blacks prove too strong and win 21–3.

In the first minute, Tana Umaga and Kevin Mealamu clear out Brian O'Driscoll from a ruck. He falls awkwardly and I can immediately tell it's serious. The Irish lads sitting next to us gasp, as it's their man who's been injured. The arrival of the stretcher indicates that it is indeed serious. I think back to when we spoke in October. I feel his hurt.

Following Brian's departure, it is now easier to support the All Blacks so unashamedly this evening. With Lawrence and Simon also injured and Martyn not selected, Brian was the only player playing whom I've been following on my odyssey.

Although it is a great night for All Black fans and I almost skip back to the car, the real winners are the Lions supporters, who've proven emphatically that being a fan isn't just about supporting a winning side.

They've shouted their support, they've draped the sides of the stands with signs of home, they've worn their team colours with pride and, throughout it all, they've made sure they have enjoyed themselves.

They are not bad losers; in fact, tonight they are going to party as if their side has won by 30 points. As we leave the ground, I'm thinking about Diane and Robert. I know that despite the result, they will have enjoyed the occasion in the Christchurch rain.

We decide not to go into the city as Steph's parents are hosting something of a first Test party. When we arrive there and take off our 12 layers of winter clothing, we partake in their festivities.

There are numerous desserts for us to savour, hot chocolate and coffee. Black flags line the lounge, while everyone is in a festive mood. I can't count the number of smiles and we all just want to talk about the rugby. It feels real and it feels one.

Some people say that New Zealanders are obsessed with rugby. Clive Woodward and his PR guru Alastair Campbell would probably be top of the list. Yet sitting here tonight in the warmth of an All Blacks' victory, I can't see how anything that brings people together can be a bad thing.

322

THE SPIN OF DEFEAT

Saturday, 2 July 2005

If ever there was a sign that rugby had moved to a new era it came when Clive Woodward appointed Alastair Campbell as the Lions' media adviser.

Campbell, for all his undoubted talent as a manipulator of message and image, adds significantly to the 14 tonnes of baggage that the Lions have brought with them to New Zealand.

Clive Woodward wants the best for his Lions and that, apparently, involves bringing with him the master spin doctor. It is rumoured that Campbell's services are costing around £500,000.

He earns a portion of his fee in the 24 hours after the first Test. Four press conferences, including one at the Lions' hotel late in the evening after the match, are held as the Lions get their message across.

Rather than concentrate on what went wrong on the field as you might expect, Clive and Alastair do their damnedest to present every possible angle on the incident leading to Brian O'Driscoll's injury.

They have a point to some degree: the incident should have been looked at by the IRB Judicial Officer, yet the fact remains that Clive has more pressing concerns, the most prominent of which being getting the Lions prepared for the second Test in Wellington.

Yet that logic seems to be overlooked as the hours fly by and the British and Irish media review the incident more times than is healthy. A number of issues get lost in the spin, most notably the biting charge that forces lock Danny Grewcock out of the tour in disgrace after he pleads guilty.

Regardless of the rights and wrongs of the incident, the spin put on the episode galvanises the All Blacks more than anything else could. In that sense, the spin backfires on the Lions and means their job of squaring the series in Wellington is now that much harder.

With Brian O'Driscoll and Richard Hill injured, the Lions have to make changes and they do. They make seven in fact, partly inspired by their performance midweek in their 109–6 thumping of Manawatu.

The game against Manawatu, a team made up of amateurs, emphasises the difference between professionals and amateurs. It also reconfirms the fact that the tours of the past, where the Lions used to play provinces up and down the country, would now not even be contests. The modern Lions have to play professional players and not earnest part-timers.

Somewhat surprisingly, the All Black selectors make three changes to their side, with Byron Kelleher getting the nod over Justin Marshall at half-back.

Yet leading into the Wellington Test, everyone is talking about the O'Driscoll injury and whether there will be any bite in the match as a result. One could argue that without Danny Grewcock playing, that is unlikely.

The All Blacks are privately seething about the way the Lions have milked O'Driscoll's injury and the lack of respect they have shown Tana Umaga.

The senior All Blacks have got around their captain and pledged their support. Richard McCaw and Aaron Mauger spoke to the team on Friday in support of Tana. If ever there was a moment when the All Blacks won the second Test, it was then.

The Lions start the Test with a hiss and a roar: stand-in captain Gareth Thomas scores and the Lions lead 7–0. Yet you get the feeling the Lions do not have the strike power to maintain this early momentum.

Then in perhaps the moment of the series for the All Blacks, Daniel Carter makes an outstanding break down the left-hand side of the field and runs and runs with the grace of a ballet dancer. When Gavin Henson tracks back and makes the tackle, Daniel feeds Tana Umaga who races over to score a magnificent try.

For a week that those in the camp describe as 'living hell' for him, Tana scores perhaps his sweetest Test try on his home ground. As Tana scores, I think about Alastair Campbell and Clive Woodward and the games that they have been playing this last week.

There are some things you can spin but the truth in rugby is as plain as the day is long: 15 blokes going out onto the field and playing for each other collectively. It is simple, it is pure and in Wellington tonight, Tana Umaga demonstrates it far better than any words that can ever be written. Priceless.

The All Blacks power on. Daniel Carter gives the performance of his young career and one of the greatest ever by an All Black first five-eight. He has not only met the standard, he's raised the bar.

Daniel scores 33 points (including 2 tries) and has the normally critical commentators humming like morning birds. They are already talking about Daniel being the greatest ever. Even former English centre Jeremy Guscott is saying that he is a more complete player than Jonny Wilkinson.

I think back to earlier this year when I asked Daniel about his likely rivalry with Jonny. Then, I figured that it would be boy against man, pretender against champion. Yet in Wellington Daniel shines and Jonny has come off. Reputations are important, yet rugby, like life, is about the moment and this one's Daniel's.

The All Blacks have won the series. It has been convincing and I for one am over the moon. Before the series began, Colin Meads had said that it was important that the Lions didn't win. If they did, he surmised, then it would be a sign to all major rugby-playing nations that to win a series you had to select 45 players and a huge management team and run the tour like a military operation.

Clive Woodward has espoused the beauty of the concept of the Lions the length and breadth of New Zealand, although it is questionable whether he has lived the talk. These are the modern Lions and I am wondering whether they have stayed true to what the Lions have represented down the years. Maybe Colin had a point and if he did, then tonight maybe he and the rugby gods would be smiling into their beer.

IF WINNING WAS ALL
THAT MATTERED

Saturday, 9 July 2005

My girlfriend Steph had a theory about the Lions series before it began. Her view, espoused on the way to Dunedin earlier in the tour, was that she hoped the All Blacks won the series, but that it was evenly contested and that we would come to Auckland for the third Test with the series on the line.

My response is not repeatable but the crux of it is that the All Blacks had to win and that, all things considered, it would be better if the men in black did it in style and racked up as many points as possible.

Yet now we are preparing for what is essentially a dead rubber, I think there is some merit to Steph's view. Along with the rest of New Zealand, I would have enjoyed looking forward to a Test series decider.

The build-up to this Test has been particularly flat. With the series lost and the promise of summer holidays, the Lions now want to be in New Zealand as much as a Westerner wants to be in modern Iraq.

The fact that there is no Carter, Mauger, McDonald or McCaw in the All Black line-up and no Wilkinson, Henson, O'Driscoll or Hill in the Lions team further reduces the intensity of what should have been a showpiece of the series.

Rather than go to Auckland and pay another NZ$370 to indulge in more corporate hospitality, I've decided to sit in my front room and watch the game all by myself and reflect on what was as much as what is.

As the teams take the field and try to get psyched up for what is essentially only a matter of pride, my mind wanders back to the players of yesteryear like they were past loves.

I'm thinking about the dynamic Harry Bowcott and that wonderful try he scored for the Lions in the third Test at Eden Park in 1930. How he must have thought of that score in his last days in late 2004.

Tonight there are other Welshmen making their mark for the Lions: Ryan Jones, perhaps the player of the tour, who runs around the field like an industrious street-sweeper; Stephen Jones and Dwayne Peel in the halfs; captain Gareth Thomas from the midfield; prop Gethin Jenkins, who makes a strong burst early in the match to set up what should have been a try.

I can't help but reflect on George Nepia, that great full-back and New Zealander, and all that he did to promote rugby. Tonight there are seven Polynesians and two Maoris in the starting line-up for the All Blacks, a reflection to some degree of his legacy.

New Zealand has changed more since 1930 than anyone could have imagined. Yet what hasn't changed is the way the All Blacks savour the symbolism of the jersey that they wear.

An All Black is an All Black and regardless of whether it is 1930 or 2005, the everlasting pride in having the opportunity to wear something so precious remains paramount. In that sense, nothing's changed.

Tonight, I'm thinking back to Bob Scott and his magnificent

drop kick on this same ground in 1950. Tonight there is a new star: five-eight Luke McAlister, from across the bridge in North Harbour, who has come in for Daniel Carter.

McAlister starts shakily, but improves as the game continues and sends through a nimble grubber kick that leads to the All Blacks' second try of the night for towering lock Ali Williams.

When Tana Umaga latches on to a perfect popped pass from McAlister near half-time to score a try, I wonder what Jack Kyle would make of this performance sitting at home in Northern Ireland.

Would he be full of admiration for the skill on display, or would his mind go back to when the Lions attacked from almost their own line in 1950, leading to Ken Jones scorching across the earth to score?

Would Jack, like me, be feeling somewhat melancholy at half-time with the All Blacks up 24–12 and looking to all and sundry as certain winners? Maybe he would think, like me, that the contest and tradition was actually bigger than who won or lost.

Three tries are scored in the second half – Umaga again, Lions flanker Lewis Moody and an outstanding individual effort by All Black wing Rico Gear.

This is a far cry from 1959, when the Lions beat the All Blacks 9–6 at Eden Park. I can't help but think about Tony O'Reilly barging over in the second half of that game, or of Don Clarke missing a penalty in the final minutes that would have drawn the match.

That too was a dead rubber but crowds thronged to the match as though it was one of the few shows in the town, which in those days it most probably was.

Such was the way the Lions played the game that a good portion of the New Zealand rugby public wanted them to win and at least have something to show for their efforts throughout the tour.

I am sure that Ken Scotland would be putting his head in his hands in Edinburgh and lamenting the way these Lions are playing. It's not necessarily the fact that the Lions are losing, it's more their style of play that's such a disappointment.

They appear to have no imagination, no sense of creativity, and they do not deserve to get close to an All Black team that has set a precedent for innovation. In that sense, the tables have turned since 1959. As Tiny Hill might say, they haven't played with much guts and it's a great shame for all lovers of the game.

With 30 minutes remaining, Justin Marshall comes on in perhaps his last match for the All Blacks. Graham Henry had hinted during the build-up to the Test that, despite heading to Britain, Justin could be around for the 2007 World Cup. Time will tell. Yet Justin is on fire and his vision leads to Tana's second try of the night that effectively seals the match.

As the final whistle goes, with the All Blacks having won the Test 38–19, I know the post-mortems will compare this Lions side with the 1966 and 1983 teams, both of which also failed to win a Test.

I smile to myself when I think about 1966 and what Willie John McBride had told me about the players preparing for the first Test in Dunedin by dodging incoming aeroplanes in the cold of Queenstown.

The 2005 Lions were at the other extreme, but the lesson was stark: it didn't necessarily matter how much money you spent on preparation, winning or losing depended on much more. In that sense, Colin Meads was right in the warning that he gave.

As the players wait for the post-match festivities, it is noticeable that the Lions stand around in ones and twos. There appears little sense of camaraderie and very little spirit. I wonder whether they ever had a chance to bond and grow as a team.

That couldn't be said for the 1971 Lions, who regularly have reunions. From the power up front of the likes of McBride, McLauchlan and Quinnell to the amazing back line containing the likes of Gibson, Edwards, John, Williams and Davies, these remain the most outstanding Lions to tour New Zealand.

I wonder what we will make of the 2005 Lions in 35 years' time? Probably not very much, as tonight I'm struggling to think of anything apart from a very good defence in the early matches of the tour.

Even some of the stars of the tour – Ryan Jones, Simon Easterby, Simon Shaw, Mark Cuerto – were not originally selected for the monster 45-man squad to tour New Zealand.

We saw moments of individual brilliance, but nothing to compare to Ian Kirkpatrick's outstanding try in 1971 at Lancaster Park, or the ongoing sublime performances of Andy Irvine for the Lions in 1977.

During the tour, it was announced that Irvine was the new president of the Scottish Rugby Union. I knew what his concerns were about the game, but I wonder whether one man could make a significant difference.

One man who would know how stand-in captain Gareth Thomas

is feeling is Ciaran Fitzgerald, captain of the vanquished 1983 Lions. Likewise, I am sure that Andy Dalton would understand how Tana Umaga is feeling. I can almost hear Ollie Campbell gushing about the performances of Daniel Carter throughout the series.

When the post-match presentation has ended, the players troop from the field like soldiers coming back from war. For the Lions, the tour is over and they will undoubtedly have a big night out before heading back home tomorrow.

As they traipse off, I can't help but wonder whether this side had any stars. More particularly, I wonder where are the individuals of the quality of Sean Fitzpatrick or Gavin Hastings, the captains in the 1993 series? The Lions tried – but where were the heroes?

Sitting here alone, I'm in tears as the coverage of the tour ends on the television in front of me and all post-game analysis aside (that will last for days), the tour and my odyssey are nearly over.

It's hit me like a thunderbolt but somehow I've finally found the perspective that throughout this tour the New Zealand rugby public has been missing.

Right now, I can see so clearly the wonderful men I've spoken to over the last 18 months and their stories: Ollie Campbell in Dublin, Andy Dalton in Auckland, Tane Norton in Christchurch, Gavin Hastings in the unfamiliar surroundings of Cardiff.

I can see Jack Kyle with a cold in Belfast; Sean Fitzpatrick obviously missing home at the St Andrews Hotel in Scotland; I can see the Kurow Kid, Richard McCaw, answering questions so sincerely; lanky Chris Jack smiling when he told me about seeing Dean Richards with dirty boots and his socks down.

I can see Willie John McBride sitting in his lounge lamenting professional rugby; Ian Kirkpatrick tucking into breakfast, still as athletic as he was when he was playing; Mervyn Davies sharing his passion for the sport; Brian O'Driscoll's cheeky grin when I suggested he would be a fine captain of the Lions.

I can see Tana Umaga displaying the ease of a champion in a Christchurch hotel and the dignity of Luke O'Donnell on the West Coast, when I realised that the Lions would have to beat four million New Zealanders and not merely the fifteen on the field.

What's more, I see so clearly now that, as time passes by and the memories fade, what is really important is the contest and the clash. Everything else, including results, is merely statistical. It has to be said: you were so right Steph and I love you for it.

EPILOGUE

Saturday afternoon in the Western Highlands, early autumn 1991, and not unusually I find myself lying in the corner of the Mushroom Field, seeped in the damp of the nearby Oban to Crinan canal. My cheek and eye are crushed into grass and mud, several half-naked strangers are piled at right angles beside and on top of me and softly, from the sea-grey sky, it starts to rain. Which is when I think, I seriously think: 'God, I love this game.'

Richard Beard, *Muddied Oafs: The Last Days of Rugger*

My odyssey ends in many ways at the same place it began: at Lincoln Domain, some 400 metres from where I grew up.

It feels like so many other Saturday afternoons of my childhood in July: icy cold, with a light wind coming from the south. The overcast sky reminds me of the grey winter days in west London that I saw last October.

I stand alone this afternoon, like so many other times in the past, although today I am on the visitors' side of the field and have been joined by a few visiting spectators.

Lincoln are playing Celtic, a club based in Ashburton, some 45 minutes south of here. When I was growing up, Ellesmere and Mid Canterbury were two separate competitions. Now, at the senior level at least, they play in one joint competition.

As a result, I'm not familiar with Celtic's lime-green jerseys, but then again I'm not familiar with the lads that are turning out for

Lincoln this afternoon either. They look so young, which is hardly surprising, as the average age must be in the early 20s at most.

The rugby is not what it used to be and, with a push, I reckon I could just about win a place on the bench. Still, there is plenty of energy and enthusiasm in this Lincoln team and I love the way they throw the ball about and enjoy themselves so much in the process.

Lincoln have their innovative gameplan rewarded and dominate the first half, much the same way the All Blacks did during their series with the Lions recently. At half-time, they lead 20–0 and the game looks over.

As the teams turn round, suck their oranges and work out second-half tactics, I look across the paddocks that used to be so imposing when I was a kid. I think about Grant Keenan and how I wanted to be like him.

I think about training on Lincoln Number One with the Under-14 side and then, the following weekend, breaking away from a maul against Prebbleton and racing away to score. Like Ian Kirkpatrick in 1971, I just kept running and no one could stop me.

I think about how this domain, this venue, has captured part of my soul and how I feel such identity with it. The players may have changed, but the red and black stripes remain as bold as ever to me.

The second half is bizarre: Lincoln score two further tries and lead 32–0 at one stage, before Celtic stage an amazing comeback and when the final whistle goes, we're only up by 32–29. I can almost hear the sighs of relief from our boys at the end.

The match has been a cracker in many respects and I've enjoyed every minute of it, despite the cold that made me shiver and the isolation of standing alone. It's light years away from the Lions series that finished last week, but not as far away as I may have initially thought.

The Lions series was a disappointment as a contest, but not as an event. The Lions supporters made the tour special and proved that the spirit of rugby was alive and well in their part of the world.

Yet what the Lions tour also proved was that regardless of how much money you spent, it did not guarantee you a series win or, even at a simple level, a tour that players and management alike would necessarily enjoy.

All week commentators have reviewed what went wrong with the Lions tour and, more particularly, the mistakes that Clive Woodward made. It seems to me that regardless of how many players Clive brought with him and how many games he had to prepare his side, the All Blacks were simply the better squad.

Throughout the last 18 months I've looked at professional rugby at various levels – player, coach, administrator, journalist, fan. I've delved into the state of the game in seven countries and addressed some of the issues facing the professional game.

I've found on the whole a mixed picture. While commercial considerations have become paramount to keep the professional game on an even keel, those franchises and clubs that have been successful have never forgotten rugby's special ethos.

The administrators that have regarded rugby solely as a business have alienated the communities they represent and have often paid the price with reduced gate-takes and sponsorship and declining spirits.

At a player level, the elite in the professional game still put their bodies on the line, just as the best players have always done. Coaches and the periphery expect them to always peak, week after week, match after match.

Despite this, it was never realistic to expect the players in the professional era to toil away without thinking of their futures, economic or otherwise. Players will always go where they are appreciated.

Yet what I have also found is that the players who have reached their goals have generally acted professionally, but have applied those fundamental virtues that have made rugby the sport that it is.

Honesty, integrity, and playing for your team and community are virtues not unique to rugby, but are at risk of being overlooked in the professional age as outside concerns become more important.

If there is one lesson that's come out of my odyssey it is that those in professional rugby who serve themselves rather than others normally come second. Ignore the history and spirit of the sport at your peril.

Despite this, there are some very real warnings for the game of rugby as we know it. The most obvious is that the elite players are fast becoming burnt out by the amount of rugby they are being asked to play.

In the northern hemisphere, they are regularly expected to peak for their club in one of the numerous competitions the club is involved with, as well as for their nation in the numerous internationals played these days.

After all that, they are expected late in the season to front up for a tour for their home nation or, once every four years, undertake a Lions tour.

In the southern hemisphere, the elite thrash themselves and each other at Super 12 level, then embark on a Tri-Nations series. The New Zealanders and the South Africans have domestic competitions to play in, before heading to the northern hemisphere for always strenuous and challenging one-off Tests.

The Lions series proved that a side that is in the middle of its season would always have an edge over a side with players nearing the end of their season and in desperate need of a holiday.

A further lesson learnt is that sometimes in rugby, less is more. Having the southern hemisphere nations travel north to play in meaningless Tests each year devalues the game's history. As Andy Irvine had told me, fillet steak is nice, but if you have it every night you will soon be crying out for baked beans.

The bastardisation of the British Barbarians, the centralisation of New Zealand's rugby talent and, from 2006, the introduction of Super 14 and an extra round of Tri-Nations games are further examples.

Administrators have a duty to protect what has gone before. Selling out to broadcasting requirements solves short-term problems, but at the cost of risking the special ethos that has made the game great.

As Robert Norster told me in Cardiff, finding the right balance between preserving the game's rich traditions and acting professionally is not easy. Yet it remains the key to a successful and healthy professional game in the years ahead.

Professional rugby has had a varied impact on the amateur game. Those amateur clubs doing well seem to have a positive relationship with their professional cousins and be working hand in hand.

Whether this is through a payout from the spoils of success, as happens in Canterbury in New Zealand, or in the clubs acting as a feeder system for the professional sides, as happens in Edinburgh, there needs to be some positive relationship.

Clubs are on the whole, however, seemingly facing tough times as bar receipts and club attendances are down and the big-name players no longer front. It is ironic that while there has never been more money in the game, most of it hasn't filtered down to the grass roots.

Senior player numbers are decreasing at most clubs, as is the number of administrators and officials needed to keep the game healthy at all levels.

Rugby, even in the heartlands of New Zealand and Wales, cannot merely rely on the rank and file who provide the backbone of the game's soul always being available.

Clubs, provincial unions and countries have to find new ways to keep people interested and a part of a game that, in the case of some countries, has become part of their national character and tradition.

Despite all of this, I have no doubt that rugby's special ethos does exist but that it is not necessarily found in the places where it used to be.

Sure enough, it can be found in the way Richard McCaw strides up and down the pitch before a match at Jade Stadium, or the way Brian O'Driscoll shares a laugh before an important international in Dublin.

It can be found in the cheery smile Tana Umaga gives a young rugby fan on the street, or when Simon Taylor picks up a struggling writer in his Land-Rover.

Yet often overlooked is the fact that this special ethos is increasingly being found at semi-professional rugby level, or within amateur rugby.

I saw it with George Naoupu, Michael Johnson and Luke O'Donnell during the 2004 NPC in New Zealand and their stories were as inspirational as that of any full professional.

I saw it in the pride that Russell Watkins in Lincoln and Ken McDonald in Blackrock showed towards their clubs, the children's eyes as they swarmed around Mick Galway at Thomond Park in Limerick.

Yet, as in the past, rugby's special ethos could be found in unlikely places: from a press conference with Rueben Thorne before a Super 12 final, to a damp corridor after a Celtic League match in Limerick or even a loud Irish bar before a Lions Test.

However, the more my odyssey progressed the more I realised that rugby's special ethos was as much about relationships as it was about the game itself.

It was about a father and son going along to the rugby like they used to, two brothers even. It was about going on a first date and eventually needing to know the score in a Test. It was about spending an amazing afternoon with a new friend talking rugby.

As it always had been, rugby's special ethos was not merely about the game or the individuals concerned. Rugby's special ethos was about relationships and about bringing people together, whether it was going along to a Test together or a feeling of warmth and unity after your national side had won a big game.

At the end of the day, we might have to look a little harder for rugby's special ethos in this professional era, but it is there waiting for us should we choose to go looking for it.

The Lions tour of New Zealand proved that all the professionalism, commercialism and money in the world will not necessarily buy you success on the field. Rather, what will increase your chances of winning is pulling together and working as a team. In that sense, rugby is and remains the perfect metaphor for life.

To be honest, my passion for the game has returned and, given my goals at the beginning, this odyssey has been a huge success. Yet my passion isn't just for the professionals, but for all rugby and its people.

It's for the people who make the afternoon teas, the club stalwarts who mark the fields, the liaison officers who take care of the teams, the referees who give up their Saturdays week after week for the glory of rugby.

Sure, it's for the professionals who regularly display the skill of champions, the old players and heroes of yesteryear, the journalists who write the reports and the professional administrators who run the game.

Yet it's just as much for the clubman who gives up a night a week for his sport, the amateur representative player who travels miles every weekend for his game.

We gripe and moan about what professional rugby is doing to our sport but the main thing is that we are passionate enough to care. The game may never be all we want it to be but at the end of the day, right or wrong, it remains our game, the winter game.